British Politics and European Elections 2004

Also by David Butler

THE BRITISH GENERAL ELECTION OF 1951
THE ELECTORAL SYSTEM IN BRITAIN 1918–51
THE BRITISH GENERAL ELECTION OF 1955
THE STUDY OF POLITICAL BEHAVIOUR
ELECTIONS ABROAD (*editor*)
THE BRITISH GENERAL ELECTION OF 1959 (*with Richard Rose*)
THE BRITISH GENERAL ELECTION OF 1964 (*with Anthony King*)
THE BRITISH GENERAL ELECTION OF 1966 (*with Anthony King*)
POLITICAL CHANGE IN BRITAIN (*with Donald Stokes*)
THE BRITISH GENERAL ELECTION OF 1970 (*with Michael Pinto-Duschinsky*)
THE CANBERRA MODEL
THE BRITISH GENERAL ELECTION OF FEBRUARY 1974 (*with Dennis Kavanagh*)
THE BRITISH GENERAL ELECTION OF OCTOBER 1974 (*with Dennis Kavanagh*)
THE 1975 REFERENDUM (*with Uwe Kitzinger*)
COALITIONS IN BRITISH POLITICS (*editor*)
POLICY AND POLITICS (*with A. H. Halsey*)
THE BRITISH GENERAL ELECTION OF 1979 (*with Dennis Kavanagh*)
REFERENDUMS (*with Austin Ranney*)
EUROPEAN ELECTIONS AND BRITISH POLITICS (*with David Marquand*)
DEMOCRACY AT THE POLLS (*with Howard Penniman and Austin Ranney*)
THE BRITISH GENERAL ELECTION OF 1983 (*with Dennis Kavanagh*)
DEMOCRACY AND ELECTIONS (*with Vernon Bogdanor*)
PARTY STRATEGIES IN BRITAIN (*with Paul Jowett*)
GOVERNING WITHOUT A MAJORITY
INDIA DECIDES (*with Ashok Lahiri and Prannoy Roy*)
THE BRITISH GENERAL ELECTION OF 1987 (*with Dennis Kavanagh*)
THE BRITISH GENERAL ELECTION OF 1992 (*with Dennis Kavanagh*)
ELECTIONEERING (*with Austin Ranney*)
FAILURE IN BRITISH GOVERNMENT (*with Andrew Adonis and Tony Travers*)
BRITISH POLITICS AND EUROPEAN ELECTIONS 1994 (*with Martin Westlake*)
BRITISH ELECTIONS SINCE 1945
CONGRESSIONAL REDISTRICTING (*with Bruce Cain*)
FIXING THE BOUNDARIES (with Iain McLean)
THE BRITISH GENERAL ELECTION OF 1997 (*with Dennis Kavanagh*)
REFERENDUMS AROUND THE WORLD (*with Austin Ranney*)
TWENTIETH CENTURY BRITISH POLITICAL FACTS, 1900–2000 (*with Gareth Butler*)
THE LAW, POLITICS AND THE CONSTITUTION: Essays in Honour of Geoffrey Marshall
BRITISH POLITICS AND EUROPEAN ELECTIONS 1999 (*with Martin Westlake*)
THE BRITISH GENERAL ELECTION OF 2001 (*with Dennis Kavanagh*)

Also by Martin Westlake

BRITAIN'S EMERGING EURO-ELITE? The British in the European Parliament 1979–1992
THE COMMISSION AND THE PARLIAMENT: Partners and Rivals in the European
Policymaking Process
A MODERN GUIDE TO THE EUROPEAN PARLIAMENT
BRITISH POLITICS AND EUROPEAN ELECTIONS 1994 (*with David Butler*)
THE COUNCIL OF THE EUROPEAN UNION
THE EUROPEAN UNION BEYOND AMSTERDAM: New Concepts of European Integration
(*editor*)
LEADERS OF TRANSITION (*editor*)
THE COUNCIL OF THE EUROPEAN UNION (*revised*)
BRITISH POLITICS AND EUROPEAN ELECTIONS 1999 (*with David Butler*)
KINNOCK: THE BIOGRAPHY
THE COUNCIL OF THE EUROPEAN UNION (*third edition, with David Galloway*)

British Politics and European Elections 2004

David Butler
Emeritus Fellow
Nuffield College
Oxford

Martin Westlake
Head of Communications
European Economic and Social Committee
Brussels

First published 2005 by
PALGRAVE MACMILLAN
Houndmills, Basingstoke, Hampshire RG21 6XS and
175 Fifth Avenue, New York, N.Y. 10010
Companies and representatives throughout the world

PALGRAVE MACMILLAN is the global academic imprint of the Palgrave
Macmillan division of St. Martin's Press, LLC and of
Palgrave Macmillan Ltd.
Macmillan® is a registered trademark in the United States, United
Kingdom and other countries. Palgrave is a registered trademark in the
European Union and other countries.

ISBN-13 978–1–4039–3585–4 hardback
ISBN-10 1–4039–3585–8 hardback

This book is printed on paper suitable for recycling and
made from fully managed and sustained forest sources.

A catalogue record for this book is available from the British Library.

Library of Congress Cataloging-in-Publication Data
Butler, David.
    British politics and European elections, 2004 / David Butler,
Martin Westlake.
        p. cm.
    Includes bibliographical references and index.
    ISBN 1–4039–3585–8
        1. European Parliament—Elections, 2004. 2. Elections—Great Britain.
    3. Great Britain—Politics and government—1997— I. Westlake, Martin.
    II. Title.

JN36.B8755 2005
324.94'0561—dc22

                                                            2005042911

10   9   8   7   6   5   4   3   2   1
14 13 12 11 10 09 08 07 06 05

Printed and bound in Great Britain by
Antony Rowe Ltd, Chippenham and Eastbourne

Contents

List of Tables, Figures, Boxes and Appendices

Tables

Figures

Boxes

Appendices to the chapters

Acknowledgements

This book has two principal authors but, as always, many people have helped in its making. We would like to thank the Warden and Fellows of Nuffield College, both officially and personally, for once again supporting an election study. We are grateful to the Nuffield Foundation for its generous, and vital, support. We would also like to place on record our gratitude to the European Parliament and, in particular, its Secretary General, Julian Priestley, and the Head of its UK Office, Dermot Scott, and the press officer, Simon Duffin, who were unfailingly helpful in fielding our requests for information. However, as always, we would like to make it clear that any opinions expressed are entirely personal.

We would like to thank those in the political parties who were generous with their time and their thoughts and suggestions. Clearly, a study of an election would be impossible without the full cooperation of the participants. We have been helped most comprehensively by the candidates, the MEPs (both old and new), MPs, ministers and frontbench spokesmen, and by a very large number of party activists, as well as journalists and political commentators who followed the campaign. To them go our grateful thanks.

A number of individuals provided detailed comment on one or more of the draft chapters in this work and we would like to put on record our particular gratitude to: Elspeth Atwool, MEP; John Biesmans; John Bowis, MEP; Lord Brittan of Spennithorne; Simon Buckby; Bryan Cassidy; Hugo Charlton; Richard Corbett, MEP; Nigel Farage, MEP; Chris Heaton-Harris, MEP; Robert Hull; Lord Inglewood; Caroline Jackson, MEP; Francis Jacobs; Lord Kerr of Kinlochard; (Lord) Neil Kinnock; Dr Caroline Lucas; Neil MacCormick; Linda McAvan, MEP; Eluned Morgan, MEP; Simon O'Connor; Dermot Scott; Pierpaolo Settembri; Manuel Szapiro; Anthony Teasdale; James Temple-Smithson; Daffyd Trystan; Lord Wallace of Saltaire; Lord Williamson of Horton; and Terry Wynn, MEP.

Our grateful thanks go to John Curtice, Stephen Fisher and Michael Steed for their punctually delivered and typically incisive statistical appendix. Our thanks go to the polling organisations who have authorised us to reproduce their work here.

In addition to penning a perceptive piece on the role of IT in the campaign, Liam Spender gave us invaluable research and administrative help. Our grateful thanks go to Fabiola Giraldo Restrepo and Sophie Philippa, who typed up some of the many tables to be found in this book, to Anna Skulavikova, who so skilfully and rapidly compiled the index, and to James Hughes, Jerome

Glass, Claire Stubbs and Kristine Timberlid, who helped compile the media journal on which Chapter 4 is in part based.

We would also like to voice our gratitude to the authors of the House of Commons library research paper (04/50) on the 2004 European Parliament Elections and the Electoral Commission's December 2004 official report on the 2004 European Parliamentary Elections. For the reader seeking chapter and verse on electoral mechanics or statistical niceties about the results, these are the reference works to plunder.

After many years of writing about elections, we should pay tribute to an extraordinary new helper – the internet. We have been spared hours of sorting through press cuttings and party leaflets by our new friends, Google, LexisNexis and the party websites, as well as by the websites of the BBC and the newspapers. The search for a fact or a date or a quotation has been enormously simplified and we must pay tribute to a host of assorted and anonymous webmasters who have contributed so much to the writing of contemporary history.

Last and never least, our grateful thanks go to our wives, Marilyn and Godelieve.

David Butler and Martin Westlake
Nuffield College, December 2004

Notes on Authors and Contributors

David Butler, Emeritus Fellow of Nuffield College, Oxford, has been associated with the Nuffield election studies since 1945, and has been the author or co-author of each one since 1951. His most recent publications include *The British General Election of 2001* (with Dennis Kavanagh). He is well known for his electoral commentaries on television and radio and has written widely on British, American and Australian politics.

Martin Westlake has served in a number of European institutions and is currently Head of Communications in the European Economic and Social Committee. He has published widely on the European institutions and British politics. His most recent publications include *Kinnock: The Biography* (2001) and *The Council of the European Union* (with David Galloway, 2004). He is a Visiting Professor at the College of Europe, Bruges, and an Associate Member of the Centre for Legislative Studies at the University of Hull.

John Curtice is Professor of Politics and Deputy Director of the Centre for Research into Social Trends at the University of Strathclyde. He has contributed to each statistical appendix since 1979.

Stephen Fisher is Lecturer in Political Sociology and a Fellow of Trinity College at the University of Oxford. He has research interests in elections and voting behaviour, especially tactical voting, neighbourhood contextual effects and turnout.

Liam Spender was recently freed from studying Politics, Philosophy and Economics at St John's College, Oxford.

Michael Steed is Honorary Lecturer in Politics at the University of Kent at Canterbury and has contributed some, or all, of the statistical appendices to the Nuffield studies since 1964.

List of Abbreviations

ACP	Africa, Caribbean and Pacific (countries)
ALDE	(Group of the) Alliance of Liberals and Democrats for Europe
AT	Austria
BA	British Airways
BBC	British Broadcasting Corporation
BE	Belgium
BNP	British National Party
BSE	Bovine Spongiform Encephalopathy
CAA	Cinema Advertising Association
CAP	Common Agricultural Policy
CFP	Common Fisheries Policy
CFSP	Common Foreign and Security Policy
Con	Conservative (Party)
CY	Cyprus
CZ	Czech Republic
DCA	Department for Constitutional Affairs
DE	Germany
DK	Denmark
DUP	Democratic Unionist Party
E	Eastern
EA	East Anglia
EC	Electoral Commission
EC	European Community
ECB	European Central Bank
ECOFIN	Economic and Financial Affairs Council
EDD	European Democracies and Diversities (group)
EE	Estonia
EEA	European Economic Area
EEC	European Economic Community
EFA	European Free Alliance
EL	Greece
ELDR	European Liberal Democrat and Reform Party
EM	East Midlands
EP	European Parliament
EPLP	European Parliamentary Labour Party
EPP	European People's Party
EPP-ED	European People's Party-European Democrats
ES	Spain
EU	European Union

EUL/NGL	(Confederal Group of the) European United Left/Nordic Green Left
EURATOM	European Atomic Energy Community
FA	Football Association
FCO	Foreign & Commonwealth Office
FI	Finland
FPC	Foreign Policy Centre
FR	France
GATS	General Agreement on Trade in Services
GB	Great Britain
GE	General Election
GM(O)	genetically modified (organisms)
HU	Hungary
IDS	Iain Duncan Smith
IE	Ireland
IGC	Inter-Governmental Conference
Ind	Independent
Ind/Dem	Independence and Democracy (Group)
IRA	Irish Republican Army
IT	information technology
IT	Italy
ITN	Independent Television News
Lab	Labour (Party)
Lib Dem	Liberal Democrat (Party)
Lon	London
LT	Lithuania
LU	Luxembourg
LV	Latvia
MEP	Member of the European Parliament
MOD	Ministry of Defence
MP	Member of Parliament
MPC	Monetary Policy Committee
MSP	Member of the Scottish Parliament
MT	Malta
NA	non-attached (members) (those elected who were not members of one of the established political groupings)
NATO	North Atlantic Treaty Organisation
NE	North East
NEC	National Executive Committee
NF	National Front
NGO	non-governmental organisation
NHS	National Health Service
NI	Northern Ireland
NI	*non-inscrit* (members) (those elected who subsequently remain outside of the EP's political groupings)

NL	Netherlands
NLP	Natural Law Party
NW	North West
OSCE	Organisation for Security and Co-operation in Europe
PAYE	Pay As You Earn
PC	Plaid Cymru
PES	Party of European Socialists
PL	Poland
PPCs	Prospective Parliamentary Candidates
PR	proportional representation
PSA	Political Studies Association
PSOE	Spanish Socialist Party
PT	Portugal
PUP	Progressive Unionist Party
Respect	Respect, Equality, Socialism, Peace, Environment, Community, Trade Unionism
SARS	Severe Acute Respiratory Syndrome
Sc	Scotland
Sc Pmt	Scottish Parliament
SDLP	Social Democrat and Labour Party
SE	South East
SF	Sinn Féin
SI	Slovenia
SK	Slovakia
SNP	Scottish National Party
SSP	Scottish Socialist Party
STV	single transferable vote
SW	South West
TEC	Treaty establishing the European Community
UEN	Union for Europe of the Nations (Group)
UK	United Kingdom
UKIP	United Kingdom Independence Party
UKUP	United Kingdom Unionist Party
UN	United Nations
US	United States
UUP	Ulster Unionist Party
VAT	value added tax
W. Assem	Welsh Assembly
WA	Wales
WM	West Midlands
WMD	weapons of mass destruction
WTO	World Trade Organisation
Y & H	Yorkshire and Humberside

1
Background

Significant ripples

On 10 June 2004 the British electorate was asked to vote in the sixth set of direct elections to the European Parliament. Participants and observers concurred that the contest had been something of a 'non-event'. Paradoxically, however, the elections did not pass imperceptibly; for, although they may have seemed but a ripple in the tide of history, they nevertheless played a significant role in the evolution of twenty-first century politics in Britain and in the European Union. Malcolm Muggeridge, a journalist and television personality of the 1950s and 1960s, was fond of remarking that 'a row is never about what it is about'. A similar remark could be made about European elections – at least as far as the United Kingdom is concerned. Clearly, what they are *not* about is a popular desire to have a say in the composition of the European Parliament. Rather, they are national contests fought largely in the national context. 'Europe' may be an electoral issue, but it is an issue in a domestic contest.

European elections in the United Kingdom – a quarter-century on

Great expectations

In September 1952 the Common Assembly of the European Coal and Steel Community, the precursor to today's European Parliament, met for the first time. The Parliament could thus be considered to be over 50 years old (Hix, Raunio and Scully, 2003; Corbett et al., 2003b). The first direct elections to the European Parliament were held in June 1979 – a quarter of a century ago. The European elections held in June 2004 were thus the sixth direct elections. The people of the United Kingdom, together with the peoples of the 24 other European Union member states – an electorate of over 420 million – were given the opportunity to participate in the world's largest ever transnational election – dubbed by some as the largest experiment in democracy that the world has ever seen.

Doubtless, historians will look back on this event – laden with post-Cold War symbolism – with wonder, but even the Parliament's best friends would admit that the June 2004 European elections were an anti-climactic disappointment. In the case of some of the newest member states, turnout was grievously low.

In the first stages of European integration direct elections tended to be seen as the key not only to the evolution of the European Parliament but to the democratic development of the European Union itself (Westlake, 1994). Progress towards a direct system was for long stymied, first by President de Gaulle's opposition to the integrationist approach and then by the search for uniformity (Butler and Westlake, 1995, 2000).

Throughout the 1960s, the Parliament remained an inconsequential institution, with only the feeblest of consultative powers, whilst the European Commission and the Council of Ministers were fast consolidating their roles and gaining more substantive powers. When, in June 1979, direct elections to the European Parliament at last occurred, there was a strong feeling that a key part of the 'jigsaw puzzle' had at last been inserted (Marquand, 1979) and consequently there were strong expectations that the directly elected Parliament would, by popularising and legitimising itself and the other institutions (the European Commission in particular was expected to bathe in its democratic glow), provide the remedy to the impression of distance and impenetrability that the incremental European integration process had cumulatively created.

These expectations have led to what one observer has described as being a 'central democratic dilemma';

> With the advent of direct elections came increased power and with that came the accusation that Europe is an emerging super state; when the European venture was primarily intergovernmental (with power vested primarily in the Council of Ministers), there was of course little or no role for the people, but thus it was accused of lacking democratic legitimacy. Balancing the involvement of people while maintaining the role of governments has not only been tricky in Europe – it has allowed Euro sceptics at home to have it both ways: either this is a super state or it is undemocratic.[1]

Those who favour the European Parliament and the European integration process have been deeply disappointed at the lack of popular political involvement in European elections and hence also in the European Union's political process. For them, European elections are a little like a soufflé that stubbornly refuses to rise, despite all of the earnest chefs' attentiveness to the recipe, instructions and equipment. Why should this be so?

Second-order national elections

As the results of those first direct elections, held in the then nine member states, were being analysed, two Mannheim empirical political scientists cast the first doubts about the potential for direct European elections to have the sort of effect the founding fathers had imagined. In a simple and enduring theory, Reif and Schmitt (1980) suggested that, far from being a fresh, pan-European departure, the nine sets of European elections belonged to a sub-category of national election – second-order national elections.[2]

Because no *national* power was at stake in such elections, the traditional electoral actors (primarily political parties but also the media) devoted far less of their scarce resources (money, activists' energies) to the contest. For the same basic reason, voters were less likely to turn out and be loyal to their party, and the media would be less interested and provide less coverage. Free of the responsibility of electing an executive, voters would be more likely to make gestures by casting their votes for 'anti-system' parties and protest movements. The closer a second-order election was held to a first-order national election (for example, a French Presidential election or a British General Election), the more it would be likely to reproduce the first-order results. But the further along in the electoral cycle second-order elections were held, the more incumbent parties would suffer and the better opposition parties would fare.

Characteristics of the British political system

Figure 1.1 is a simple representation of the electoral cycle in the United Kingdom since 1979. It demonstrates graphically how well the second-order theory holds for European elections, particularly if a few specific characteristics of the British political system are factored into the equation.

A first characteristic is that Labour voters have, traditionally, been less likely to turn out and vote. As a consequence, Labour tends to do less well on lower turnouts – this is a phenomenon that holds true for all types of elections. This has meant that, since European election turnout in the UK has been low, the Labour Party has been at a natural disadvantage in this sort of contest.

A second, linked, characteristic is that, from 1979 to 1986–87, the Labour Party's basically negative stance towards the European integration process made it additionally difficult for the party to motivate its activists in European electoral contests – let alone its voters. This was particularly the case in the June 1979 European elections, which followed close on the heels of Labour's drubbing in the May General Election (Butler and Marquand, 1980).

A third is that, until the 1999 European elections, Britain used its traditional first-past-the-post electoral system (with single member constituencies) for the European elections. This tended to stifle the electoral performance of third parties – at least in terms of seats won. The Liberal Democrats, for example, only won their first seats (just two) to the European Parliament in 1994. And in the June 1989 European elections, held midway between the 1987 and

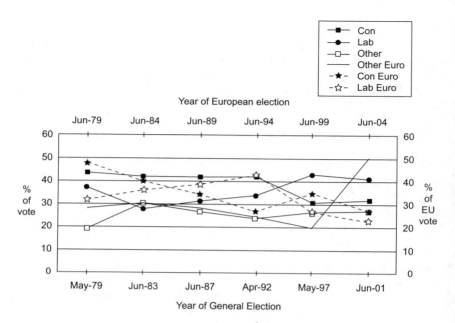

Figure 1.1   Second-order elections in the United Kingdom

Source: Authors' compilation.

1992 General Elections, the Green Party won no less than 15% of the vote (though no seats).

Until the momentous switch to PR in 1999, third parties – and hence third-party voters – acted more as spoilers, whether or not this was their intention. In the 1994 European elections, for example, strong performances from the UK Independence Party, anti-Maastricht candidates and the Green Party all deprived the mainstream Conservative and Labour Parties of seats they might otherwise have won (Butler and Westlake, 1995, pp. 267, 269, 270–1).

The 1999 switch to PR on the other hand gave voters the opportunity to give more positive illustrations of the second-order theory at work; in 1999 the Liberal Democrats won ten seats, whilst the UK Independence Party (three), Green Party (two) and Plaid Cymru (two) all won European seats for the first time, and the SNP, having won an additional seat at a 1998 by-election, maintained its representation of two seats. Regional representation became more distinct and, Labour's anti-marketeer performances in 1979 and 1984 apart, anti-integrationism won a first, significant, toehold in the UK political system.

A fourth specific characteristic of the British political system – the absence of a mainstream Christian Democratic tradition and the dominance of the

Conservative Party – is linked to a more general consideration about the nature of European elections.

The absence of European political parties

'All politics', former House Speaker Tip O'Neill famously remarked, 'is local.' The very term, *European* elections, strongly implies that these particular electoral contests are fought and won on *European* issues – and by European parties. Though this may one day be the case,[3] there is clearly still a very long way to go. Transnational European party federations have steadily evolved and European political parties now exist in European law – although arguably more in legal and financial terms than in political practice (see below). But even the most ardent of European federalists would admit that political parties as they would be understood at the national level – that is, aggregations of popular interests fighting for political/executive power on pan-European issues – do not yet exist, and this for several reasons.

The first is the general decline of the mass political party as a basic component of the modern political process. Ironically, the European Parliament seems to have won something akin to a full panoply of its legislative, budgetary and political powers (Corbett et al., 2003b) at precisely the moment when the paradigm on which it was modelled (parliamentary democracy, political parties, and so on) has entered an accelerated decline.

The second is the absence of a European 'demos'. The literature on the European Union's cultural challenges, of which Joseph H.H. Weiler (1999) is a notable exponent, has considered at length and in great detail this particular aspect of the so-called 'democratic deficit'. There is no popular sense of Europeanness, goes the basic argument, as there is, say, Britishness or Frenchness. There are hence no cultural foundations on which collective institutions, such as the European Parliament, can be built.

Primarily because of that lack of a demos, but also because of the Union's linguistic complexity, there is, with such partial exceptions as, for example, the *Financial Times* (Anglophone), the *European Voice* (Anglophone and Brussels-centric) and *Euronews* (mainly Francophone), no European media. When therefore the European Union's political parties – even the embryonic European political parties, fight for publicity, they do it through the national media, and they tend to do it mainly on national issues or national slants on European issues.

The third is the absence of any linkage between executive power and European elections. This is an issue which has much exercised minds, not least in the context of the convention on the future of the European Union (see below).

Some observers argue that the definition of a political party must evolve with the times and that, if a more modern definition is elaborated, then it becomes clear that European political parties do exist and are becoming more relevant (for example, Jansen, 2001, although even he would admit that this is something of a self-fulfilling prophecy).

One political scientist has forcefully argued that political parties in all systems are evolving into self-serving administrative organisations which, increasingly dependent on state funding, fight for state resources in order to maintain their own bureaucracies (Mair, 1995); in this context it should be noted that the two largest political groups within the European Parliament already have over 250 'temporary' officials on their payrolls.

Notwithstanding such critiques, within the European Union the evolution of European political parties, building on the existing pan-European party federations and mirroring the political groupings within the European Parliament, has generally been considered to be a desirable development. The 1991 Maastricht Treaty introduced a new Article, 191, which argued that 'Political parties at European level are important as a factor for integration within the Union. They contribute to forming a European awareness and to expressing the political will of the citizens of the Union.' The introduction of this Article was the direct result of a joint initiative of the three largest European political groupings of Socialist/Social Democrat, centre-right, and Liberal (respectively known as PES, EPP and ELDR).

Though such European political parties, in the sense of Article 191, did come into being, they did not differ markedly from the pan-European party federations that had preceded them. Clearly, in the absence of old-style mass membership or other forms of support, financial support could be a major contributory factor to their development. The 2001 Nice Treaty amended Article 191, providing that:

> The Council, in accordance with the procedure referred to in article 251 (co-decision), shall lay down the regulations governing political parties at European level and in particular the rules regarding their funding.

On 4 November 2003, after protracted negotiations, the European Parliament and the Council adopted a Regulation on 'the regulations governing political parties at European level and the rules regarding their funding'.[4]

The Regulation, which entered into force *after* the June 2004 European elections, lays down that, to achieve recognition and hence funding, a European party must be represented in at least one-quarter of the member states (currently 7 of 25), by members of the European Parliament or in the national parliaments or regional parliaments or in the regional assemblies. Alternatively, a European party must have received, in at least one-quarter of the member states, at least 3% of the votes cast at the most recent European elections. A European party must have participated in elections to the European Parliament, or have expressed the intention of so doing. The European Union's budget will make available €8.4 million per year for the funding of recognised political parties. Of this sum, 15% will be distributed in equal shares among all the parties, while the rest will be distributed in proportion to the number of members elected to the European Parliament. To receive such funding, a European political party must file an application with the European Parliament each year. Any money thus received may only be used to cover expenditure directly linked to the objectives set out in its political programme and may not be used for the direct or indirect funding of national political parties.

Though of no direct relevance to the 2004 campaign itself, the 2004 Regulation represents a new departure in European electoral politics. The clear intention is to 'force' European political parties as a gardener would force early rhubarb, and it may be that the 'Nuffield study' of the 2009 European elections will find more encouraging evidence of a European-level campaign. The Regulations conditions and generous rewards will certainly concentrate minds and influence the formation of Groups within the European Parliament itself.[5]

The continued pre-eminence of national politics and parties

Even though European political parties exist, all would agree that until now European election campaigns have remained resolutely national in character. At their best, European political parties have acted as umbrella organisations, bringing together kindred ideological spirits and encouraging cooperation at European level and in European contexts (such as, for example, the pre-European Council 'summits' which all of the main political families now regularly organise – see, for instance, Hix and Lord, 1997). But it is the component parts of the European parties/federations – national political parties, that have fought the European elections in national political contexts and it is the national media that have covered the campaigns. There was no reason to suppose that the 2004 European elections would be any different.

Political parties, political science teaches, are best regarded as rational actors with scarce resources that they must husband to maximise advantage. From their point of view, maximum advantage is to be gained in the national context through national power. It is therefore entirely rational for them not only to limit their expenditure of resources in second-order contests, but also to regard such second-order elections as a means for maximising advantage in the first-order context. From this perspective, European elections are but punctuation marks in the national political cycle (and hence the electoral cycle runs from General Election to General Election) and, as the ubiquitous second-order theory predicted, will remain so for as long as national politics predominate.

European politicians and national politics

At the same time, members of the European Parliament, divided into political groupings based on party affiliations, have conscientiously pursued their role as they understand it. Numerous statistics exist to demonstrate the prodigious work rate of the Parliament – a rate achieved notwithstanding the obligation forced upon it (by the member state governments) to meet and work in two places (Brussels and Strasbourg), with part of its administration in a third (Luxembourg).

The European Parliament's concerns are not about winning or losing elections and thus controlling executive power but about the quality and nature of legislation and about the holding of various parts of the European Union's executive machinery (the Commission, the Council, the Central Bank) to account. A large majority of the Parliament's membership is also concerned about the continued construction of the European Union – and until recently that concern has also included an assertion of the Parliament's own role as a – if not the – primary democratic counterweight within the system.

In order to exercise its powers, the Parliament has adopted a consensual methodology. This is in part due to exogenous factors (particularly the majority requirements set down in the treaties), but in part due also to the nature of the so-called 'Community method'. The rules of procedure of all of the main institutions – the Parliament, the Commission, the Council – set out basic majority requirements, yet in all of them great efforts are made in practice to achieve the broadest possible consensus, thus going beyond the majorities the rules require. The Parliament's *rapporteurs* (the authors of its legislative reports) make considerable efforts to win consensual support at the committee stage (without, however, necessarily yielding too much ground on issues of political principle). In the budgetary sphere, the larger political groups have committed themselves to so-called 'technical agreements', designed to enable the *Parliament*, rather than any political groupings within it, to exercise its powers vis-à-vis the Council and the Commission. (This prevails somewhat less in general legislative votes, where there can be – and are – shifting majorities on a left–right spectrum.) To this should be added the fact that there is a natural majority within the European Parliament in favour of extending the 'Community method' so that co-decision prevails over all areas of the EU's legislative competence.

This consensual methodology (to say nothing of the causes espoused) is alien to the Westminster model, where there is a relatively stable constitutional settlement and where heavily whipped government and opposition parliamentarians work in a majoritarian and confrontational style. In the European Parliament, majorities are not so predictable and no effective system of monolithic party whipping exists in the political groups (as distinct from the national delegations within them).

Thus, for five years, divorced from the domestic political cycle and only intermittently noticed by the domestic media, members of the European Parliament labour to improve draft European legislation and to hold the European executive to account but then, in order to seek re-election, they are plunged back into an essentially domestic context and a domestic system.

The result is a periodic dialectic between European politicians and national politics. One MEP remarked:

> In general I think commentators simply do not realise how 'stakeholders' (to use the jargon) now see the European Parliament as the place policy is made in a growing number of areas, rather than Westminster. We receive much more lobbying than ever we did in the Commons and both industry and NGOs seem to know to come to us – particularly on co-decision issues. The British public and media are blissfully unaware of this. (Exchange with the authors)

When the inter-relationship between the European and domestic political systems is examined it becomes difficult to understand why this dialectic is quite so strong. After all, draft European laws are also scrutinised by national parliaments (though this scrutiny work, which some would argue is less than thoroughgoing, passes largely unnoticed by the general public); they are adopted or approved by national ministers (meeting together in the Council) as well as members of the European Parliament (the Parliament is the other half of the European Union's legislative authority); they are implemented by national administrations; and frequently European legislation has to be transposed, via implementing (secondary) legislation, into national law. Far from being divorced, therefore, European and national politics are part of the same continuum. But somehow that continuum remains stubbornly invisible to the average voter.

When election time comes, most incumbent members of the European Parliament would understandably like to fight on their record and on the record of their party grouping. However, to the extent that the tide flows at all, they find themselves caught up in a domestic contest, fought primarily on domestic issues and for domestic political ends. Bowing to the inevitable, European parliamentarians and candidates 'knuckle down' and 'fight the good fight' while, just as understandably, privately expressing their frustration at the impossibility of contesting the election on their own ground and on their own issues. This has become an immutable characteristic of direct European elections in the United Kingdom.

Ironically, the 1999 switch to proportional representation exacerbated the situation. Until then, British members of the European Parliament, consciously modelling themselves on their Westminster *confrères*, adopted the constituency MP approach, even though their constituencies were composed of roughly half a million voters. The introduction of multi-member regional constituencies made this model largely impossible to follow and research would seem to indicate that British members of the European Parliament have not yet found an alternative representational model – certainly not one with which they are comfortable (Scully and Farrell, 2003).[6]

All of the foregoing does not mean that there is a complete lack of media interest in European elections. But what interests domestic observers is, naturally, not so much the implications of the British part of the European elections for the European Union but, rather, the implications of European politics for the domestic political scene. Nor does the attitude of domestic political parties mean that such elections are devoid of domestic consequences; on the contrary, and as this study will show, they can be of great importance.

A constitutional laboratory and a political testing ground

The 1997 new Labour government's announcement that the 1999 European elections in the United Kingdom would be fought for the first time on a proportional representation system was generally seen as part of Tony Blair's new progressive constitutionalism but also as a pragmatic gesture. Mixing constitutional reform with political considerations had come to be considered a characteristic Blairite formula.[7] At the time, Mr Blair enjoyed close relationships with Paddy Ashdown, the then leader of the Liberal Democrats, and with the late Lord Jenkins of Hillhead, who were both powerful proponents of a new centre-left coalition that would, it was argued, be able to keep the Conservatives out of power for a lengthy period. There was much talk about the possibility of introducing proportional representation for Westminster elections, since this would, it was reasoned, guarantee numerical superiority to the centre-left. Indeed, Lord Jenkins was commissioned by the government to draft a report on PR and to make recommendations (the report was published on 29 October 1998). The introduction of proportional representation for the 1999 European elections was both a gesture to Mr Ashdown and a first experiment in the use of PR on a nationwide scale (Butler and Westlake, 2000, pp. 31–5).[8]

When in 2004 the government announced that, despite the various misgivings expressed (see Chapter 2), it would go ahead with full postal ballots in four regions for the 2004 European elections, there was a similar sense of the European elections being used as a sort of constitutional laboratory. In particular, the government had announced its intention of holding regional referendums (a possibility set out in the Regional Assemblies (Preparations) Act 2003) with a view to the establishment of regional assemblies.

Knowing from experiments at local election level that turnout could be greatly increased by the use of full postal balloting, the government intended to use such a method for its envisaged referendums. Using full postal balloting for the regions in the European elections was considered a useful way of familiarising voters with the method before the referendums were held (at the time, this was generally expected to be in the autumn of 2004). It also represented a dry run for the electoral authorities, enabling them to identify and iron out any practical problems. On this occasion, therefore, it was the regional aspects of the European elections that loaned them to the role of constitutional laboratory.

Another aspect of the second-order phenomenon is the way in which the mainstream political parties have come to see the European elections as a useful testing ground for ideas and tactics that can then be either used or discarded in the General Election context.

Britain and Europe – a change in public opinion?

Undoubtedly the biggest 'story' of the 2004 European elections in the United Kingdom was the strong electoral performance of the United Kingdom Independence Party, which took 12 seats of the 78 seats on offer. In European electoral terms, a party that calls into question the country's basic relationship with the European Union corralled almost one-sixth of the country's European parliamentary seats. Could this phenomenon be regarded as an inconsequential flash in the pan? Or was its strong performance symptomatic of an underlying phenomenon, growing Euroscepticism in British public opinion and, increasingly, a readiness to call into question the nature of the United Kingdom's relationship with the European Union?

In effect, however, the question of the United Kingdom's basic relationship with the European Union had already been put – by the British Prime Minister, in his pre-campaign promise to hold a referendum on the draft Constitutional Treaty, and this whether or not it had already been voted down in a referendum elsewhere. As in 1997, it seemed that, to be sure of (re-) election, Tony Blair had decided to concede a possible future referendum. Indeed, linked to his promise of a referendum on the draft constitutional treaty was the evident fact that the referendum on British membership of the single currency was now postponed so far into the distance as to have become an academic prospect, if not altogether invisible (see below). The strong pro-European stance of the Prime Minister, which gave such hope to the pro-European camp when he was first elected in 1997, appeared to have given rise to little more than a set of hypothetical conditionals. In the meantime, the anti-integrationist camp had grown in strength and conviction.

Britain and Europe, 1999–2004

From the very outset, the United Kingdom has always had a complex and ambivalent relationship with the European integration process. The Nuffield Studies of the 1994 and 1999 European elections dealt in some detail with the history of this troubled relationship, and the reader is referred to these for the longer-term view (Butler and Westlake, 1995, pp. 1–9, 2000, pp. 3–13; see also Geddes, 2004).

The 1999–2004 period saw a number of European themes constantly interwoven with the British domestic political scene – namely, the single currency, enlargement, fraud (in various guises), constitutional reform at

European Union level, and the role of the European Commission. These all created fresh challenges and contexts for the government, and for opposition parties. As will be seen, they all converged on, and hence fed into the dynamics of, the June 2004 European election campaign.

The euro

The three-stage timetable leading to the introduction of the European single currency had been set out in the 1991 Maastricht Treaty. To most of the member states the single currency seemed a logical consequence of the establishment of the European single market. But in Britain this was no foregone conclusion. In objective terms, the entry of sterling – a formerly oil-based currency linked to a major financial services centre and a radically liberalised economy – would be a very different proposition from, say, that of the Italian lira or the Spanish peseta. There were genuine concerns about how the British economy and its cycle could be synchronised in such a way that sterling might join. Linked to these objective concerns, however, were important political sensitivities. The idea of a strong pound had traditionally been as much a part of the British political psyche as the independent nuclear deterrent and the United Kingdom's seat on the United Nation's Security Council.

It was only under political duress – and then on her own valuation of the pound – that Margaret Thatcher had agreed to the entry of sterling into the European Exchange Rate Mechanism (which the Maastricht Treaty would subsequently transform into the first stage of the economic and monetary union process). Her successor, John Major, negotiated hard to win a specific status for sterling. Dubbed an 'opt-out', this arrangement might more accurately be described as a 'holding' clause, since it would effectively enable a British government to hold back from entry into the euro even if the economy were to respect the convergence criteria and other entry conditions. Then, on 16 September 1992, sterling was ignominiously forced out of the European Exchange Rate Mechanism, and though John Major's government laboured on until 1997, it never really recovered its reputation for sound economic management. John Major himself became increasingly sceptical about the single currency, and sterling's membership became a distant and academic prospect.

In marked contrast, Tony Blair seemed genuinely favourable towards the euro. During the 1997 General Election campaign, the Labour leader (boxed in by similar undertakings given by the Liberal Democrats and then by John Major's Conservatives) promised a referendum before sterling could join, but the new Labour government's early actions all seemed clearly to indicate that, as far as Mr Blair and his Chancellor, Gordon Brown, were concerned, it was no longer 'if' but 'when'. One of Mr Brown's earliest acts was to transfer interest rate management to the Bank of England (establishing an independent central bank is a necessary condition for euro membership), and in September 1997 share prices surged to a record high, following rumours that the government would seek entry for sterling as soon as possible after 1999 (the starting date for the third stage of Economic and Monetary Union – irrevocably fixed exchange rates).

On 28 October 1997 Gordon Brown declared that there was no constitutional barrier to joining the single currency. Having set out five tests,[9] he said that sterling would join when those conditions were right, probably early in the next Parliament. On 10 November 1997, Gordon Brown presented proposals for making British business 'euro-friendly'. Thereafter, the government reportedly began working quietly towards the informal deadline of the year 2002, when euro notes and coins were scheduled to come into circulation in the euro-zone. Most notably, on 23 February 1999 (the single currency having formally come into being on 1 January 1999), Tony Blair announced a national changeover plan for the euro. The government's 'prepare and decide' stance was contrasted favourably with the 'wait and see' approach of the previous Conservative government.

The then German Chancellor, Helmut Kohl, was so impressed by this new approach that he promised to keep a seat free for a British representative on the board of the European Central Bank, and the promise was backed by the French government at the 6–7 November 1997 Anglo-French Canary Wharf summit.

Domestic pro-euro politicians were equally impressed by the new resolve. On 14 October 1998, Kenneth Clarke – one of the Conservative Party's 'big beasts' and still, at the time, a potential future leader – joined together with Michael Heseltine (another 'big beast'), Charles Kennedy, Tony Blair and Gordon Brown at the Imax cinema in central London to launch a cross-party 'Britain in Europe' campaign. 'The launch of the campaign', said Lord Marshall, its Chairman, 'is a truly historic moment. We have the political leaders; we have the support of most British companies. Together we will win this debate' (*Financial Times*, 14 October 1999). It was intended that the campaign would work very closely with the veteran European Movement.

As promises of support and finance from business (the Confederation of British Industry was a notable supporter) flooded in, it really did seem only a matter of time before the referendum would be held, although opinion polls consistently showed that a majority of 2:1 would vote against membership. On 14 May 1999 in Aachen, at a Charlemagne Prize acceptance speech, Tony Blair confirmed his 'real' intention to enter the euro-zone and his desire to resolve UK ambivalence towards the European Union for once and for all.

No single event postponed the government's promised decision, but somehow the prospect of a referendum on the euro in the lifetime of the 1997 Labour government evaporated. A large part of the explanation surely lay in the relationship between Prime Minister Blair and his Chancellor. Although always denied, it was strongly rumoured that Tony Blair and Gordon Brown had agreed to a division of responsibilities between them that granted the Chancellor policy primacy on all matters economic and financial. Certainly, Gordon Brown established a unique policy dominance as Chancellor. From the beginning it became clear that the decision about whether the five conditions had been met would be taken by the Chancellor, acting on the Treasury's assessment. (This was more explicitly stated in a June 2003 assessment – see below.) Thus, despite Mr Blair's growing, though measured, personal enthusiasm, the decision was shifted further from his direct responsibility.

A second probable explanatory factor lay in Mr Blair's (and Mr Brown's) determination to win a second term in office. As that prospect came closer, so probably grew the government's determination to avoid any potentially dangerous distractions. Tony Blair was renowned for his sensitivity to public and media opinion, and opinion polls (which had shown consistent 2:1 majorities against membership of the single currency over a ten-year period) and the Labour Party's private focus groups indicated clearly that the single currency was an unpopular issue.

Meanwhile, opponents of the euro had not been idle. 'Business for Sterling', launched in 1998, claimed the support of 'approximately 16,000 businesses' and boasted of having 'over 1,000 leading figures from business on its council – including over thirty chairmen or chief executives of FTSE 100 or FTSE 250 companies'. On 2 March 1999, ten days after the Prime Minister's announcement of a changeover plan, David Owen, Denis Healey and Jim Prior (all now in the Lords) launched a cross-party 'New Europe' Group that was pro-European but anti-euro. This cross-party platform, including, in Denis Healey, a former Labour Chancellor, generated considerable media interest and rapidly gathered momentum. Malcom Rifkind and Nigel Lawson were also among the ex-Cabinet ministers to join its ranks, and its website boasted an impressive array of senior diplomats and civil servants, together with academics and journalists.

In September 2000 a 'No' campaign, 'in favour of continuing membership of the European Union but opposed to euro membership for the foreseeable future', was launched. In coalition with New Europe (and to be joined in 2002 by the Green Party and a 'Labour Against the Euro' grouping), the 'No' campaign gathered momentum and confidence. The campaign seemed well-organised and comfortably financed.

On 28 September 2000, the Danish people voted 53.1%–46.9% against joining the euro, thus setting a precedent. Moreover, despite the Cassandras who had predicted dire consequences for the City if sterling were not in the single currency from the beginning, London's financial services industry continued to flourish. A few international companies made vaguely threatening noises about relocating to the euro-zone, but there was certainly no stampede to the Continent. After its 1999 creation, the euro's value against the dollar slipped badly, reaching a low of 82 cents in October 2000, whilst sterling remained consistently strong.

In other words, taking all of this together, the case for *not* making a case grew stronger.

Throughout 2000 and early 2001, the Prime Minister occasionally made positive remarks (for example, on 7 January 2001, on BBC television's *Breakfast with Frost*, he opined that joining the euro was 'sensible in principle') but by then a General Election was in the offing. On 7 February 2001 the Prime Minister set a new deadline for reassessing the five tests, to within two years of the beginning of the new Parliament. On 16 February, for good measure, he declared that a decision on the single currency was too big an issue to be wrapped up in an election campaign. Through these pronouncements Mr Blair simultaneously demonstrated decisiveness, gave the pro-euro camp some hope and, perhaps above all, booted the single currency issue well into the long grass of a second term.

The 7 June 2001 General Election produced another Labour landslide, and the pro-euro campaign took fresh heart. The next day Lord Haskins declared that 'Labour's resounding victory gives the government the mandate to initiate a national debate on British membership of the euro. It is encouraging to see early indications that this is what they intend to do.' On 23 August a 'government adviser' told the *Daily Mail* that 'We are ready to go ahead at any time and we think a date for a referendum could come as early as next year. We have been told to be ready for a quick, hard-hitting campaign and this is what we have done.'

The January 2002 introduction of euro notes and coins would, David Milliband told the *Daily Telegraph* (17 December), 'probably have much more effect over the next few months', and Jack Straw opined that 'As people become familiar with the reality they are likely to become more receptive to it. Since we support it in principle I hope that is the case' (*Financial Times*, 15 December 2001). Simon Buckby, the Director of Britain in Europe, believed that there would be 'another rise in support in the summer when many people will spend the euro for the first time on holiday. Familiarity is breeding consent' (*Independent*, 12 April 2002).

But the promised reassessment was very slow in coming, and the momentum of the pro-euro camp again waned. Then, in the spring of 2003, the mood music of the Prime Minister and the Chancellor seemed to give fresh hope. Tony Blair told a 22 May 2003 press conference: 'This is a debate that I think will go through many stages, and as we have seen it is possible for opinion polls to change and I simply think that in any event, whatever comes out of the assessment on 9 June, there is a big debate that will happen in this country about Europe. I relish that, and I relish being part of it.' On 5 June Gordon Brown declared that 'We are now in a position to announce our decisions in the House of Commons on Monday and *I look forward to the debate in the country that will follow it.*'

On 9 June 2003, Chancellor Brown delivered the promised reassessment of the five tests. It was remarkable for his unambiguous assertions about the benefits of membership of the single currency: 'I have no doubt: first, about the potential benefits to Britain and the British people of joining; second, the potential risks of delaying the benefits of joining; and third, the advantages inside the euro area of greater influence over policy towards the euro and thus Europe.' The reassessment was also remarkable for the 18 Treasury studies that accompanied it (though sceptics saw these as window dressing). But the Chancellor's conclusion was that only one of the five tests had been fully met, and that further flexibility and sustained and durable convergence was required. The Chancellor set out a series of reforms designed to encourage flexibility and convergence, stating that 'We will report on progress in the Budget next year. We can then consider the extent of progress and determine whether on the basis of it we make a further Treasury assessment of the five tests which – if positive next year – would allow us at that time to put the issue before the British people in a referendum.'

For that reason, Mr Brown promised the publication of a draft Referendum Bill in the autumn; the introduction of further paving legislation; the publication of a full and complete version of the British National Changeover Plan (including a possible timetable for a changeover); and a number of other preparatory measures. Collectively, it seemed an impressive declaration of intent, but the media, noting that the autumn of 2004 would be close to another General Election year, were sceptical, portraying the reassessment as, in effect, a form of postponement *sine die*.

Did the government overestimate the impact of the Chancellor's unambiguous statement in favour of the euro? On 10 June 2003 Peter Mandelson declared to the *Daily Telegraph* that 'The great euro verdict has come – and in my view it takes us further in the direction of entering.' 'Euro roadshows' were launched, as a way of dispelling misapprehensions about the single currency, but these soon petered out. There was a sense of anti-climax, and the Britain in Europe campaign, which had been 'on hold' since 1999, began to deflate. The problem, it was generally argued, was a lack of effective government involvement. On 25 June 2003 Ian Taylor, a former Conservative minister and now a Britain in Europe board member, declared that 'Britain in Europe and the European Movement would be very happy to work closely with the government in putting across the positive European case, but we have not yet seen any eager signs of them wanting to start.' Britain in Europe's director, Simon Buckby, who had initially been criticised by some for being too close to the government and Labour's 'Millbank machine', was now subject to another sort of criticism. 'Downing Street', the 25 August *Daily Mirror* reported, 'is said to be furious that Simon Buckby, the man they put in charge of the campaign, has failed to set it alight.' A 'government source' added: 'We have to gear up for the euro and the feeling is that Britain in Europe is no longer capable of turning around public opinion.' On 9 September Mr Buckby announced his resignation; 'When I came here I was told Tony Blair would attack anti-European prejudice ... One speech every six months does not a campaign make.' He argued that the government had failed to agree a consistent strategy to fight anti-European prejudice; 'Stop–go is not good enough.'

On 14 September 2003 a further dangerous precedent was set when the Swedish people voted against membership of the single currency by 56% to 42% (with 2% of voters 'undecided') on a high turnout and despite a high-profile establishment campaign in favour of membership. The next day, the *Independent* reported this as bad news for Britain's euro supporters, since it illustrated to Mr Blair how difficult it could be to win a referendum. The *Daily Telegraph* declared:

> deep down, even the most fanatical supporters of the euro must now recognise that it isn't going to happen. Their two main contentions – that the euro is inevitable, and that Britain is too small to go it alone – have been blown away by Sweden's 'nej' ... Instead of always wanting to be at the heart of Europe, never quite making it, sulky and resented, Britain could become the leader of an alternative grouping of non-federalist, peripheral states.

On 10 December 2003 the government went ahead with the publication of its draft Referendum Bill, setting out the question the nation would be asked: 'Should the United Kingdom adopt the euro as its currency?'

As he had promised, the Chancellor returned to the single currency case in his 17 March 2004 budget. Having favourably compared British growth rates (an average of 2.5%) with those in the euro-zone (1.6%), Mr Brown declared that the government did 'not propose that a euro assessment be initiated at the time of this Budget', but that 'the Treasury will again review progress at Budget time next year and report to the House' (Hansard, Column 324). A week later, the 'No' campaign announced that it was suspending its activities, on the grounds that there was no chance of a referendum being held in the near future. Mr Brown's announcement of a 'rolling assessment' made it most unlikely that a referendum could be held much before spring 2008, the campaign calculated.

A final blow came in April 2004 when, as will be seen below, Prime Minister Blair conceded a referendum on the draft European Constitution. Since a referendum on the euro could not be held before, and since no referendum was expected on the draft Constitution before 2006 at the earliest, sterling's membership of the single currency died as a political issue. In effect, the euro went from being a near prospect in 1997 to a distant prospect in 2004.[10] In his resignation remarks, Simon Buckby made two significant observations with implications for the 2004 European elections. First, he argued that the 'fundamental problem' was that anti-European prejudice was more deep-seated than many admitted; 'We have seen it in our focus groups, showing that racism and xenophobia come to the fore quite quickly.' Second, 'the anti-Europeans have opened a second front by arguing that the new European constitution represents a super state ... It seems to me that this is code for Britain getting out of Europe altogether ...' In retrospect, the shadow boxing around the shimmering prospect of a referendum on the single currency seemed to have been a limbering-up exercise for a more fundamental debate.

Enlargement

After the fall of the Berlin Wall in 1989 successive British governments consistently supported moves to allow the former communist states of Central and Eastern Europe to accede to the European Union. There was a strong moral argument for admitting these countries to a prosperous club from which they had previously been excluded through the vagaries of the Cold War. But traditionally many in British governments also had a more pragmatic reason for supporting a new wave of accessions; enlargement ('widening'), it was believed, would inevitably slow down further integration ('deepening').

The Central and Eastern European countries soon enjoyed Association Agreements similar to those that Turkey (1963), Malta (1970) and Cyprus (1972) had enjoyed for some time. At the 1993 Copenhagen European Council meeting, the Heads of State or Government agreed that 'the associated countries in Central and Eastern Europe that so desire shall become members of the European Union'. Enlargement was no longer a question of 'if', but 'when'. The Copenhagen meeting set down criteria (democracy, rule of law, and so on) that candidate countries had to achieve. The 1995 Madrid European Council added conditions concerning adequate administrative and judicial structures.

In 1998 the European Commission adopted opinions recommending that accession negotiations begin with Hungary, Poland, Estonia, the Czech Republic, Slovenia and Cyprus and in 1999 with Romania, the Slovak Republic, Latvia, Lithuania, Bulgaria and Malta. By December 2002 the European Commission was able to recommend closing the negotiations with ten of these countries (all but Bulgaria and Romania, which were expected to follow in about 2007). Behind this process lay a political debate about whether the Union should adopt a 'big bang' approach to accession or whether, rather, countries should join at their own pace. The debate strengthened the resolve of the candidate countries to accelerate and consolidate their reform processes, and the 'big bang' proved something of a self-fulfilling prophecy.

On 16 April 2003 in Athens an accession treaty was signed with each of the ten countries, and it was agreed that the new member states would join the European Union on 1 May 2004, once the accession treaties had been ratified. Though no referendums were required in the existing 15 member states, nine of the ten accession states held referendums in the course of 2003. On 1 May 2004, on the eve of the European elections, the ten new member states duly took up their places as fully-fledged members of the European Union. Transitional arrangements had been agreed in Athens whereby 'observers' from the new member states had already participated in the

Union's institutions (for example, the European Parliament and the Council), though with no voting rights. The impact of this largest-ever enlargement wave was therefore softened, as far as daily life in Brussels, Strasbourg and Luxembourg was concerned.

In the early days of the enlargement process the British media portrayed it generally as being a 'good thing'. Enlargement would result in the admission of countries with which the United Kingdom had historical or sentimental links (Poland, the Czech Republic); it would create a market of some 480 million citizens in which British business could ply its trade, aided by the predominance of English as a second language in most of the new member states; and it would slow down attempts to integrate Europe still further – or so it was thought.

In the closing stages of the accession negotiations, the British government became embroiled in a festering dispute with the French government over the positioning of a refugee centre at Sangatte, close to Channel ferry ports and the entrance to the Channel Tunnel. The British media reported at great length on the efforts of refugees (many of them more probably economic migrants) to smuggle themselves into the United Kingdom.

The dispute was settled in November 2002, and it was agreed that the Sangatte centre would be closed down (it closed on 14 December 2002), but the media reporting had clearly created the impression of a country under a sort of siege from would-be economic migrants, and this was inevitably linked with the larger issue of impending enlargement. The impression was further enhanced by a series of tragic accidents involving foreign workers, many of them illicit. As enlargement day approached, these impressions seemed to feed into an atmosphere of growing apprehension about the prospect of free movement of workers and people from Central and Eastern Europe. Newspapers published interviews with Europeans planning to come seeking their fortune, and with British workers afraid for their jobs. Whilst the government continued to make welcoming noises, there was a groundswell of apprehension that was far from receding by the time of the European elections.

Constitutional Reform at European Union level

Amsterdam and Nice

Despite successive British governments' belief that enlargement would slow down the integration process, the prospect of ten new member states joining the Union – the largest ever wave of enlargement – inevitably raised questions about the functioning of the Union's institutions. How, for example, could a European Commission, designed for nine Commissioners (from six member states) in 1957, cope with 30 or more members 50 years on? The 1997 Amsterdam Treaty – the first Inter-Governmental Conference in which the new Labour government participated – was portrayed as a first attempt to rationalise and reform the Union's institutions, but enlargement was too distant a prospect to concentrate minds. Nevertheless, a 'Protocol on the institutions with the prospect of enlargement of the European Union' provided for another Inter-Governmental Conference to be convened 'at least one year before the membership exceeds twenty'. Its task would be to carry out 'a comprehensive review of the provisions of the Treaties on the composition and functioning of the institutions' and it provided explicitly for the larger member states (including the United Kingdom) to lose their second Commissioner, provided that the weighting of votes in the Council of Ministers had been modified in such a way as to compensate them for this loss.

As seen above, enlargement negotiations got underway already in 1998 and so at the June 1999 Cologne European Council it was agreed that the new Inter-Governmental Conference should be convened in early 2000 and closed at the December 2000 Nice European Council.

The Cologne summit also provided for a Charter of Fundamental Rights to be drafted through a new mechanism, a Convention bringing together representatives of the governments, the European Parliament and national parliaments and the European Commission. The Convention method delivered on time a consensual and well-prepared document which was 'solemnly proclaimed' by the EU institutions at the Nice Inter-Governmental Conference. Suggestions that the Nice IGC might incorporate it into the Treaties were met with criticism from many quarters in the United Kingdom, including the Conservative Party, primarily on the grounds that it would represent a further extension of the primacy of EU law and the Luxembourg-based European Court of Justice over domestic law, but they also argued that it would clash with UK domestic case law based on the European Convention on Human Rights and judgments of the Strasbourg-based European Court of Human Rights. As will be seen below, this issue was to return in the run-up to the June 2004 European elections.

The closing meeting of the Nice Inter-Governmental Conference was a lengthy and ill-tempered affair. President Chirac and the French EU Presidency more generally was alleged to have muscled through agreements, pushed its own views too strongly and to have brow-beaten smaller member states. The candidate countries were roughly treated. The Inter-Governmental Conference was perceived as having been ill-prepared and the narrow view of member states' governments was harshly criticised by the European Parliament, among others. More significantly from the British point of view, President Chirac let it be known that, in the face of continued resistance to change from the British and other governments, he would be prepared to countenance forging ahead with more advanced bilateral integration outside the EU structure. (The Nice atmosphere was not helped by the notoriously poor relationship between Mr Blair and Mr Chirac.) Joschka Fischer, Germany's foreign affairs minister, seemed to deliver a similar message. Such pronouncements set in relief the Blair government's repeated efforts either to join the Franco-German club and form a '*directoire*' or to establish the United Kingdom, in alliance with the other larger member states, Italy and Spain, as an alternative source of EU leadership. Thus, although the Chirac–Fischer statements may only have been crude negotiating tactics, the remarks were widely reported and analysed in the British media.

In the end, the Nice IGC did achieve the required results – after a fashion (Galloway, 2001). According to its narrow initial remit, it did take decisions concerning modifications to the institutions which would enable enlargement to go ahead. But by the time the IGC took place, expectations had exceeded this narrow remit, and there was widespread (though misplaced) disappointment that the member states had not agreed on simplifying and rationalising the Treaty structures or even 'constitutionalising' the Treaties. However, there was a general recognition that more work on rationalisation and simplification needed to be done, and a declaration attached to the Nice Treaty provided for another Inter-Governmental Conference to be convened before enlargement occurred.

From the British point of view, it was confirmed that the UK would lose its second Commissioner in 2004 (though this change was explicitly linked to the rebalancing of voting rights in the Council) and it was agreed that the number of British members of the European Parliament would be reduced from 87 to 78. Perhaps more profoundly, and despite a 30 November preparatory pre-IGC summit between Tony Blair and Jacques Chirac, the British public had witnessed crude attempts to bully the British government – the government itself had certainly taken good note. There was a widespread feeling among Heads of State or Government that the Nice experience should not be repeated. The European Parliament was among those calling for better and more representative preparation of the next Inter-Governmental Conference, which was portrayed as being the European Union's last chance seriously to rationalise the complex treaty structures before a Union of 25 or more.

The European Convention

The European Parliament had called for the Union to adopt the successful Convention method used to draw up the Charter of Fundamental Rights.[11] The 2001 Laeken European Council declared:

> In order to pave the way for the next Intergovernmental Conference as broadly and openly as possible, the European Council has decided to convene a Convention composed of the main parties involved in the debate on the future of the Union ... it will be the task of that Convention to consider the key issues arising for the Union's future development and try to identify the various possible responses.

Those issues were identified as: a better division and definition of competences in the European Union; simplification of the Union's instruments; more democracy, transparency and efficiency in the European Union; and moves towards a 'Constitution for European citizens'. Former French President Valèry Giscard d'Estaing was appointed as chairman and, significantly, the former head of the British Diplomatic Service and former British permanent representative to the European Union, Sir John (now Lord) Kerr, was appointed head of the Convention's secretariat. The Convention was to be composed of 15 representatives of the member states' governments, 30 of national parliaments of the member states, 16 members of the European Parliament and 2 Commission representatives, plus 13 representatives from the candidate countries and 26 from their parliaments and observers from the Union's other consultative organs and institutions (European Economic and Social Committee, Committee of the Regions), the social partners and the European Ombudsman. The British representatives are set out in Table 1.1.

Table 1.1   British representatives to the European Convention

	Members	*Alternates*
Government representatives	Peter Hain	Baroness Scotland
Representatives of national parliaments	Gisela Stuart (Praesidium member)	Lord Tomlinson (Former MEP)
	David Heathcoat-Amory	Lord Maclennan of Rogart
Representatives of the European Parliament	Timothy Kirkhope	The Earl of Stockton
	Andrew Duff (Praesidium member)	
	Linda McAvan	Neil MacCormick

The Convention was set a tight timetable; it had to report within a year, starting from its inaugural meeting on 1 March 2002. A forum was to be established so that the Convention could consult as widely as possible. The Convention established its own three-phase (listening, deliberating, proposing) working method and encouraged written and oral contributions.

From the outset of the Convention's work, it was clear that M. Giscard d'Estaing was determined to forge consensus and present a single text for the consideration of the Heads of State and Government, and it was this, against the odds, that he was able to do, presenting a text, in the form of a draft Constitutional Treaty, to the Thessaloniki European Council meeting on 19 June 2003. The presentation of a single text was not an obligation (the Laeken declaration spoke of 'either different options ... or recommendations if consensus is achieved') but the former French President was a canny negotiator who, it was alleged, had his eye on history. M. Giscard d'Estaing knew that the presentation of options rather than a single consensual text would have weakened the Convention's proposals and enabled the member state governments to reopen negotiations on any number of areas.

Consensus, then, was a considerable achievement, but it came at a cost. Whilst the chairman encouraged debate and contributions, he was reportedly ruthless at taking (some would say 'imposing') majority decisions and squeezing minority opinions to the margins. Minority opinion holders, such as Danish June Movement MEP Jens-Peter Bonde, recognised the logical consequences of Giscard d'Estaing's decision to try hard to propose a single consensus text but regretted the weakening of one of the Convention's avowed roles, which was 'to pave the way for the next Inter-Governmental Conference as broadly and openly as possible'.

But a surprise came when, after M. Giscard d'Estaing's Thessaloniki presentation of the results of the Convention's work, Gisela Stuart, House of Commons' representative and a previously enthusiastic member of the Praesidium, publicly criticised the Convention's methodology and its results (Stuart, 2003a, 2003b). Notwithstanding its noble and honest intentions, she insisted, the Convention had somehow failed to engage the European people in a popular debate. Moreover, national parliaments, although directly represented in the Convention, had failed (or were unable) to represent its deliberations back to the people they purportedly represented. The result was a step-change in European integration with no accompanying understanding and support from European citizens.[12] Gisela Stuart's was, though, a lonely dissenting voice,[13] with most Convention members arguing for a rapid and full approval of its proposals by the member states.

The 2003–04 Inter-Governmental Conference and the draft Constitutional Treaty

On the basis of the European Convention's recommendations the 29–30 September 2003 European Council gave its agreement to the opening of an Inter-Governmental Conference which formally began in Rome on 4 October. It rapidly became clear that there was general agreement on much of the proposed text, but that there remained a few difficult issues. The British government was swift to lay down the 'red lines' which it was not prepared to cross. These were set out in the September 2003 White Paper *A Constitutional Treaty for the EU – the British Approach to the EU IGC 2003*:

> We will insist that unanimity remain for Treaty change and in other areas of vital national interest such as tax, social security, defence, key areas of criminal procedural law and the system of own resources (the EU's revenue-raising mechanism). Unanimity must remain the general rule for CFSP, as proposed in the final Convention text.

Silvio Berlusconi's Italian EU Presidency was nevertheless confident that it could reach agreement before the end of 2003 but, despite the success of a 'conclave' of Defence Ministers in Naples in November, the 13 December 2003 IGC meeting resulted in a stand-off between Poland and Spain and the other member states on the esoteric issue of voting weights and blocking minorities in the Council. In early 2004, the Irish EU Presidency took up the cudgels. The Irish Prime Minister, Bertie Ahern, a renowned deal-maker, made several tours of the European capitals and was prudently circumspect about the prospects of success.

It was suspected that the December setback suited the British government; in the absence of any final agreement, the issue of a European Constitution and its contents would be safely postponed beyond the June 2004 European elections – perhaps indefinitely. But the tragic Madrid bombings in March 2004 led to the unexpected defeat of José-Maria Aznar's government, which had been one of the major blocks on progress. Bertie Ahern was therefore able to set his sights on winning agreement before the end of the Irish Presidency (30 June 2004). There were rumours of a Blair–Ahern deal, whereby the Irish Prime Minister would soft pedal until the European election campaign was out of the way. If this was true, Mr Ahern demonstrated a poker player's skills, since the overall deal would also be linked to the nomination of the next President of the European Commission (see below). In the event, on 18 June 2004 – just a week after the European elections, the Heads of State or Government agreed to a document which gave full satisfaction to the British government and its 'red lines', as well as answering the objections and preoccupations of the Spanish and Polish governments and other member states.

The draft Constitutional Treaty largely took over the text proposed by the European Convention. There was, perhaps, less to it than met the eye. In particular, its work of rationalising the previous Treaty structure was far from comprehensive and, to take one example, even its admirers were critical of the confusing profusion of arrangements for the Presidency of the Council. Nevertheless, the draft Constitution was seen as a progressive compromise which deserved to be adopted – as M. Giscard d'Estaing put it himself, the results of the Convention were 'unsatisfactory but far better than had been expected'.

As Bertie Ahern made quiet progress, the quandary arose for the Labour government as to how to 'sell' the anticipated result. Was the draft a major new constitutional departure – if so, the case for a referendum would be strong – or was it more a matter of putting into order existing provisions and a relatively modest preparation for enlargement? The government, wary of stirring latent Euroscepticism and of committing itself to a further referendum, opted for the latter approach. The message went out to government spokesmen and party activists that this was no new major constitutional departure but, rather, a 'tidying up' exercise (and this message was delivered loyally until Prime Minister Blair's volte-face on the eve of the European election campaign). Sceptics argued that the government felt more comfortable with its large parliamentary majority than with the unknown of a referendum campaign.

As Simon Buckby had presciently pointed out in his resignation comments, polls seemed to indicate that in the 1999–2004 period a groundswell of opposition to the single currency had been diverted and joined up with a deeper underlying opposition to further European integration, as symbolised by the prospect of a draft European Constitution. As with the 'No' campaign against the single currency, this deeper opposition was given organisational expression through a campaigning organisation, Vote 2004, which described itself as a 'pro-democracy coalition'. Vote 2004 was well-organised and seemed well-resourced. A number of figures who had been active in the 'No' campaign were also active in Vote 2004. The campaign's strategy was simply to bring pressure to bear on the government to 'give the people a referendum'. It set up an attractive and dynamic website, listed its supporters, identified those MPs and political parties which had already come out in favour of a referendum, organised targeted poster campaigns, developed free literature and videos and commissioned opinion polls.

The polls, linked with judiciously timed press releases, were probably the campaign's most effective activity. On the morning of the 12–13 December 2003 Brussels Inter-Governmental Conference, the *Guardian* published an article with the headline 'Labour risking seats on euro poll'. Vote 2004 argued that Labour could lose as many as ten European parliamentary seats because of the government's refusal to agree to a referendum on the draft Constitution and produced convincing polling evidence to support its argument. An ICM poll of 1,000 voters had shown that 83% thought that there should be a referendum. The poll showed that 79% of Labour voters backed a referendum and it also showed that 64% of respondents would be 'quite' or 'very angry' if the government refused to hold a referendum. Asked about voting intentions for the European elections, 39% would vote Labour (compared to 30% Conservative and 24% Liberal Democrat), but asked how they would vote if they knew that the Conservatives and the Liberal Democrats favoured a referendum, the figure became 34% Labour (34% Conservative and 24% Liberal Democrat). Labour's focus groups were telling a similar story.

When the U-turn came (see Chapter 3), Vote 2004's website adopted a quietly satisfied tone. 'Job done', it declared; 'Vote 2004 has now ceased operations following its success in campaigning for a referendum…' It was redolent of the similarly triumphant announcement that had appeared on the 'No' campaign website ('"no" suspends active campaigning after Budget announcement ends prospect of referendum in foreseeable future').[14]

The 1999–2004 Prodi Commission

The 1999 Prodi Commission came into office in the wake of the Santer Commission's resignation. Reform was necessarily at the heart of its agenda and Britain's two Commissioners were intimately involved in the process. Former Labour leader Neil Kinnock, a Commission Vice-President, drove through a programme of root-and-branch reform of the administration and, together with Budget Commissioner, Michele Schreyer, of the Commission's financial procedures. It was a thankless task and one which Mr Kinnock undertook with a heavy heart (Westlake, 2001, p. 699). It engendered a long period of introspection and a diversion of human resources towards internal procedures. But by 2004 Mr Kinnock could claim that most of the reform programme – essential to the Commission's future role – had been achieved. The British media eagerly focused in on Mr Kinnock when a senior Commission official, Marta Andreasen, was suspended, apparently for publicly criticising the Commission's accounting system. Mr Kinnock defended the Commission's position – reforms were well under way, Marta Andreasen had not respected her statutory responsibilities (it was strongly argued that she had been hired to sort out the very problems to which she had drawn attention), but Mrs Andreasen found some support in the European Parliament, particularly in the person of Conservative MEP Christopher Heaton-Harris, who had specialised in anti-fraud and anti-corruption issues.

The former Conservative Party Chairman Chris Patten had meanwhile acted as head of the Commission's external relations portfolio. It was a difficult role in a difficult period. Mr Patten, too, drove through a major reform of the European Union's external aid policy. In previous Commissions his portfolio responsibilities had been divided between a number of Commissioners, and because of the huge scope of his responsibilities Mr Patten was obliged to travel extensively. He also had to 'co-habit' with the new High Representative of the EU's Common Foreign and Security Policy, former Spanish Foreign Minister and NATO Secretary General, Javier Solana. Mr Patten, who brought large quantities of plain language and common sense to his role, made occasional forays into journalism. He won much respect on the Continent for his criticism of the United States' unilateralist tendencies. In March 2003 he was elected to succeed Lord Jenkins as Chancellor of Oxford University, and it seemed that his political career was over, but there was to be a momentary spark in the embers ...

History may be kinder to the Prodi Commission than contemporary commentary. Romano Prodi himself became the butt of much criticism in the British media. His English was heavily accented and his manner donnish (he was a Bologna University economics professor). He was prone to 'gaffes'. He could be outspoken. He was said to have his heart in Italian politics and to harbour ambitions to return as the leader of a centre-left coalition able to oust Silvio Berlusconi – and indeed, it later transpired that at least part of his heart *had* remained in domestic Italian politics. The British media was also swift to report his federalist utterances and to portray him as a centraliser in the Delors mould.

Despite all of this, the Prodi Commission could point to an impressive record of achievements. The transition to the third stage of economic and monetary union, with the introduction of euro notes and coins and the rapid phasing out of national currencies, had been achieved on time and without any major hitches. The steely Competition Commissioner, Mario Monti, had taken on and won against some of the major concentrations in the world.

The negotiations leading to the unprecedented 2004 admission of ten new member states had been ably managed by the Commission. A major new policy towards the European Union's 'new neighbours' had been elaborated and implemented. Trade Commissioner Pascal Lamy had helped the World Trade Organisation's Doha Round of trade liberalisation talks reach a successful preliminary conclusion. Antonio Vitorino had taken on the Commission's fresh responsibilities in the new policy area of cooperation in justice and home affairs with aplomb. And all of this – and much more – had been achieved whilst Vice-President Kinnock was driving through major administrative and financial reforms. It was a considerable set of achievements, but the Commission was nevertheless seen as having been weakened politically and critical articles continued to surface in the British media.

In early 2004 speculation grew about the likely identity of Romano Prodi's successor. By the time the June 2004 European election campaign began, the speculation had reached a crescendo. Until 1999, the President of the European Commission was nominated unanimously by the member state governments, then subjected to a vote of approval in the European Parliament before member states, together with the President, nominated the other members of the college and the President-elect attributed portfolios (subject to the agreement of the college). The college as a whole was then subject to a confirmation vote in the Parliament. By 2004 two rules of the game had changed. In formal terms, the Nice Treaty changes meant that the nomination of the President could now be made by qualified majority. In informal terms, the leader of the EPP-ED Group (numerically the largest) in the European Parliament, Hans-Gert Poettering, made a number of increasingly assertive comments about how the choice should reflect the results of the forthcoming European elections – which were widely expected to give the Christian Democrats continued status as the largest grouping. In making these demands Mr Poettering was anticipating the provisions of the draft European Constitution. Though the Irish Presidency, which had primary responsibility for finding a suitable candidate, publicly refused to acknowledge such a condition, it was clearly an important consideration. There were other traditions: presidents from large member states were traditionally followed by presidents from small ones; from the left by from the right. From the early 1990s onwards there was also an unwritten agreement among member states that the candidate should be an acting or former Prime Minister.

Taken together, these conditions greatly narrowed the field. A number of attractive potential candidates – Antonio Vitorino notable among them – fell by the wayside because they did not satisfy all of the conditions. Other potential candidates who satisfied all of the conditions – most notably Luxembourg Prime Minister Claude Juncker and Irish Prime Minister Bertie Ahern – repeatedly ruled themselves out. For a long time Belgian Prime Minister Guy Verhofstadt appeared to be a frontrunner, but in due course his candidature was reported to have been vetoed by Mr Blair. Then, in May, the

EPP's leaders, meeting in Meise, decided to push Chris Patten as a compromise proposal, apparently with British government backing, only for him to be vetoed by President Chirac – ostensibly on the grounds that his French language abilities were insufficient. But there was general recognition that it would be impossible for an Englishman to be President of the European Commission for as long as sterling had not joined the single currency.

The speculation about a Patten candidature had a knock-on effect on the speculation about who would be the United Kingdom's Commissioner (the Nice Treaty had reduced the number of Commissioners from the five larger member states from two to one). Early frontrunners included Helen Liddell (there was pressure on member state governments to nominate more women) but she accepted the government's nomination to become High Commissioner to Australia. Robin Cook who, following his resignation from the government on principle (see below), had presided over the pan-European Party of European Socialists, was considered a strong potential candidate, but since that point of principle was the American invasion of Iraq, of which he was still very critical, his chances seemed slim. London-based journalists speculated that the beleaguered Defence Secretary, Geoff Hoon (a former MEP), might be sent to Brussels (with Patricia Hewitt taking his place), and then that Patricia Hewitt might be sent instead. The rumours swirled up to the House of Lords (Baroness Amos and Baroness Scotland) and then out to the business world ('a businessman').

All this time, though, an eminently suitable potential candidate was waiting in the wings. Peter Mandelson had twice been forced to resign from the government benches and it was felt that the way back had been permanently barred. Soon after his second resignation in January 2001, rumours began to circulate that Mr Mandelson was being thought of as a potential successor to Neil Kinnock and Chris Patten ...

The European Parliament, 1999–2004

Main developments

The 1999–2004 Parliament differed from its predecessors in one important respect. From 1984 through to 1999, the two largest groups within the Parliament, the Socialists and the Christian Democrats, had worked together on the basis of a 'technical agreement'. This enabled the Parliament to achieve the absolute majorities it required in order to use its legislative and budgetary powers. It also enabled the two groups to engage in a systematic share-out of the major patronage prizes in the Parliament, from the Presidency through to the rapporteurship on the budget. As far as the Presidency was concerned, the two groups agreed to alternate. But in 1999 the electoral mathematics changed. The EPP became the largest political group in the Parliament for the first time since 1979, and it was able to forge a new agreement with the liberals (ELDR) whereby an EPP Presidency (Nicole Fontaine) in the first half of the mandate would be followed by an ELDR Presidency (Pat Cox) in the second half of the mandate. Mrs Fontaine's Presidency was considered uneventful, but Pat Cox, an amiable, charismatic and eloquent Irishman, was elected (his main opponent was David Martin) on a reform and communication platform, and over the next two and a half years he put his skills to good use, generally raising the profile of the Parliament but insisting that agreement had to be reached on the vexed issue of the common statute for members (see next chapter).

The British contingent in the 1999–2004 Parliament was more varied than in previous Parliaments (see Table 1.2); there was British membership of five political groups (see Table 1.3).

Table 1.2 European Parliament election results in the United Kingdom, 1979–99[a]

	Con	Lab	Lib/Lib Dem	PC/SNP	Other	Total
Share of vote (%):						
1979	48.8%	31.6%	12.6%	2.4%	4.9%	100%
1984	38.8%	34.8%	18.5%	2.5%	5.4%	100%
1989	33.5%	38.7%	5.9%	3.3%	18.5%	100%
1994	26.9%	42.6%	16.1%	4.1%	10.2%	100%
1999	33.5%	26.3%	11.9%	4.6%	23.8%	100%
Seats won:						
1979	60	17	0	1	3	81
1984	45	32	0	1	3	81
1989	32	45	0	1	3	81
1994	18	62	2	2	3	87
1999	36	29	10	4	8	87

[a] For relative votes in Scotland and Wales, 1999–2004, see Table 6.4.

Source: Parliamentary Research Services, *British Electoral Facts 1832–1999*.

The Conservatives

The Conservatives continued with their semi-detached alliance with the EPP Group (the so-called Malaga Agreement – see Chapter 3) and they were able to win some influence from their status as the second-largest national contingent within the group. Nevertheless, their effectiveness as a group was hampered by the strongly Eurosceptical line taken by the Hague and Duncan Smith leaderships and by the divisions between Eurosceptics and Euro-enthusiasts within the contingent itself. The leadership of Edward McMillan-Scott was considered to be an important stabilising influence, but in December 2001 he was displaced by an alliance between Europhiles and Eurosceptics which, it was reported, enabled former Conservative Under-Secretary of State Jonathan Evans to grab the leadership (by one vote) and the more Eurosceptical Theresa Villiers to become his deputy. However, Mr Evans proved to be an equally stabilising influence and his personal friendship with Michael Howard proved a

Table 1.3   British membership of European Parliament political groups (in 2003)

Political group	British political parties	No. of seats
Group of the European People's Party (Christian Democrats) and European Democrats (EPP-ED)	Conservative Party	36
	Ulster Unionist Party (UUP)	1
Group of the Party of European Socialists (PES)	Labour Party	28
	Social Democrat and Labour Party (SDLP)	1
European Liberal, Democratic and Reformist Group (ELDR)	Liberal Democrats	11
Group of the Greens/European Free Alliance	Green Party	2
	Scottish National Party (SNP)	2
	Plaid Cymru	2
Europe of Democracies and Diversities (EDD)	UK Independence Party (UKIP)	2
Non-attached members	Democratic Unionist Party (DUP)	1
	Independent (ex-UKIP)	1

vital factor in maintaining the Tories' loose pragmatic relationship with the Christian Democrats in the run up to the elections. Among British Tory office-holders in the European Parliament during the period should be noted: James Provan, who served as a Vice-President of the Parliament; Caroline Jackson, who proved a high-profile Chair of the influential Environment Committee; Struan Stevenson, Chair of the Fisheries Committee; James Elles, a Vice-President of the EPP-ED Group; Giles Chichester, John Corrie and Roy Perry, who served as Group Coordinators (a little known but very influential policy coordination role); Edward McMillan-Scott, President of the Inter-Parliamentary Delegation with the European Economic Area; Robert Sturdy, President of the EU-Canada (1999–2002) and EU-Australia and New Zealand Inter-Parliamentary Delegations (2002–04); Christopher Beazley, President of the EU-Estonia Inter-Parliamentary Delegation (2002–04); and John Corrie, President of the ACP-EU Joint Assembly (2002–04). It should also be noted that Roy Perry was a frontrunning, though ultimately unsuccessful, candidate for the position of European Ombudsman.

Labour

In numerical terms, Labour MEPs' influence had waned in comparison with the 1994–99 Parliament, but the contingent was more cohesive than its Conservative counterpart. There were no tensions behind the surprise resignations of Alan Donnelly and then Simon Murphy as EPLP leaders, though the dysfunctional aspects of the Parliament's peripatetic lifestyle gave all food for thought. The experienced Gary Titley provided a safe pair of hands and, like his predecessors, worked well with the Labour government. Among British Labour office-holders in the European Parliament during the period should be noted: David Martin, who served as Vice-President until 2002 and was a strong candidate for the Parliament's Presidency in that year; Terry Wynn, who provided authoritative chairmanship of the Parliament's Budgets Committee (and was spoken of as a potential candidate for the 2004–06 Presidency of the Parliament); Eryl McNally, Stephen Hughes, Brian Simpson and Richard Corbett, who acted as Group Coordinators; Mel Read, President of the EU-US Interparliamentary Delegation (1999–2002); Gary Titley, President of the EU-Lithuania Inter-Parliamentary Delegation (1999–2002); Gordon Adam, President of the EU-Lithuania Inter-Parliamentary Delegation (2002–04); and Glenys Kinnock, who acted as an influential and highly visible President of the ACP-EU Joint Assembly (2002–04).

The Liberal Democrats

With their ten members (eleven after William Newton Dunn's defection – see Appendix 1.2), Britain's Liberal Democrats seemed to be on a roll. In early 2002, Graham Watson was elected to the leadership of the ELDR Group, following Pat Cox's election to the Presidency of the Parliament. Given the post-1999 'technical agreement' between the EPP and the numerically inferior ELDR Groups, this frequently gave Mr Watson a power-broking role for the second half of the mandate. Diana Wallis was elected leader of the British Liberal Democrat contingent to succeed him. Among British Liberal Democrat office-holders in the European Parliament should be noted: Graham Watson who, until 2002, served as an influential President of the Committee on Civil Liberties and Home Affairs; Baroness Ludford, Chris Huhne, Diana Wallis, Nick Clegg, Elspeth Attwooll and Andrew Duff, who acted as Group Coordinators; Baroness Emma Nicholson, President of the EU-Australia and New Zealand Inter-Parliamentary Delegation (1999–2002) and then President of the Inter-Parliamentary Delegation with the United States (2002–04); and Diana Wallis, President of the Inter-Parliamentary Delegation with the European Economic Area (2002–04). Andrew Duff's energetic role as a learned and committed member of the Praesidium of the Convention gave him a high media profile.

The Greens, the SNP and Plaid Cymru

The two Scottish and one Welsh Nationalist MEPs found themselves in the novel situation of sharing group membership with the two British Green MEPs, but there was recognition from the outset that the alliance could only work if it remained sufficiently loose and there were therefore no major frictions. Caroline Lucas (Green), Jean Lambert (Green), Neil MacCormick (SNP) and Eurig Wyn (Plaid Cymru) all acquitted their roles as Group Coordinators with energy and commitment. Like the Liberal Democrat Andrew Duff, Neil MacCormick's role as a member of the Praesidium of the Convention gave him a high media profile.

The UK Independence Party

Dogged initially by internal tensions, the three-man UK Independence Party contingent elected in 1999 was reduced to just two when Michael Holmes withdrew from the Group in March 2000. The two remaining UK Independence Party MEPs wielded little influence in the EDD Group, where Dane Jens-Peter Bonde was, as leader, by far the more dominant component. Graham Booth's arrival in 2003 (see Appendix 1.2) came too late for the UK Independence Party to augment its influence, but influence in Brussels and Strasbourg had never been the UK Independence Party's main aim. As Nigel Farage put it:

> Jeffrey Titford and I, helped by Graham Booth for the last 18 months, would regard our major achievement during that time not in terms of what was done in Brussels and Strasbourg. We spent the five years touring the UK, using the MEP title and speaking at literally hundreds of events. Our focus was ... to build our membership. (Correspondence with the authors)

Nevertheless, Jeffrey Titford (Budgetary Control) and Nigel Farage (Fisheries) acted as their group's spokesmen.

The 1999 European elections in the United Kingdom

Despite the introduction of PR on a nationwide scale for the first time, the 1999 European elections were a quiet affair (see Table 1.4). Turnout was just 23%: only 6.3% of Britain's total electorate voted Labour, 8.3% for the Conservatives. For the first time since 1992 and just two years after their crushing 1997 General Election defeat, the Conservatives beat Labour in a national election. In England, they topped the poll in seven out of the nine regions (Labour led them only in London and the North East). Counting the votes on a Westminster constituency basis, the Conservatives 'won' 352 seats to Labour's 261 and the Liberal Democrats' 3 – which would have represented a Conservative 'gain' of 144 seats from Labour and 40 from the Liberal Democrats compared with the 1997 General Election.

William Hague's Conservative Party inevitably portrayed the result as a victory, though it soon became clear that this had been an autumnal break in the clouds rather than spring sunshine. The 'victory' dispelled questions about Mr Hague's leadership for a while but the Eurosceptical tack the party had taken was insufficiently salient to the electorate to give the party a fighting chance at the next General Election.

The 1999 result caused some resentment among those sitting Labour MEPs who lost their seats but felt that they would have been returned if first-past-the-post had been retained. But Labour emotions had mainly focused on the preceding selection process, where a number of incumbent MEPs had failed to gain a winnable slot on the regional lists. The outcome of the

Table 1.4 Results of the 10 June 1999 European elections in the United Kingdom

	Votes	%	MEPs
Great Britain:			
Conservative	3,578,203	35.8	36
Labour	2,803,820	28.0	29
Liberal Democrat	1,266,549	12.7	10
Plaid Cymru	185,235	1.9	2
SNP	268,528	2.7	2
UKIP	696,055	7.0	3
Green	625,378	6.3	2
BNP	102,644	1.0	
Others	475,841	4.7	
Total votes cast	10,002,253		84
Turnout		23.1	
Northern Ireland: (1st pref. votes)			
DUP	192,762	28.4	1
SDLP	190,731	28.1	1
UUP	119,507	17.6	1
Sinn Féin	117,643	17.3	
PUP	22,494	3.3	
UKIP	20,283	3.0	
Alliance Party	14,391	2.1	
NLP	998	0.1	
Total votes cast	678,809		3
Turnout		57.0	

Source: Parliamentary Research Services, *British Electoral Facts 1832–1999*.

election played its part in the postponement of the Labour government's proposed referendum on the single currency (see above), but was otherwise insignificant, as the 2001 General Election result demonstrated crushingly.

At face value, the Liberal Democrats fared well, winning ten seats, but they had lost one sitting MEP and, in Westminster terms, had 'won' just three constituencies. They won 55,000 fewer votes than the combined totals of the UK Independence Party and the Greens. Nevertheless, PR had at last delivered them a significant platform within the European Parliament.

The Scottish National Party performed well, coming within 15,000 votes of toppling Labour from first place, but the party was still 5 points down on its vote share in the 1994 European elections. Plaid Cymru did very well, winning 25,000 more votes than in the 1997 General Election, despite a much lower turnout. But the real winners in 1999 were the United Kingdom Independence Party and the Green Party, which won three and two seats respectively. The UK Independence Party won the sixth seat (out of seven) in the South West region; the eighth seat (out of eleven) in the South East; and the last seat in the Eastern region. It was a highly significant but nevertheless tenuous breach. The Greens won the last seats in the London and the South East regions.

In Northern Ireland Sinn Féin increased its share of first-preference votes by 7.4 points compared with the 1994 European elections. Over the same period support for the Ulster Unionist Party fell by 6.2 points. Dramatically, the SDLP's John Hume came within just 2,000 votes of displacing the DUP leader, Ian Paisley, as the politician with the greatest number of votes.

The result was a false dawn for the Conservatives, but one trend was to continue into the following General Election. The low turnout in June 1999 foreshadowed the lowest turnout in a General Election since 1918; only 59.1% of the electorate voted in June 2001. Such low levels of participation raised serious questions about the state of the nation's political health. Was low turnout a function of contentment or, more worryingly, indifference or cynicism? Whichever, the Labour government was deeply concerned by a trend which could, if continued, undermine the legitimacy of British governance.

Appendix 1.1: Chronology, 1999–2004

1999

10 Jun	UK European elections: 36 Con, 29 Lab, 10 Lib Dem, 3 UKIP, 3 Green, 2 SNP and 2 PC. Turnout only 23%.
12 Jun	British troops enter Kosovo.
20–23 Jul	New European Parliament elects Nicole Fontaine President.
21 Jul	New Prodi Commission informally presented to the EP.
1 Aug	EU lifts ban on British beef exports; France and Germany continue ban.
4 Aug	G. Robertson appointed NATO Secretary-General.
9 Aug	C. Kennedy succeeds P. Ashdown as Lib Dem Leader.
8 Sep	Outgoing 'caretaker' Santer Commission meets for the last time.
15 Sep	EP votes to approve the new Prodi Commission. Vice-President N. Kinnock is responsible for administrative reform.
4 Oct	Austria's far-right Freedom Party comes second in Austrian General Elections.
11 Oct	Cabinet reshuffle: P. Mandelson NI Sec.; G. Hoon to Defence.
29 Oct	European Commission orders France to lift its ban on British beef exports.
15 Nov	600 Hereditary Peers mark their last day as members of the House of Lords.
16 Nov	European Commission launches case against France over British beef ban.
21 Nov	J. Archer stands down as Con Candidate for Mayor of London.

21 Nov	Sitting Con MEP W. Newton Dunn defects to Lib Dems.
29 Nov	NI Executive established with D. Trimble as First Minister.
10–11 Dec	Helsinki European Council decides on agenda of Inter-Governmental Conference on the 'Amsterdam leftovers'.
13 Dec	C. Kennedy ends joint Cabinet Committee meetings with Labour.
15 Dec	A. Donnelly, leader of Labour's MEPs resigns. Replaced as MEP by G. Adam.
17 Dec	European Fisheries ministers agree large reductions in EU fishing quotas.
31 Dec	B. Yeltsin announces resignation and Russian President, V. Putin succeeds him.
31 Dec	P. Green resigns from EP. Replaced as MEP by M. Honeyball.

2000

1 Jan	UK switches to metric measurements in shops.
12 Jan	S. Murphy elected new leader of Labour MEPs.
30 Jan	P. Kilfoyle resigns from government to become 'critical friend'.
9 Feb	A. Michael resigns as Welsh First Secretary and is succeeded by R. Morgan.
11 Feb	P. Mandelson suspends NI Executive and restores direct rule from London.
14 Feb	Special ministerial meeting launches the 2000 Inter-Governmental Conference.
17 Feb	M. Portillo appointed Shadow Chancellor.
20 Feb	Lab selects F. Dobson 51%–49% over K. Livingstone to stand for London Mayor.
27 Feb	Labour Party celebrates centenary.
29 Feb	NI Executive resumes office on IRA promise to put arms 'beyond use'.
1 Mar	European Commission adopts White Paper on Commission reform.
23–24 Mar	Lisbon European Council meeting.
27 Mar	V. Putin wins Presidential election with 52.5% of the vote.
4 Apr	K. Livingstone deemed to have expelled himself from the Labour Party.
4 May	K. Livingstone elected as London Mayor.
4 May	Lib Dems win Romsey by-election. Cons advance in local elections.
9 May	45 Lab MPs defy government over privatising air traffic control.
20 May	T. Blair's son, Leo, born.
7 Jun	T. Blair slow hand-clapped as he speaks to the WI Annual Conference.

27 Jul	Government publishes ten-year plan for the NHS.
3 Aug	Chancellor G. Brown marries.
8 Sep	Blockade of fuel depots causes crisis and Labour poll slump.
28 Sep	Danish public reject joining the euro in a referendum: 53.1%–46.9%.
2 Oct	European Convention on Human Rights incorporated into English law.
5 Oct	S. Milosevic deposed as President of Yugoslavia.
11 Oct	Labour's Scottish First Minister D. Dewar dies. Succeeded by H. McLeish.
11 Oct	C. Kennedy calls for abolition of tuition fees.
13–14 Oct	Biarritz informal European Council meeting debates Austria, the IGC and endorses the EU Charter of Fundamental Rights against background of UK government concerns.
17 Oct	Hatfield train crash causes massive disruption.
7 Nov	US Presidential election produces unclear result.
29 Nov	Political Parties Elections and Referendums Act becomes law.
30 Nov	J. Chirac and T. Blair in pre-Nice IGC summit meeting.
7–9 Dec	Nice European Council meeting 'proclaims' the EU's Charter of Fundamental Human Rights and agrees Treaty modifications.
15 Dec	A. Gore concedes Presidential victory to G. Bush.

2001

7 Jan	T. Blair on *Breakfast with Frost* says joining euro 'sensible in principle'.
18 Jan	Fox hunting ban passes Second Reading by 387 to 174.
19 Jan	UK Electoral Commission formally established.
20 Jan	G. Bush succeeds W. Clinton as US President.
24 Jan	P. Mandelson resigns over Hinduja passports affair.
28 Jan	Con Shadow Chancellor M. Portillo announces changes to taxation politics.
29 Jan	C. Kennedy refuses a Lib-Lab electoral pact for the General Election.
2 Feb	Treasury Committee criticises Chancellor's dominance.
5 Feb	R. Cook endorses euro in *Times* interview.
7 Feb	T. Blair promises euro decision in two years.
14 Feb	W. Hague vows to restore grammar schools.
16 Feb	T. Blair says euro is too big an issue to be wrapped up in election campaign.
20 Feb	First confirmed outbreak of foot-and-mouth disease at an Essex abattoir.
23 Feb	T. Blair has first meeting with President Bush at Camp David.
7 Mar	G. Brown delivers his fifth budget.
9 Mar	Hammond Report clears P. Mandelson over Hinduja passports.

14 Mar	Unemployment falls below 1 million for first time in 25 years.
2 Apr	T. Blair announces local elections will be delayed until 7 June.
25 Apr	G. Brown warns European Commission against 'over-reaching itself' in budgetary matters.
8 May	T. Blair announces General Election for 7 June.
13 May	S. Berlusconi wins Italian General Election.
17 May	Labour launches General Election manifesto.
22 May	At a Conservative rally Mrs Thatcher says she would never scrap sterling.
23 May	EU Commission document calls for greater tax harmonisation.
26 May	Race riots in Oldham.
28 May	L. Jospin speaks of a European *arte de vivre* and calls for a stronger EU.
29 May	R. Prodi calls for EU-wide tax to cover the union's £60 billion a year costs.
29 May	Lib Dems claim opposition role.
7 Jun	General Election: Lab 413 seats, Con 165, Lib Dem 52. Record low turnout.
8 Jun	W. Hague announces resignation.
8 Jun	Reshuffle: J. Straw to Foreign Office; D. Blunkett to Home Office; R. Cook Commons Leader.
12 Jun	P. Hain appointed Minister for Europe.
15–16 Jun	Gothenburg European Council meeting marred by protesters.
7 Jul	Bradford race riots.
14 Jul	Stoke-on-Trent race riots.
16 Jul	100 Labour MPs rebel over Whips' removal of two Select Committee chairmen.
19 Jul	J. Archer found guilty of perjury and sentenced to two years.
6 Aug	IRA agrees a means of decommissioning its weapons.
28 Aug	Teacher shortage declared worst in 40 years.
7 Sep	W. Duisenburg (European Central Bank) warns that growth forecasts too high.
11 Sep	Terrorist attacks on World Trade Center and the Pentagon.
13 Sep	I. Duncan Smith elected Conservative leader.
1 Oct	War on Afghanistan declared.
8 Oct	H. McLeish resigns as Scottish First Minister.
16 Oct	Lord Skidelsky resigns Tory Whip citing 'hysterical' Europhobia.
13 Nov	Kabul captured.
26 Nov	US economy declared to be in official recession.
27 Nov	J. McConnell elected to succeed H. McLeish as Scottish First Minister.
10 Dec	Sitting Labour MP P. Marsden defects to Lib Dems.
14–15 Dec	Laeken European Council meeting launches European Convention process.

2002

1 Jan	Euro notes and coins begin circulating in twelve EU member states.
14 Jan	Government declares that the UK is officially free of foot-and-mouth disease.
29 Jan	President Bush labels Iran, Iraq and N. Korea as an 'axis of evil'.
3 Feb	T. Blair pledges that 'wreckers' will not prevent public service reform.
5 Feb	C. Kennedy calls for voting age to be reduced to 16.
6 Feb	Queen Elizabeth II celebrates the fiftieth anniversary of her accession.
12 Feb	Colin Powell speaks of investigating how to topple Saddam Hussein.
13 Feb	Scottish Parliament outlaws hunting with hounds in Scotland.
14 Feb	President Bush announces his laxer alternative to the Kyoto Protocol.
27 Feb	German statisticians declare German economy to be in recession.
28 Feb	V. Giscard d'Estaing opens the Convention on the Future of Europe in Brussels.
5 Mar	Sitting Labour MEP R. Balfe defects to Cons.
5 Mar	President Bush imposes tariffs of up to 30% on European steel.
18 Mar	Gibraltarians protest as Spain and the UK begin talks on the island's future.
30 Mar	Queen Mother dies.
6 Apr	J-M. Durao Barroso sworn in as PM of Portugal.
16 Apr	Dutch government resigns over 1995 Srebrenica episode.
21 Apr	J-M. Le Pen leads L. Jospin in first round of the French Presidential Election.
5 May	President Chirac wins second term, defeating Le Pen 81%–18%. A. Winterton sacked from Shadow Cabinet after making racist joke.
6 May	Charismatic Dutch populist P. Fortuyn assassinated.
10 May	Potters Bar rail crash kills 77.
17 May	B. Ahern re-elected as PM of Ireland.
28 May	Transport Secretary S. Byers resigns. A. Darling succeeds him.
28 May	P. Boateng as Chief Sec. is first black Cabinet minister.
1 Jun	Four days of celebrations begin for the Queen's Golden Jubilee.
11 Jul	Home Secretary D. Blunkett reclassifies cannabis from Class B to Class C.
16 Jul	IRA publishes a full apology to the families of all its victims.
23 Jul	D. Davis replaced as Conservative Chairman by T. May.
3 Aug	As part of EU membership bid, Turkey abolishes the peace-time death penalty and allows Kurdish broadcasting.

26 Aug	A ten-day UN Summit on Sustainable Development opens in Johannesburg.
27 Aug	Leader of Labour MEPs S. Murphy resigns, citing onerous travel obligations.
4 Sep	G. Titley elected new leader of Labour MEPs.
11 Sep	C. Kennedy becomes first Lib Dem Leader to address TUC annual conference.
12 Sep	President Bush at UN General Assembly calls for rapid action on Iraq.
15 Sep	G. Persson re-elected as PM of Sweden.
22 Sep	G. Schroeder re-elected as German Chancellor.
22 Sep	Countryside Alliance protests at Westminster against banning fox hunting.
24 Sep	In dossier on Iraq T. Blair says that WMD can be used in 45 minutes.
7 Oct	T. May declares Conservatives are seen as 'the Nasty Party'.
12 Oct	183 people killed in Bali Bomb attack.
14 Oct	J. Reid suspends Home Rule in Northern Ireland.
17 Oct	R. Prodi brands the 1997 Stability and Growth Pact as 'stupid'.
19 Oct	Irish Referendum approves the Treaty of Nice.
24 Oct	Education Secretary E. Morris resigns. C. Clarke succeeds her. J. Reid becomes Party Chairman. P. Hain becomes Wales Secretary.
26 Oct	127 people killed when Russian troops storm hijackers in a Moscow theatre.
28 Oct	European Convention publishes its draft constitution. D. MacShane named as new Europe Minister.
4 Nov	J. Bercow resigns from Shadow Cabinet refusing to prevent adoption by gay and unmarried couples.
5 Nov	European Court of Justice rules that bilateral aviation treaties between members and the US violate common market.
8 Nov	Security Council passes Resolution 1441, returning weapons inspectors to Iraq.
13 Nov	Firefighters commence 48 hours of strike action.
21 Nov	Prague NATO summit asks seven Eastern European countries to join the Alliance.
24 Nov	W. Schüssel re-elected Chancellor of Austria. Freedom Party drops to 10%.
2 Dec	EU Health Ministers approve tobacco advertising ban.
3 Dec	EU Finance ministers approve new regulations banning insider trading.
7 Dec	Iraq publishes a 12,000-page denial of WMD.
10 Dec	Cherie Blair apologises over lack of clarity about purchase of two Bristol flats.
11 Dec	Firefighters' union suspends planned eight-day strike.

| 14 Dec | Red Cross camp at Sangatte closes permanently. |
| 17 Dec | Polls show lowest Con ratings for four years. |

2003

5 Jan	Metropolitan Police raids on two London addresses reveal ricin.
21 Jan	Firefighters begin 24-hour strike.
1 Feb	NASA's *Columbia* space shuttle disintegrates in the upper atmosphere.
1 Feb	Treaty of Nice enters into force.
3 Feb	Government publishes its second dossier on Iraqi WMD.
6 Feb	Colin Powell says Iraq is in 'material breach' of UN resolutions.
15 Feb	1 million people march in London in protest against invading Iraq.
17 Feb	Congestion charging scheme begins in London.
24 Feb	Britain, the US and Spain table Security Council resolution on Iraq action.
7 Mar	UK presents new draft Resolution calling for Iraqi compliance by 17 March.
12 Mar	Firefighters' union's executive recommends rejection of employers' offer.
17 Mar	UK, US and Spain attempt to get UN backing for invasion of Iraq.
17 Mar	R. Cook resigns from the government on point of principle.
18 Mar	Commons passes resolution authorising use of British military in Iraq: 412–149.
20 Mar	Bombing of Baghdad begins.
6 Apr	British troops enter Basra.
7 Apr	US troops enter Baghdad after days of heavy bombing.
9 Apr	Statue of Saddam Hussein toppled in centre of Baghdad.
2 May	C. Blunt calls for motion of no confidence in I. Duncan Smith.
12 May	International Development Secretary C. Short resigns.
12 May	Suicide bombers kill 35 at a Riyadh housing complex for Western workers.
13 May	I. Duncan Smith pledges Cons will abolish tuition fees.
20 May	Firefighters' union and employers reach agreement on staged pay offers.
29 May	In BBC *Today* broadcast, A. Gilligan quotes anonymous source to claim government 'sexed up' its September 2002 dossier on Iraq's WMD.
1 Jun	A. Gilligan newspaper article again claims government 'sexed up' dossier.
4 Jun	Israel and Palestine formally adopt the American 'roadmap' to peace.

6 Jun	PM's spokesman A. Campbell complains to the BBC about A. Gilligan's claims.
9 Jun	Treasury assessment of the five tests for joining euro says only one met so far.
12 Jun	Firefighters' union accepts government pay package.
12 Jun	A. Milburn unexpectedly resigns as Health Secretary: J. Reid succeeds; Lord Falconer becomes last Lord Chancellor; Peter Hain becomes Leader of Commons.
19 Jun	A. Gilligan appears before Commons Foreign Affairs Committee.
25 Jun	A. Campbell appears before Commons Foreign Affairs Committee.
26 Jun	A. Campbell issues fresh demand for apology from the BBC.
30 Jun	Government scientist D. Kelly admits speaking to A. Gilligan.
7 Jul	Foreign Affairs Committee concludes A. Campbell did not 'sex up' dossier.
9 Jul	D. Kelly confirmed as A. Gilligan's source by the Ministry of Defence.
15 Jul	D. Kelly appears before the Commons Foreign Affairs Committee.
16 Jul	D. Kelly appears before Commons Intelligence and Security Committee.
18 Jul	D. Kelly found dead near his Oxfordshire home.
18 Jul	T. Blair, in Tokyo, announces Hutton Inquiry.
22 Jul	S. Hussein's sons Uday and Qusay killed by US soldiers in Northern Iraq.
1 Aug	Hutton Inquiry opens into circumstances surrounding Kelly's death.
13 Aug	A. Gilligan appears before Hutton Inquiry.
19 Aug	Massive truck bomb blows up UN HQ, killing top UN envoy S. de Mello.
19 Aug	A. Campbell appears before the Hutton Inquiry.
28 Aug	T. Blair appears before the Hutton Inquiry.
11 Sep	Swedish Foreign Minister A. Lindh stabbed to death in Stockholm.
14 Sep	Sweden votes against the euro, 56–42.
15 Sep	WTO talks in Cancún, Mexico, fail after rich and poor countries cannot agree.
25 Sep	Hutton Inquiry concludes. Lord Hutton begins writing his report.
08 Oct	Arnold Schwarzenegger elected Governor of California.
10 Oct	T. Blair admitted to hospital after suffering heart palpitations.
13 Oct	Standards Commissioner to investigate I. Duncan Smith's office expenses.

24 Oct	Concorde makes its last scheduled flight from New York to London.
28 Oct	Tory leadership election triggered.
29 Oct	Tory leader I. Duncan Smith loses vote 75–90.
6 Nov	M. Howard elected new leader of the Cons Party unopposed.
7 Nov	M. Portillo announces he will stand down as an MP at the next election.
10 Nov	M. Howard announces first Shadow Cabinet reshuffle. D. Davis is Shadow Home Sec., O. Letwin is Shadow Chancellor; L. Fox and C. Saatchi become chairmen.
11 Nov	Cons announce plans to sell lease on Smith Square headquarters.
20 Nov	Two suicide bombers kill British consul and 25 others in Istanbul.
23 Nov	England victory over Australia in Rugby World Cup final.
4 Dec	President Bush repeals US steel tariffs to prevent EU retaliation.
14 Dec	Saddam Hussein captured by US soldiers.
17 Dec	I. Huntley convicted of murdering Jessica Chapman and Holly Wells.
19 Dec	Libya renounces its WMD.
25 Dec	UK space probe *Beagle II* fails to land on Mars.
26 Dec	Earthquake in Bam, Iran, kills 15,000.

2004

3 Jan	Department of Transport orders BA to cancel flight 223.
4 Jan	T. Blair visits UK troops in Basra.
4 Jan	NASA's *Spirit* rover successfully lands on Mars.
6 Jan	Letter bomb explodes in the office of leader of Labour MEPs, Gary Titley.
6 Jan	K. Livingstone readmitted to the Labour Party.
8 Jan	Queen officially launches the *Queen Mary II* from Southampton.
9 Jan	BBC presenter R. Kilroy-Silk sacked for controversial comments on Arabs.
23 Jan	Lib Dem spokeswoman J. Tonge sacked after comments on suicide bombers.
25 Jan	NASA's *Opportunity* rover lands on Mars.
27 Jan	T. Blair wins Commons vote on top-up fees for university education 316–311.
28 Jan	Hutton Report published.
28 Jan	G. Davies, Chairman of the BBC Governors, resigns.
29 Jan	G. Dyke, Director-General of the BBC, resigns.
31 Jan	A. Gilligan resigns as BBC reporter.

1 Feb	President Bush agrees to an independent inquiry on the use of intelligence.
2 Feb	T. Blair announces a British inquiry under Lord Butler.
4 Feb	House of Commons debates the Hutton Report.
16 Feb	Shadow Chancellor O. Letwin lays out plans on tax and spending.
23 Feb	D. Blunkett says accession country migrants free to work, but not to get benefits.
25 Feb	M. Rifkind selected as prospective Con candidate for Kensington & Chelsea (Portillo's seat).
27 Feb	Widespread criticism of former International Development Secretary C. Short after she reveals secret Cabinet papers and alleges Kofi Annan was bugged.
9 Mar	Government approves the first commercial production of GM maize.
11 Mar	199 people killed in Madrid train bombings.
14 Mar	PSOE wins Spanish General Election.
15 Mar	V. Putin re-elected in Russia with 68% of the vote.
15 Mar	New Spanish PM J.L. Rodriguez Zapatero orders Spanish troops out of Iraq.
17 Mar	G. Brown delivers eighth budget.
21 Mar	C. Kennedy dismisses attacks of poor health, but looks ill at party conference.
23 Mar	European Parliamentary Elections Regulations (SI 2004–293) come into force.
25 Mar	M. Campbell regretted not standing in 1999 Lib Dem leadership race: 'for 10 minutes a day'.
31 Mar	Government succeeds on tuition fee increases: 316–288.
1 Apr	Immigration Minister B. Hughes resigns over 'dodgy visas' affair.
1 Apr	Bill on postal voting areas enacted after ping-pong with Lords.

Appendix 1.2: Switches, resignations, replacements and milestones

The 1999–2004 period saw an unusually large number of switches, resignations and replacements in the UK's EP membership.

Unexpectedly, on 15 December 1999, the leader of the European Parliamentary Labour Party, Alan Donnelly, suddenly announced his resignation, not only from the post of leader but from the European Parliament altogether.[15] Mr Donnelly, who had made a significant mark in a short period of time, cited the unreasonable amount of travel involved. His place as an MEP was taken by Gordon Adam, who had been an MEP from 1979 until

June 1999. On 12 January 2000 Simon Murphy was elected as Mr Donnelly's successor to the leadership.

In the meantime, on 31 December 1999, the former leader of the socialist grouping in the Parliament, Pauline Green, announced her resignation from the Parliament. In simple numerical terms the Labour contingent returned in 1999 was insufficient to maintain her in the leadership position (which went to Enrique Baron Crespo, a former President of the Parliament) and her political standing was undermined by the complex situation surrounding the resignation of the Santer Commission. Her outspoken criticism of the Parliament's failure to adopt a members' statute had also lost her support from the German Social Democrats (Butler and Westlake, 2000, pp. 192–3). Unlike Mr Donnelly, Mrs Green was not lost to public life, becoming Chief Executive and General Secretary of Co-operatives UK (formerly the Cooperative Union), and in the 2003 New Year's Honours List she was made a Dame. Her seat in the Parliament was taken up by Mary Honeyball.

In March 2000, following internal disputes, former UK Independence Party leader Michael Holmes MEP (South West region) left the party and joined the 'non-aligned' members within the Parliament. Mr Holmes subsequently suffered a stroke and, battling health problems, finally gave in his resignation as an MEP on 16 December 2002. His place was taken by longstanding UK Independence Party activist and former Party Vice-Chairman, Graham Booth.

On 21 November 1999 sitting Conservative MEP William ('Bill') Newton Dunn, first elected in 1979, defected to the Liberal Democrats, in protest at William Hague's 'hard swing to the right'. Mr Newton Dunn was known to be pro-European and pro-euro and his defection was indicative of the mood within the Conservative Party. Mr Hague, he argued, presided over an 'intolerant and dogmatic' party (*Guardian*, 22 November 2000).

In March 2001 Scottish newspapers reported that Labour MEP David Martin had been forced, on a technicality, to withdraw his candidature for the nomination to become Labour's candidate for the Scottish Parliament seat of Strathkelvin. A by-election was triggered by the decision taken by the incumbent Labour MP, Sam Galbraith, to step down from politics. Mr Martin, an MEP for 17 years, twelve of them as Vice-President, was told by Labour's national executive that he should have asked permission from the executive before throwing his hat into the ring. 'Party sources', reported the *Herald* (28 March 2001), 'said he had fallen victim to internal rivalries between followers of the Chancellor, Gordon Brown, and others.' The successful candidate, Brian Fitzpatrick, was 'widely seen as the favoured candidate of Mr Brown'. The *Herald* reported that 'If Mr Martin had succeeded he would have been seen immediately as ministerial material and possibly as first minister.'

On 5 March 2002, sitting Labour MEP Richard Balfe announced his defection to the Conservative Party, citing the Labour Party's 'growing arrogance and dishonesty' (*European Voice*, 7–13 March 2002). He was the first Labour politician to 'cross the floor' to the Conservatives in 25 years. Mr Balfe was one of the few MEPs who had sat without interruption since 1979. He had scraped into Labour's fourth London seat in 1999, and it was uncertain as to whether the fourth-placed candidate would be returned in 2004. Latterly, he had specialised as one of Parliament's Quaestors, but he had angered the PES Group and EPLP hierarchy by successfully standing twice for election as an 'independent' (thus taking a position which had been promised to another political group), and disciplinary proceedings had been begun against him. He had first left to sit with the non-aligned members in the Parliament 'on a temporary basis to contemplate my future'. But, wrote Michael White in the *Guardian* (7 March), 'the strange case of a pro-European MEP willing to defect to one of the most Eurosceptic groups in the parliament also raised some questions about his motives ...' A 'war of words' broke out in the British press, with Mr Balfe claiming he had been subjected to strong-arm tactics and various Labour figures arguing that Mr Balfe had disqualified himself through his actions.

On 27 August 2002 Simon Murphy resigned his position as leader of the European Labour Party, citing 'the incompatibility of the demands of a young family coupled with the stress of political life'. He announced that he would not stand in the 2004 European elections. On 4 September Gary Titley was elected to succeed him.

On 29 September 2003, Conservative MEP Lord Bethell resigned for health reasons. He had been an MEP for the London constituency since 1999 and previously for the London North West constituency from 1979 to 1994. He was replaced by Ian Twinn, who was the Conservative MP for Edmonton from 1983 to 1997.

Other MEPs unsuccessfully sought election to offices outside the Parliament. Following the 18 June 2003 death of sitting Brent East Labour MP Paul Daisley, Robert Evans MEP was selected as Labour's candidate, but in the 18 September 2003 by-election was sensationally defeated by a 29% swing to the Liberal Democrats. It was Labour's first loss of a parliamentary seat in a by-election for 15 years. A by-election for the elected mayor of North Tyneside took place on 12 June 2003, following the resignation of Conservative mayor Chris Morgan. The by-election returned roughly the same result as the first election a year earlier. Linda Arkley won for the Conservatives with an increased majority of 4,800 votes, ahead of Labour candidate Gordon Adam (who may, it is speculated, have lost some popularity through already being an MEP).

In August 2002 Labour MEP Eryl McNally announced that she would not be seeking re-election. The vast majority of voters in her region had no idea who she was, she argued.

In December 2002, Liberal Democrat East Midlands MEP Nick Clegg, who was considered to be one of the party's brightest prospects in the Parliament, let it be known that he also would not be seeking re-election. Young, charismatic and eloquent, he had previously worked as a member of the Cabinet of the then Sir Leon Brittan, the Trade Commissioner. On 27 November 2003, an op-ed article appeared under Nick Clegg's byline in the *Guardian* under the headline 'Why I am quitting Europe'. Mr Clegg explained that, after a mere three years in the Parliament he had decided not to stand again (he was later selected as the prospective parliamentary candidate for the Westminster seat of Sheffield Hallam) because all of the important European political issues would be resolved 'where all politics begins and ends – at home'. Mr Clegg was one of several 'bright young things' in the 1999–2004 Parliament who turned to domestic politics, triggering much introspection about the attractiveness and effectiveness of the Parliament's work. In the summer of 2004 it was announced that Mr Clegg had joined a Brussels-based consultancy.

On 17 May 2003 London Conservative MEP Theresa Villiers was selected by the Chipping Barnet Conservative Association as its Prospective Parliamentary Candidate to replace Sir Sydney Chapman as the Conservative candidate at the next General Election. On 14 June 2003 South East Liberal Democrat MEP Christopher Huhne was selected as the prospective Parliamentary Candidate for Eastleigh, where the sitting MP, Lib Dem David Chidgey, had announced that he would be retiring at the next General Election. Both Ms Villiers and Mr Huhne were nevertheless selected as candidates for the June 2004 European elections.

As the 1999–2004 European Parliament drew to a close, two major political figures announced that they would not be standing again. In January 2004 DUP leader Ian Paisley announced that he would not be standing in order to concentrate his energies on the next round of the Good Friday peace process talks. In February Foyle MP John Hume announced that he was stepping down altogether from public life on medical grounds. Both Mr Paisley and Mr Hume had served as MEPs since 1979. Mr Hume, who received the Nobel Peace Prize jointly with Ulster Unionist leader David Trimble in 1998, was described by the Parliament's President, Pat Cox, as one of the Parliament's 'most outstanding, respected and longstanding members', with a 'dogged commitment to non-violent conflict resolution'. Mr Hume had stood down from the SDLP leadership in November 2001, citing health reasons. In their different ways, both MEPs had been major figures in the European Parliament.

Notes

1. Simon Buckby, in 7 September 2004 correspondence with the authors.
2. Though Lord Wallace of Saltaire has argued to the authors that the real problem might be distance rather than the second-order nature of the elections: 'Even in the developed federal system of the United States popular attitudes towards remote government in Washington are highly ambivalent.' According to this argument, anti-system parties would tend naturally to do better ...

3. And then, as the authors like to point out, the title of this series would change from 'British Politics and European Elections' to 'European Elections and British Politics'!

4. *Official Journal of the European Union*, L 297, 15.11.2003, pp. 1–4.

5. The decision of the EP's bureau setting out details of the rules governing European political parties was published in OJ C 155 of 12 June 2004. The EP also published two calls for tender for the funding of political parties for (1) 20 July to 31 December 2004 inclusive, and (2) the whole of 2005 (see OJ C 161 of 18 June 2004). To be eligible for funding in 2004, parties had to forward applications by 23 July 2004. For funding in 2005, the deadline was 15 November 2004.

6. Although several MEPs observed to the authors that MEPs are becoming more aware of the possibility of forming cross-party links to deal with regional issues (for example, Scotch whisky and fishing). Another MEP pointed out that, where a party has more than one MEP to a region, MEPs are increasingly dividing up the region so as, in effect, to create 'mini-constituencies'. One MEP argued strongly that 'I do not agree with you about MEPs not knowing what they are doing under the new system. We do. We are representing our regional parties. Our relationship with the national party is dwindling away.'

7. Though there was also a 'European' reason – the obligation to avoid distortion. See Chapter 2.

8. At least one MEP was convinced it was also a deliberate way of kicking PR for Westminster elections into very long grass.

9. 1. Are business cycles and economic structures compatible? 2. If problems emerge, is there sufficient flexibility to deal with them? 3. Would joining economic and monetary union create better conditions for firms making long-term decisions about investment in Britain? 4. What impact would entry into the single currency have on the competitive position of the UK's financial services industry, particularly the City's wholesale markets? 5. Will joining economic and monetary union promote higher growth, stability and a lasting increase in employment?

10. In this context Lord Wallace of Saltaire observes that 'It is extremely difficult to sell the idea of joining a currency zone which has a growth rate considerably lower than your own country, and the behaviour of the French and German governments in undermining the stability pact made the case for joining even more difficult to argue.' This was to have knock-on consequences when the Convention came to consider whether to include the Charter of Fundamental Rights in the Constitutional Treaty – which it did.

11. One of the major debates during the Convention's work concerned the inclusion of social 'rights'; in particular, the argument about whether rights which are not directly enforceable nor justiciable in a court of law should be included.

12. As a national politician sympathetic to Gisela Stuart's views put it to the authors: 'The Convention was perceived as very un-English, and as being presided over by a Machiavellian Frenchman who obviously had, as part of his agenda, the doing down of John Bull. By the time the *Daily Mail* et al. had finished with it, it was discredited in the eyes of the public.'

13. And, to fellow 'Conventioneers', a puzzling one. As one MEP put it: 'Something happened between Gisela's speech at the close of the Convention and her Fabian pamphlet. What was it?' Richard Corbett, a Labour MEP, later issued a pamphlet seeking to rebut Mrs Stuart's arguments (see Corbett, 2004a). For Mrs Stuart's converted view, see Stuart (2003a).

14. On the relationship between Mr Blair's apparent failure to push the pro-European case and the Eurosceptical Murdoch press there has been considerable speculation, some of it seemingly informed. The press pointed in particular to a visit to Downing Street by Mr Irwin Stelzer, a sort of Murdoch envoy, shortly before Mr Blair's referendum decision …

15. Mr Donnelly became the managing director of his own consultancy company. Two former Labour MEPs, Carole Tongue (1984–99) and Baroness Billingham (1994–99) are fellow board members.

2
Framework

The complexity of a dual framework

All elections take place in a framework provided by a combination of law, regulation, tradition and habit. European elections are no different in this respect; but the framework within which they take place is rendered more complex by the fact that, as pointed out in Chapter 1, the elections take place in both a European and a national context. This chapter describes both frameworks.

The European framework

Direct and uniform elections

History

The 1957 Treaty of Rome provided that the (initially nominated) Parliament should 'draw up proposals for elections by direct universal suffrage in accordance with a uniform procedure in all Member States' (TEC Article 190). The Union's 'founding fathers' clearly expected direct elections to take place soon after the Rome Treaty entered into force and hence a directly elected Parliament to play its democratic role in the process of European integration. But the immediate prospect was blocked by the return to power in France of Charles de Gaulle (for whom all supranational tendencies were anathema). Even after de Gaulle's 1969 departure discussions continued to be dogged by the twin conditions of directness and uniformity. In 1975 the Parliament proposed separating off the principle of uniformity, which would remain a longer-term goal, from that of directness. This proposal led directly to the breakthrough which enabled the first direct elections to the European Parliament to go ahead in June 1979, some 20 years later than originally envisaged. (Box 2.1 provides a chronology of direct and uniform elections from the Treaty of Rome to 2004.)

Box 2.1   Chronology of direct and uniform elections, 1957–2004

15 Mar 1957	Treaty of Rome signed. EEC comes into being
29 May 1958	President de Gaulle comes to power
Oct 1958	EEC Parliamentary Assembly establishes Working Party to draft Convention – Article 138(3) – now Article 190
10 May 1960	Parliamentary Assembly adopts draft Convention (Dehousse Report)
20 June 1960	Convention forwarded to the Council of Ministers
Nov 1961	First Fouchet Plan
Jan 1962	Second Fouchet Plan
30 May 1962	European Assembly decides to call itself 'European Parliament'
Mar 1969	Parliament 'reminds' Council of its duties
28 April 1969	President de Gaulle resigns
2 Dec 1969	Hague Summit decides to give 'further consideration' to the question of direct elections
1 Jan 1973	UK accedes to the European Community
Jun 1973	Parliament decides to redraft its convention
10 Dec 1974	Paris Summit announces wish that Council should act in 1976, with a view to holding of direct elections 'in or after 1976'
14 Jan 1975	Parliament adopts Patijn Report, which distinguishes between uniformity and directness and sets target date of May 1978
5 Jun 1975	UK referendum votes 67% 'Yes' for continued EC membership
17 Feb 1976	UK government publishes Green Paper
13 Jul 1976	Brussels European Council reaches agreement on number and distribution of seats
3 Aug 1976	Commons Select Committee expresses preference for first-past-the-post
20 Sep 1976	European Assembly Elections act signed. It sets May–June 1978 as period for first direct elections
23 Mar 1977	Lib-Lab Pact
1 Apr 1977	Government publishes White Paper – Cabinet favours regional list system
13 Dec 1977	Commons votes in favour of first-past-the-post (with STV for Northern Ireland)
8 Apr 1978	Copenhagen European Council recognises delay and sets 7–10 June 1979 as period for first direct elections
5 May 1978	UK Direct Elections Bill receives Royal Assent
10 Mar 1982	Parliament adopts Seitlinger Report, which calls for PR in multi-member constituencies. Council fails to act
14–17 Jun 1984	Second direct elections
28 Feb 1985	Bocklet Report on a uniform system adopted in committee, but Parliament ultimately unable to adopt new Convention
15–18 Jun 1989	Third direct elections
10 Oct 1991	First de Gucht Report adopted (rules out identicality)
10 Jun 1992	Second de Gucht Report adopted (recommendations on number and distribution of members)

▶

10 Mar 1993	Parliamentary Resolution abandons uniformity in favour of principle of 'general guidelines'
19 May 1993	Plant Working Party on electoral reform recommends PR for Euro-elections
30 Sep 1993	Shadow Home Secretary Tony Blair promises reform of Euro-elections system if Labour comes to power
1 Nov 1993	Maastricht Treaty enters into force. Article 190 amended to give Parliament assent (veto) powers over draft Convention
9–12 Jun 1994	Fourth direct elections
21 Jul 1994	Tony Blair elected Labour Party Leader
5 Mar 1997	Firm agreement reached by joint Labour-Liberal Democrat Consultative Committee on a regional list system for Euro-elections
1 May 1997	Labour's landslide General Election victory
11 Jun 1997	Home Office Minister Lord Williams declares government has no plans to introduce PR for 1999
1 Jul 1997	Tony Blair and Paddy Ashdown reportedly reach agreement on PR for 1999 Euro-elections during flight back from Hong Kong handover ceremony
15 Jul 1997	Euro-Parliament adopts Anastassopoulos Report. Draft Convention foresees common system for 2004 Euro-elections
17 Jul 1997	Home secretary Jack Straw announces that time will, after all, be found to legislate for PR during first parliamentary session
29 Oct 1997	European Parliament Elections Bill published, providing for PR and closed regional lists
19 Nov 1998	Registration of Political Parties Act receives Royal Assent
14 Jan 1999	European Parliamentary Elections Act receives Royal Assent
28 Apr 1999	European Parliamentary Regulations come into force
1 May 1999	Amsterdam Treaty enters into force. Article 190 amended so as to foresee uniformity or 'principles common to all Member States'
10–13 Jun 1999	Fifth direct elections
25 Jun 2003	The Council, with the European Parliament's assent, adopts a decision amending the 1976 Act, notably introducing common principles. The long search for 'uniformity' is over.

Agreement on the number and distribution of seats was reached at the July 1976 Brussels European Council, and in September 1976 the Act Concerning the Election of the Representatives of the European Parliament by Direct Universal Suffrage was signed by the representatives of the member state governments. The Act built largely on the Parliament's detailed preparatory work. The Parliament was to be elected for a five-year term. The member states would each fix the date for their European elections, but would agree on a common Thursday-to-Sunday period within which all would have to take place. Votes would not be counted until after the close of polling in all member states. Article 7(2) provided that, 'Pending entry into force of a uniform electoral procedure and subject to the other provisions of this Act, the electoral procedure shall be governed in each Member State by its national provisions.'

The problems in finding a uniform procedure were as old as the provision itself, but the 1973 accession of the United Kingdom, with its *sui generis* first-past-the-post electoral tradition, exacerbated matters. Nevertheless, various British governments signed up to the full provisions of the Treaty of Rome and the 1976 Act. Since other member states' systems were broadly similar, it was clear that the United Kingdom would sooner or later have to make some obeisance to the Continental PR tradition. Nevertheless, after a protracted passage through the British Parliament, the initial implementing legislation provided firmly for the first-past-the-post system to be used, with the exception of Northern Ireland where, because of its particular circumstances, the single transferable vote was preferred.

The June 1979 UK European elections provided immediate proof of the distorting effects of first-past-the-post, with the Conservatives winning 60 of the 78 mainland seats, to Labour's 17. Although they won 12.6% of the vote, the Liberals won no seats. Together with three token Danish Conservatives the British Conservatives were able to form the third largest grouping in the 1979–84 European Parliament, displacing the Liberals. This and other distortions created resentments and a desire for change within the European Parliament. Several proposals were put forward throughout the 1980s by the European Parliament but were stymied, primarily by British resistance to any departure from first-past-the-post.

In the early 1990s the European Parliament adopted a fresh approach, seeking to establish 'general guidelines' rather than a perfectly uniform system. As the Parliament's rapporteur at the time, Belgian Liberal Karel de Gucht, put it, the object of the exercise was to make it 'as difficult as possible for the UK to say no', even extending to provisions which would have allowed for the traditional over-representation of Scotland and Wales. But little progress was made in the Council, and the 1994 European elections were therefore held under the same diverse conditions as the 1979, 1984 and 1989 elections.

The 1993 Maastricht Treaty amended TEC Article 190, granting the European Parliament assent powers (that is, a veto) over any draft Council decision for a uniform procedure. Henceforth the Parliament would, at the least, be master of its own destiny. The Amsterdam Treaty further amended TEC Article 190 by providing that the European Parliament should draw up a proposal for direct elections either in accordance with a uniform procedure in all member states *or* 'in accordance with principles common to all member States'. Thus encouraged, in 1997 the European Parliament made a further set of proposals (the Anastassopoulos Report). The Anastassopoulos Report was effectively a declaration of preference for common principles over a uniform procedure. The report also recognised that progress and convergence would be more likely to come in small steps rather than a single 'big bang'.

Like its predecessors, the Parliament's report was forwarded to the Council for consideration.

The introduction of PR in the UK

There had meanwhile been significant developments on the domestic front. Neil Kinnock, Labour Party Leader until 1992, had personally come to favour PR. In 1990, at his impulse, the Labour Party set up a Working Party under Raymond (later Lord) Plant to consider all elections. The majority opinion in the 1993 Plant Report recommended that a regional list system should be used for European elections. Tony Blair, then Shadow Home Secretary, promised the September 2003 Labour Party Conference that the voting system for the European Parliament would be reformed. In March 1997 a joint Labour-Liberal Democrat Consultative Committee, jointly chaired by Robin Cook and Robert Maclennan, was able to announce that firm agreement had been reached on a regional list system and, at a subsequent press conference, Robin Cook declared Labour's intention, were it to be elected, of introducing PR in time for the 1999 European elections. Following Labour's 1997 landslide victory, the need for cooperation with the Liberal Democrats proved less evident. Mr Blair nevertheless went ahead with his commitment, despite the certain knowledge that the new system would cost several sitting Labour MEPs their seats (Butler and Westlake, 2000).

The draft Bill proved controversial. It provided for the election of MEPs through closed lists in eleven regions using the d'Hondt system,[1] with STV retained for Northern Ireland. There were protracted discussions over the definition of regions and the number of members attributed to them. By far the most heated debate related to the closed list system, which critics saw as favouring party machines over voters' preferences. After a fraught and turbulent passage through Parliament, with the Bill being taken hostage by the Lords, it was guillotined through Parliament in December 1998, leaving little time for implementation before the June 1999 European elections. One of the casualties of the accelerated process was a Commons' amendment promising a review after the 1999 election. In the event, there was little appetite to look at the system again, and so the basic framework for the 2004 European elections remained the same.

The European-level framework in 2004 – uniformity in diversity

Whilst there was reluctance at the domestic level to review this recent piece of constitutional reform, there was significant progress at European level. On the one hand, the British government's decision to switch to PR had removed the single most important distortion in the European elections; on the other, Parliament's 1997 report had already recognised that the imminent enlargement of the Union to absorb ten new member states would make the adoption of an entirely uniform procedure even less likely. This new pragmatism, as embodied in the general principles set out in the Anastassopoulos Report, allowed the Council of Ministers to make quiet progress.

Finally, in 2002 the Council, with the formal assent of the European Parliament, adopted a decision amending the 1976 Act (Council Decision of 25 June and 23 September 2002 amending the Act concerning the election of the representatives of the European Parliament by direct universal suffrage – 2002/772/EC, EURATOM). The Act was necessary, declared the Council, in order to 'enable members to be elected by direct universal suffrage in accordance with principles common to all Member States while leaving Member States free to apply their national provisions in respect of aspects not governed by the Decision'. There were some significant changes, but the basic approach was effectively to allow more openly for the differences in national systems. The 2002 Act referred explicitly to TEC Article 190 and received the required assent of the European Parliament. This meant, therefore, that the long search for uniformity, as originally enshrined in the 1957 Rome Treaty, was over.

The saga had ended in anticlimax but the 1999–2004 Parliament's attention had in any case meanwhile become more directly focused on the constitutional reform talks, first in the European Convention and then in the Inter-Governmental Conference (see Chapter 1). Significantly, the draft European Constitution provisions on the European Parliament speak only of direct universal suffrage – there is no longer any reference to uniformity, which has effectively been enshrined as a principle by the Council's 2002 Decision.

The resulting situation, as Table 2.1 demonstrates, was a mixture of commonality, similarity and differences. The variety of different election dates provides a further example of the continuing diversity; Sunday 13 June was chosen as the election date by 17 of the 25 member states, but the Netherlands and the United Kingdom, which traditionally vote on Thursdays (see below), opted for 10 June, while Ireland chose 11 June and Latvia and Malta 12 June. The Czech Republic and Italy, meanwhile, decided to vote 11–12 June and 12–13 June respectively.

Most of the member states designated a single constituency covering the whole of their national territory, whilst seven had a number of constituencies; four in Ireland, five in Italy, eight in France, eleven in Great Britain, thirteen in Poland, and sixteen in Germany (where lists could nevertheless be drawn up at either Länder or federal state level. Belgium had three electoral colleges (French, Dutch and German speaking). The majority of member states had no minimum threshold, but nine had a 5% threshold, two 4% and one 3%. Fourteen member states allowed voting for candidates from different party lists or preferential voting for one or more candidates. Others, including the UK, applied systems of closed lists and in Ireland, Malta and Northern Ireland, seats would be decided using the single transferable vote (STV) system.

Table 2.1   Electoral systems for the June 2004 European elections[a]

Member states	Number of MEPs	Electoral system	Can people choose between MEPs in the same party?	Number of constituencies	Electoral threshold (%)
Austria	18	List-PR	•	1	4
Belgium	24	List-PR	•	3	–
Cyprus	6	List-PR	•	1	–
Czech Republic	24	List-PR	•	1	5
Denmark	14	List-PR	•	1	–
Estonia	6	List-PR	•	1	–
Finland	14	List-PR	•	1	–
France	78	List-PR	x	8	5 (in each region)
Germany	99	List-PR	x	1[b]	5
Greece	24	List-PR	x	1	3
Hungary	24	List-PR	x	1	5
Ireland	13	STV	•	4	–
Italy	78	List-PR	•	5[c]	–
Latvia	9	List-PR	•	1	–
Lithuania[a]	13	List-PR	x	1	5
Luxembourg	6	List-PR	•	1	–
Malta	5	STV	•	1	–
Netherlands	27	List-PR	•	1	–
Poland[a]	54	List-PR	x	13	5
Portugal	24	List-PR	x	1	–
Slovakia	14	List-PR	•	1	5
Slovenia	7	List-PR	•	1	–
Spain	54	List-PR	x	1	–
Sweden	19	List-PR	•	1	4
UK–Britain	75	List-PR	x	11	–
UK–Northern Ireland	3	STV	•	1	–

[a] A more detailed analysis of this variety is given in Corbett et al. (2003a).
[b] But with the possibility of Länder lists.
[c] Although candidates are presented in the five regions in Italy, for the purpose of allocating seats to parties the votes from the regions are pooled in one national constituency.

Source: Authors' compilation.

Table 2.2 shows the member states' numbers of citizens per MEP.

These and other differences were the natural corollary of the absence of a uniform system. They were also a powerful expression of the fact that European elections remain primarily national contests fought in national arenas. Reflections on how to create pan-European actors (for example, European political parties) and pan-European issues (for example, election of the Commission President) are dealt with in Chapter 1 and below, but it seems almost as though, as a basic rule of thumb, the more uniformity is achieved, the more alien it may seem to the voter.

Table 2.2   The differing numbers of citizens per MEP

Member state	Electorate	Number of MEPs	Electors per MEP
Germany	63,627,000	99	642,697
Spain	34,563,545	54	640,066
Italy	49,309,064	78	632,167
United Kingdom	44,118,453	78	565,621
Poland	29,374,800	54	543,978
France	42,000,000	78	538,462
Netherlands	11,855,330	27	439,086
Greece	8,912,901	24	371,371
Sweden	6,939,860	19	365,256
Portugal	8,670,378	24	361,266
Hungary	8,155,498	24	339,812
Czech Republic	8,100,000	24	337,500
Austria	5,847,605	18	324,867
Belgium	7,343,366	24	305,974
Finland	4,221,000	14	301,500
Slovakia	4,174,097	14	298,150
Denmark	4,012,440	14	286,603
Slovenia	1,683,502	7	240,500
Ireland	2,836,596	13	218,200
Lithuania	2,638,886	13	202,991
Estonia	1,067,430	6	177,905
Latvia	1,399,795	9	155,533
Cyprus	475,913	6	79,319
Malta	297,247	5	59,449
Luxembourg	343,800	6	57,300

Source: European Parliament.

The 1976 Act and the 2002 Amending Decision

The 1976 'Act Concerning the Election of the Representatives of the European Parliament by Direct Universal Suffrage (Annexed to Decision 76/787/ECCS, EEC, *EURATOM Official Journal* L 278, 08/10/1976 P. 0005–0011) set down such basic principles as: the basic five-year term of office of MEPs; the period/dates in which European elections may be held; MEPs' independence, privileges and immunities; and set out a list of incompatible offices (MEPs may not, for example, be a member of any other European institution), though member states are free to make additional provisions regarding incompatible posts.

The 2002 Amending Decision introduced a number of minor modifications and one highly significant change. It provided for member states to set a minimum threshold, for example, but it also provided that this could not be above 5%. Other such provisions included: enabling member states to set ceilings on campaign expenses; enabling member states to establish constituencies; and enabling the count of votes to begin immediately after the polling booths had closed – but also providing that member states could not 'officially make public the results of their count' before polling booths throughout the European Union had closed. This provision meant that in the UK, where previously the vote was on Thursday but the count was not able to begin until the Sunday evening, results could be known far more rapidly.

Article 5 of the 1976 Act baldly declared that the office of representative in the Parliament was compatible with membership of the Parliament of a member state; that is, dual mandates were allowed. However, as the work rate of MEPs steadily increased, a number of member states forbade dual mandates through national legislation (and were thus almost certainly in contradiction with the primary law). In addition, a large number of political parties either forbade it formally in their statutes or informally in practice. Recognising the by now very full-time nature of an MEP's work, the 2002 Amending Act explicitly abolished dual mandates, though with two curious exceptions, further providing that:

> From the European Parliament elections in 2004, the office of member of the European Parliament shall be incompatible with that of member of a national parliament.
>
> By way of derogation from that rule and without prejudice to paragraph 3:
> – members of the Irish National Parliament who are elected to the European Parliament at a subsequent poll may have a dual mandate until the next election to the Irish National Parliament, at which juncture the first subparagraph of this paragraph shall apply;
> – members of the United Kingdom Parliament who are also members of the European Parliament during the five-year term preceding election to the European Parliament in 2004 may have a dual mandate until the 2009 European Parliament elections, when the first sub-paragraph of this paragraph shall apply.

This provision was an apparent concession to: the two incumbent United Kingdom MEPs who were also members of the House of Lords and wanted to stand again in the European elections;[2] and several members of the Irish Dail who intended also to stand in the European elections. In the best spirit of the Anastassopoulos Report, convergence was to be achieved through slow, pragmatic progress. That progress will, however, be irreversible; when British political parties come to select their candidates for the 2009 European elections, members of the House of Lords will be excluded from consideration.

The 2002 Amending Act's provisions included one major sea-change. As amended, the 1976 Act now provides that 'In each Member State, members of the European Parliament shall be elected on the basis of proportional representation, using the list system or the single transferable vote.' Article 7 now states that 'the electoral procedure shall be governed in each Member

State by its national provisions'. However, the Article goes on to declare that 'These national provisions, which may if appropriate take account of the specific situation in the member states, shall not affect the essentially proportional nature of the system.' From one point of view this was simply a statement of the status quo. But, by being part of the *'acquis'*, it meant that any and all future member states would have to ensure that their system for European elections complied with the basic condition of proportionality. It also meant that proportional representation for the European elections in the United Kingdom was now effectively a permanent fixture, since it had been ring-fenced in a basic European Act.

The 'allowances affair' and the continuing saga of a common statute for MEPs

Like its 1994–99 predecessor, the 1999–2004 European Parliament was beset by a number of high-profile allegations of malpractice by its members. These culminated, in the run-up to the elections themselves, in a very high-profile campaign by an Austrian former Social Democrat and now independent MEP, Hans-Peter Martin, who took and published photographs of MEPs, including two UK MEPs (Gordon Adam and Eryl McNally), engaging in allegedly incorrect practices connected to MEPs' allowances (see below). Similar allegations were made about a large number of MEPs, though there was no documentation and the allegations were fiercely denied. Herr Martin's allegations and photographs were enthusiastically taken up by the British press, which published such headlines as 'A quick hit gives MEPs a fast buck' (*Sunday Times*, 25 April 2004). As Chapter 4 recounts, the allegations were to be revived with a vengeance in the opening days of the European elections campaign in the UK.[3]

The word 'allegedly' is used advisedly because the MEPs concerned argued forcefully that their practice was entirely correct.[4] In the case of the UK MEPs, the issue revolved around the use of the €262 flat-rate subsistence allowance to which MEPs are entitled for attendance at the Parliament. Various MEPs were photographed signing into the register in Strasbourg early on Friday mornings after plenary sessions (which always finish on the Thursday) and shortly afterwards boarding planes back to the UK. Herr Martin alleged that the MEPs were incorrectly claiming the subsistence allowance for the Friday mornings. The MEPs concerned argued that their work had obliged them to stay on in Strasbourg for an extra night and hence they were fully entitled to the allowance.

The allegations were manna from heaven for Eurosceptics and critics of the Union's institutions, although ironically UK MEPs had been at the forefront of – largely successful – efforts to tighten up Parliament's internal rules and regulations. Indeed, as Chapter 1 recounted, Pauline Green's failure to be re-elected to the Presidency of the PES Group in 1999 was at least partly linked to her outspoken criticism of the Parliament's failure to equip itself with an overall body of such rules and regulations. Box 2.2 sets out all allowances to which MEPs are entitled, together with the conditions which must be satisfied in order to qualify for them.

Box 2.2   MEPs' allowances

In the absence of a common statute, British MEPs receive the same monthly salary as a Westminster MP – £4,790.42 on 1 April 2004, taxed at the same rate. MEPs are additionally eligible for a number of allowances, paid via the European Parliament's budget (and not taxed in the UK)[a] as follows.

General expenditure allowance
This is intended to cover constituency office management costs, telephone and postal charges, computer equipment (purchase and maintenance) and the cost of travel within the UK. The flat-sum amount is €3,700 per month, but this is halved if, for no valid reason, members do not attend half of the plenary sittings in a given year.

Subsistence allowance
A flat rate allowance of €262 per day is paid for each day of attendance at official meetings of Parliament bodies on which the member serves, and is paid only if the member has signed the official attendance register. The allowance is intended to cover accommodation, meals and all other expenses. During plenary sessions in Strasbourg and Brussels, the amount is reduced by half in the case of members who have not taken part in half of all roll call votes called during the session in question.

Secretarial assistance allowance
The European Parliament pays up to €12,576 per month to cover the expenses arising from the engagement or employment of one or more assistants. The allowance is paid either directly to the assistant(s) or to a paying agent.

Travel allowance
This is to cover the cost of travel undertaken by members within the European Union in order to attend official meetings of the European Parliament. It is also intended to cover associated expenses, such as accommodation, meals and taxis. For air travel, the allowance awarded is the cost of an economy class unrestricted fare between the airport nearest to the member's residence and the airport of the place of work concerned (a boarding pass must be presented). For rail travel or private car, €0.67 per km for the first 500 km is awarded (a rail ticket or a personal travel declaration must be presented). In addition, a distance allowance is paid: €112 for 500–1,000 km; €268 for 1,000–1,500 km; €357 for 1,500–2,000 km; €447 for 2,000–2,400 km; €558 for more than 2,400 km.

Annual travel allowance
This is intended to cover expenditure incurred in travelling anywhere in the world in performance of an MEP's duties (for purposes other than official meetings) and is paid on presentation of supporting documentation: up to €3,652.

[a] It should be pointed out that UK MPs receive similar, untaxed allowances.

The European Parliament has consistently argued that the root of the problem lies in the very different status and salaries of MEPs who, under the terms of the 1976 Act, receive the same basic salary as an equivalent national MP. A common statute for all MEPs would resolve the issue. In implicit recognition of this shortcoming, the draftsmen of the Amsterdam Treaty introduced a new and innovative provision whereby the Parliament, with the unanimous approval of the Council, should 'lay down the regulations and general conditions governing the performance of the duties of its members'. In anticipation of the ratification and implementation of the Amsterdam Treaty before the 1999 European elections, the Parliament adopted a draft Common Statute for all MEPs on 3 December 1998 and forwarded it to the Council. Although media attention focused on the provisions regarding MEPs' salaries, the draft statute covered a wide range of subjects, including incompatible offices, rules to be applied when a seat became vacant, and parliamentary immunity.

On 26 April 1999 the Council adopted its own position on the draft Statute. There were considerable divergences over fundamental issues, including the tax status of MEPs and retirement age. Many MEPs argued that the Council's preference for MEPs to pay national taxes rather than a European tax undermined the principle of equal treatment and status. On 5 May 1999, at its last plenary session before the European elections, the Parliament reluctantly rejected the Council's amended draft and called for further negotiations. 'Euro MPs,' declared the *Daily Mail* (6 May 1999) 'keep their gravy train on track'. To some it seemed that the Council was trying to rush the Parliament into accepting a disadvantageous draft; to others, including most British MEPs, it seemed the Parliament had very publicly scored an own goal. Just as bad, there seemed no obvious way out of the impasse, and there were fears that the lack of a common statute, and hence also the horror stories about alleged malpractice, would haunt the European Parliament in 2004 and 2009.

The 2001 Nice Treaty gave the European Parliament a heavy steer, amending Article 190(5) so that only a qualified majority would be required to approve the statute, *except* on rules and conditions relating to the taxation of MEPs, where unanimity would still be required. In January 2002 Pat Cox was elected President of the Parliament. He had declared the resolution of the impasse on the common statute as one of the major priorities of his Presidency. Under his impulse, Parliament returned to the matter and in June 2003 it produced a new draft.[5] However, the Council objected on three points: the proposed retirement age for MEPs; the tax arrangements for their salaries; and questions to do with privileges and immunities, which it said could only be changed on the basis of inter-governmental negotiation.

The Parliament responded by voting again in December 2003, when it decided to remove all three bones of contention. Accepting the wish of several governments, which wanted to be able to levy national income tax on MEPs' salaries even though these were now to be paid from the Union's budget, the Parliament effectively removed the taxation provisions from its draft. The only condition was that there should be no double taxation, a point accepted by the Council. The Parliament agreed to deal with immunities and privileges separately, asking the member states to revise the 1965 Protocol on which current immunities and privileges were based. Lastly, MEPs proposed a compromise on the retirement age, which the then Italian Presidency of the Union had indicated would be acceptable: MEPs would be entitled to a pension from the age of 63 (rather than 65 as the Council wanted or 60 as the Parliament had proposed in June).

Twenty-five years after the first direct elections to the European Parliament, it seemed that all of its members might at last be governed by the same set of rules. Unexpectedly, and at the very last minute, during the 26 January 2004 Council meeting which was due to adopt the Common Statute, a number of ministers objected to the level of the proposed salaries of MEPs, which had been set at half that of a judge at the European Court of Justice, and which until then had been unopposed. Domestic developments impinged on the Council's position. In particular, German opposition was hardened by the fact that the government had just implemented a package of cost-cutting reforms, making salary rises for MEPs unpalatable. In the end, Germany joined with France, Sweden and Austria in opposition. In the absence of a qualified majority, no vote was taken. Despite last-ditch efforts by President Cox to forge a compromise, the draft was again kicked into touch just before the June 2004 European elections. For Pat Cox, it was *the* setback of his Presidency. For the European Parliament, it was the worst-case scenario MEPs had feared back in 1999. Once again, the media were full of the sort of headlines the Parliament needed the least: for example, 'EU gravy train rumbles on as MEPs' pay deal blocked' (<www.eubusiness.com>).

Voting rights for EU citizens and candidate eligibility

The 1991 Maastricht Treaty introduced the concept of citizenship of the European Union (TEU Articles 17–22) for the first time. As part of these provisions, Article 19(2) declared that 'every citizen of the Union residing in a member state of which he is not a national shall have the right to vote and to stand as a candidate in elections to the European Parliament in the Member State in which he resides, under the same conditions as nationals of that State'. The Article went on to declare that the right could only be exercised once 'detailed arrangements' had been agreed unanimously by the Council. These were duly set out in Council Directive 93/109/EC of 6 December 1993, in time for the June 1994 European elections. On that occasion the UK's Home Office devoted some money to an information campaign, but few non-nationals were aware of their right and very few exercised it. In 1999 and 2004 there was no specific information campaign on this right.

In contrast to national elections, members of the House of Lords (and even the Queen) may vote in European elections.

A few non-nationals have been elected to the European Parliament since the 1993 provisions were enacted. Daniel Cohn-Bendit, a German national elected in France, is the best-known example. In the UK, any Commonwealth or Irish citizen may stand, though no non-nationals have been elected in the UK since 1999[6] and no non-nationals were to be elected in 2004. Clearly, the presence of a non-national in a European election campaign can have a highly symbolic and pedagogic effect. This was the case, for example, of Olivier Dupuis, a Belgian elected in Italy in 1994. Perhaps the best-known example precedes the Maastricht Treaty's provisions; in 1989 French political scientist Maurice Duverger, author of a renowned work on political parties, was elected as an Italian MEP.

The election date and timetable

One essential element in the uniformity of European elections related to the date on which they took place. Even on this subject, from the outset, it was a question of uniformity through diversity. The 1976 Act establishing direct elections to the European Parliament laid down that for all member states the elections should take place 'within the same period starting on a Thursday morning and ending on the following Sunday'. It was left to the Council to decide when that period should be. However, once it was chosen, the Act declared that subsequent elections should take place in the 'corresponding period' thereafter. The Council settled for the second week of June, and all five sets of European elections since 1979 have occurred in that same period. For 2004, they would take place between 10 and 13 June.

In March 1998, the Portuguese government wrote to the British Presidency to point out that Portugal had important holidays on 10 and 13 June and to request that alternative dates be found. Portugal had not been an EU member state when the June period was chosen. The Council decided that there could be no change for 1999, but a Council Working Party was asked to look into possible alternatives for 2004. A consensus gradually emerged in favour of the second Sunday in May and the three days preceding it, but this caused various problems: the French had a holiday on 9 May; Britain traditionally held local elections in the first week of May and would be reluctant to switch to the second week; Ireland didn't want to move its local elections forward from June. Nevertheless, there was an informal sense that the period for direct elections in 2004 might change.

The Council Working Party subsequently returned to the issue. There was now a fresh impetus in favour of a switch to May. As seen in Chapter 1, the UK's political establishment had been shocked by the very low turnout in the 1999 European elections and the 2001 General Election. Combining local and European elections was one of the recommendations for encouraging higher turnout that the government had received from various learned and expert sources, and so the UK delegation to the Council Working Party relaunched the question. In the event, the inertia in favour of maintaining the status quo outweighed the momentum for change. As will be seen below, the British government subsequently decided that the 'Mohammed' of local elections would have to go the 'mountain' of European elections …

Information money (EU level) and the EP London Office's information campaign

The European Parliament traditionally allocated funds to political groups to enable them to publicise their work in the European Parliament. The amounts involved were calculated on the basis of a quota for each member of a group. Following various European Court of Justice rulings, there could be no direct subsidy for electioneering. On the contrary, the Parliament imposed strict rules on how the information money could be spent. Expenditure had to be accounted for in detail and the money could not be used for party propaganda. These rules are enforced by systematic auditing, and where the auditor feels expenditure was inappropriate the MEP, Group or party concerned may be asked to reimburse the sums involved. The Parliament's political groups are entitled to devise their own rules for the disbursement of the funds allocated to them. Most balance expenditure by individual MEPs with an amount held back for centralised use by both national parties and the European Parliament's political groupings.

In election years, the Parliament imposes a cut-off date on itself; one month before the elections all disbursement of information fund money must stop. Nevertheless, the amounts of money involved are cumulatively important. Access to information money and office allowances are significant benefits of membership of the Parliament, particularly for smaller political parties.

The European Parliament's London Office organised a general information campaign about the European Parliament and European elections, starting in the autumn of 2003. The new Financial Regulation governing all EU financial actions imposed a certain rigidity, but the Office was able to launch a call for tender and select a communications agency to help it with its campaign. As in 1999, the campaign involved a hot air balloon, which was considered a 'mixed blessing' in terms of visibility and symbolism! Moreover, bad weather during the campaign frequently kept the balloon grounded. The Office's campaign was determinedly regional in emphasis. The communications agency produced a selection of promotional material (for example, beer mats, posters). A specific Euro-elections website was set up. Comedian Eddie Izzard offered his help, though in a whistle-stop sort of way. The EP's central services had prepared a promotional video, produced to cinematic standards, and the London Office helped to ensure that it was screened in cinemas before the main feature (60% of UK cinemas in the two-week period prior to the 10 June elections). The Cinema Advertising Association objected to the revealing of a woman's nipples during the short (and by Continental standards innocuous) opening sequence showing breast feeding. Following a 'leak' of the objection, considerable media coverage was generated, most seeing the CAA's objection as exaggerated.

Although the UK Office campaign focused on the elections, it clearly saw these as an opportunity to pursue the longer-term strategic aim of creating lasting awareness in the UK about the EP's role and powers. Thus the Office, which made full use of quantitative and qualitative research, including focus groups and opinion polling, saw its activities in the election context as a small contribution at the beginning of a very long haul. Nevertheless, as an internal report later demonstrated, the Office could feel that it had invested well, particularly with regard to the media. Though empirical evidence is not available, anecdotal evidence would suggest that journalists had at least begun to realise the distinct role and potential of the European Parliament.

The Institute for Citizenship ran a 'Get the Vote Out!' campaign, with funding from the UK Office of the European Parliament and the Electoral Commission. The aim was to conduct a series of public meetings with representatives of civil society (local authorities, NGOs, and so on) in each of the twelve electoral regions, with the participation of MEPs and candidates. The meetings, which took place from November 2003 to April 2004, were followed by a series of four regional receptions to meet those who had expressed an interest in following up the initiative. The conferences and the receptions were well attended.

The domestic framework

The introduction of proportional representation for the 1999 European elections was a major constitutional change, with far-reaching practical, cultural and political consequences.[7] By contrast, in 2004 there was no basic change to the electoral system, but there were a number of significant developments that nevertheless changed the electoral landscape.

The Electoral Commission

A main innovation was the creation of an Electoral Commission, which came into being under the Political Parties, Elections and Referendums Act 2000.[8] Its remit is to 'increase public confidence in the democratic process within the United Kingdom, and encourage people to take part, by modernising the electoral process, promoting public awareness of electoral matters, and regulating political parties'. Among its many tasks, the Commission had to cope with the need under proportional representation to define and register political parties. The task had been undertaken reluctantly by the Registrar of Companies for the Scottish and Welsh Assembly elections of May 1999 and for the European elections a month later, but was handed over to the Electoral Commission when it was established in February 2001, with Sam Younger appointed as its first head.

The Electoral Commission, which was given an advisory role rather than administrative status, undertook research in many areas, focusing particularly on the problem of low turnout.

Party finance

The Commission was also allocated a major regulatory role on national and local party finance. For the European elections, the monetary ceiling was hardly a problem; no party was likely to spend anything near to the prescribed limits, but there were accountancy rules to be complied with. Moreover, if, as seemed probable, the next General Election occurred in May 2005, then expenditure on the European elections would fall within the same twelve-month period in which every party's campaign expenditure faced a statutory limit of £20 million.

The Electoral Commission's rules on publicity for party finances also had an impact on fund-raising; donors found it imprudent to reveal their munificence lest they be accused of buying influence. Party workers, meanwhile, shied away from accepting offices which imposed meticulous bookkeeping duties on them.

Reducing the number of British MEPs

In the 2003–04 period the Electoral Commission faced three special challenges connected with the European elections. First, in the 1999 elections, twelve regions had chosen 87 MEPs under the d'Hondt method (and STV for Northern Ireland). But, in order to allow for the enlargement of the EU from 15 to 25 member states without creating an unmanageably large Parliament, the 2001 Nice Treaty reduced the number of UK, French and Italian MEPs from 87 to 78. The Electoral Commission was required by statute to make recommendations on how this reduction could be implemented in the UK. It issued a discussion paper suggesting four methods for calculating the most equitable way of deciding which regions should forfeit seats (clearly, such reductions would have knock-on consequences for the electoral hopes of lower-placed candidates and incumbents). On 31 October 2003, the Commission finally recommended that one MEP should be taken from each region except the South West, the East Midlands and Northern Ireland (see Table 2.3). The Commission abandoned all suggested methods of calculation in favour of the Sainte-Laguë quotient which had been put forward by academics during the consultation period. The 2003 European Parliament (Representation) Act implemented the reduction from 87 to 78 MEPs, and the Commission's recommendations were given effect in the European Parliament and Local Elections (Pilots) Act 2004, passed on 1 April 2004.

Gibraltar

A second future challenge for the Electoral Commission emerged when, on 18 February 1999, the European Court of Human Rights ruled (*Matthews* v. *United*

Table 2.3 Implementing the Nice Treaty reduction in the number of seats

| | Changes in regional seat allocation | | |
	1999	2004	Change
North East	4	3	−1
North West	10	9	−1
Yorkshire and the Humber	7	6	−1
East Midlands	6	6	0
West Midlands	8	7	−1
East	8	7	−1
London	10	9	−1
South East	11	10	−1
South West	7	7	0
Wales	5	4	−1
Scotland	8	7	−1
Northern Ireland	3	3	0
UK	87	78	−9

Source: Authors' compilation.

Kingdom, 1999) that it was contrary to the provisions of the 1950 European Convention on Human Rights (of which the UK was a signatory) for the inhabitants of Gibraltar, a part of the European Union, to be denied voting rights in the European Parliament elections. Gibraltar had been excluded from the provisions of the 1976 Act establishing direct elections in the UK. In 1980, a group of six British MEPs, three Conservative and three Labour, was set up to represent Gibraltar in European matters. This informal arrangement was ratified by the House of Assembly in Gibraltar, but not by the Foreign Office in London nor the House of Commons. It was in any case intended only as a stop-gap measure.

For 20 years the people of Gibraltar pressed for their right to elect their own MEP, or at least to be joined to an existing UK constituency. The Foreign Office argued consistently that Gibraltar was an 'autonomous territory' – not part of the United Kingdom, with no representative in the Commons, and with its own legislature. There were also practical (the small size of the population, the distance) and political (from 1986 onwards Spain was a fellow EU member state) considerations. When the European Parliamentary Elections Bill 1999 was introduced, Gibraltarians and their supporters again pressed their case, and an amendment was introduced and subsequently rejected by the government.

After the court ruling, however, the government had no option but to concede the point. The 2003 European Parliament (Representation) Act (see Box 2.3) therefore made provision for Gibraltar to be included in one of the English regions, and it was left to the Electoral Commission to recommend which region that should be. After extensive consultations and representations (including bids from London and from the West Midlands), the Commission recommended that the South West would be the most appropriate region to represent the 20,000-odd electors of Gibraltar. The government gave this effect by Statutory Order 1245 of 2004.[9]

Box 2.3   The 2003 European Parliament (Representation) Act

The European Parliament (Representation) Act, which secured Royal Assent on 8 May 2003, was required in order to enable the UK to meet two separate legal obligations.

Under the terms of the Treaty of Nice, the number of seats for the existing 15 member states was reduced in order to accommodate the accession states without rendering the EP unwieldy. In the case of the UK, the number of MEPs was reduced from 87 to 78. Part 1 of the Act therefore enabled the UK to adjust the number of MEPs.

In 1999 the European Court of Human Rights found the UK to be in breach of the European Convention on Human Rights for excluding Gibraltar from elections to the European Parliament. Part 2 of the Act enfranchises Gibraltar by allowing it to become part of a UK 'combined region' for European Parliament elections.

Addressing low turnout – all-postal ballots

The third and most controversial task that faced the Electoral Commission concerned the choice of region(s) where all postal voting might most appropriately be tried in the European elections. The Electoral Commission, reflecting the political establishment's concern, had conducted research on various possible ways of enhancing turnout in elections.[10] Since 2000, in every local election season (except 2001) there had been experiments with voting arrangements in a small selection of local authorities. These ranged from electronic voting to setting up polling booths in supermarkets.[11] In 2001 the Electoral Commission took over the evaluation and reporting on these experiments. By 2003 it seemed clear that the only innovation that increased turnout significantly was postal voting. In some cases it doubled the turnout (see Electoral Commission, 2002, 2003a). (Early and extended voting added little to turnout, though it performed a useful public service.)

Between 2001 and 2003 responsibility for electoral legislation had been reorganised. The task was passed partly to the Lord Chancellor's Department and its successor, the Department of Constitutional Affairs, but it was still left partly with the Office of the Deputy Prime Minister; the Electoral Commission stood in the wings as adviser. In September 2003 the government brought forward the European Parliamentary and Local Elections (Pilots) Bill, which had been carried over from the previous session. The Bill had a tortured passage, coming before the Lords and the Commons 24 times (and occupying 600 columns of Hansard!) before it was passed on April Fool's Day 2004.

Ministers, led by John Prescott, became increasingly enthusiastic about the further development of postal voting. In September 2003 the Electoral Commission was asked to consider which regions would be most suited to a full-scale trial of either postal voting or electronic voting in the June 2004 elections. Three regions were ruled out from the beginning: London (because of the complexities of Mayoral and Greater London Council voting); the South West (because of the inclusion of Gibraltar in its electorate); and Northern Ireland (because of its different voting system). In December 2003, the Electoral Commission recommended against any electronic voting but named two regions, the North East and the East Midlands, as being most suitable for any experimentation with full postal voting. The Commission also identified four other regions as being possible candidates for such experimentation.

Having received this advice, the government accepted the two regions recommended but decided that it would prefer the inclusion of two further regions, the North West and Yorkshire & Humberside. John Prescott, as Deputy Prime Minister, was sponsor of three referendums on the setting-up of Regional Assemblies in the North East, the North West, and Yorkshire & Humberside which were tentatively scheduled to be held in the autumn of 2004, and he was keen on trying out postal voting in these areas, despite the reservations of the Electoral Commission about the North West (based on objections from the Returning Officers).[12] Time was running out and on 4 March and 25 March the Commission sent urgent letters to the Office of the Deputy Prime Minister laying out the case for restricting the trials to at most three regions. Sam Younger wrote firmly: 'We are not persuaded of the merits of piloting in four regions.'

The European Parliamentary and Local Elections (Pilots) Bill had passed the Commons on 17 December 2003, but in February 2004 the Lords, by 169 to 110, decided to limit the pilots to three regions. Both the opposition parties supported the Electoral Commission's position on the number of regions. The Bill then ping-ponged between the Lords and Commons to decide whether three or four regions should have postal ballots. On 30 March the government was rebuffed for the fourth time by 136 votes to 130 but the next day, 1 April, moderates in the Lords decided that this was not the right issue for a fundamental struggle between the chambers; the government got its way by 138 votes to 108 and the Bill received the Royal Assent that evening. The authorities in the North West protested at the shortness of time remaining when the regulations were promulgated on 27 April, barely six weeks before the elections themselves.

As part of the 'ping-pong' legislative process, the Commons accepted a Lords amendment which made provision for all postal ballot papers to be signed by a witness. Critical observers would later argue that this had reduced the secrecy of the ballot, diminished the ease of voting (voters now had to seek out a witness) and, paradoxically, increased the chances of fraud and/or intimidation. There was certainly empirical evidence that the condition had significantly reduced the potential increase in turnout.[13]

Addressing low turnout – combining the European, local and Mayoral elections

In the same context of addressing low turnout, the dates of the 2004 local elections and the Greater London Authority elections (including that of Mayor), initially due to be held in May 2004, were changed to 10 June 2004 under the provisions of the Local Government Act 2003, so that they would coincide with the European elections. The Act gave the same power to the National Assembly of Wales so that the date of the Welsh local elections could also be shifted to 10 June (which, following a consultation, it belatedly was). One of the explanations given for the low turnout in the 1999 European Elections had been voter fatigue – the difficulty of enthusing party workers or ordinary people a mere five weeks after the local elections. No local elections were due in Scotland in 2004, but over half the rest of the country had to choose councillors. The widespread belief that a high turnout would favour Labour allegedly reinforced the government's enthusiasm for synchronous elections. Local elections, it was thought, would do more to encourage European turnout than vice versa, and voting on the same day offered some assurance of an improvement on the calamitous 24% turnout in the 1999 European elections. Table 2.4 shows the extent of combination by electoral region.

Table 2.4   Electoral regions and extent of combination

Region	No. of MEPs	Eligible electorate	Geographic size (sq. km)	No. of local authorities	No. of authorities holding elections 2004	Local authorities holding elections 2004 (%)
North East	3	1,905,132	8,592	23	6	26.09
North West	9	5,151,488	14,165	43	33	76.74
Yorkshire & Humberside	6	3,719,717	15,400	21	13	61.90
East Midlands	6	3,220,019	15,627	40	6	15.00
West Midlands	7	3,957,848	13,004	34	18	52.94
Eastern	7	4,137,210	19,110	48	28	58.33
London	9	5,054,957	1,572	33	1[a]	100.00
South East	10	6,034,549	19,096	67	31	46.97
South West	10	3,845,077	23,829	44	10	22.73
Wales	4	2,218,649	20,764	22	22	100.00
Scotland	7	3,839,952	78,772	32	0	0
Northern Ireland	3	1,072,669	14,144	26	0	0
Total	78	44,157,267	101,600			

[a] The elections for the London Assembly and London Mayor are classed in law as local elections; although only a single 'authority' was holding an election, responsibility for administration was shared by all London boroughs.

Source: Editorial Commission, 2004b.

Domestic electoral provisions

The first part of this chapter described provisions governing the European elections at European level. That European electoral framework was matched and complemented by a number of provisions at the national level.[14]

Eligibility to vote

All European Union citizens (that is, recognised citizens of an EU member state) were entitled to vote. Regardless of citizenship of other member states, electors could only vote once. Voters had to be over 18 years of age. They could not already have cast a postal ballot in a different region. Indeed, it is a criminal offence to have 'double voted' within the meaning of the Representation of the People Act (1983). Under the European Parliament Elections Act (2002), all voters were eligible to apply for a postal vote. The European Parliamentary and Local Elections (Pilots) Act (2004) removed the right of voters to cast proxy ballots or vote at a polling station if they were registered in one of the four regions.[15] Voting is not compulsory.

The design of the ballot paper

Basic provisions concerning the design of the ballot paper were set out in European Parliamentary Elections Regulations (2004; SI-293). In the 1999 European elections a Home Office publicity campaign explaining the design of the ballot paper was the source of some controversy (Butler and Westlake, 2000, pp. 231–2). In 2004 there was to be no such information campaign and hence no such controversy.[16] The design of a ballot paper is always a potential source of complaint, from the ordering of the candidates to the use of symbols. There were fewer such complaints in 2004, but there *were* vociferous complaints about the sheer size of the ballot paper in some regions, particularly in London, where the paper was combined with the local and Greater London Authority (plus Mayoral) elections.[17] This was an inevitable consequence of the decision to synchronise the local and European elections.

Returning Officers in some areas reported that the ballot papers were at the maximum dimensions for printing machines. The sheer size of papers also required the provision of more ballot boxes. The Electoral Commission's 2004 report listed a number of 'near misses' but in the end there were to be no major hitches.[18] The ballot paper provided some material for a media seeking human interest stories during a dull and flat campaign, but the only real problems were the printing of postal ballot papers at short notice and a lack of familiarity on the part of voters.

Eligibility to stand

All EU citizens resident in the UK (and UK citizens resident abroad for less than 15 years) aged 21 or over on the day of nomination and in full possession of their civic rights in their member state of origin may stand for election.

However, the European Parliamentary Elections Regulations (2004; SI-293) lay down a number of exclusions:

- members of the government or of the House of Commons
- Lords of Appeal in Ordinary
- disqualification from standing to a House of Commons constituency in the region in which the individual is seeking the office of MEP
- having committed an offence under the Representation of the People Act (1981), or the Corrupt Practises Act (1873)
- running as a candidate for election in another region or Member State
- membership of 'certain European bodies' (as defined by Council Decision 76/787, amended in 2002)
- disqualification from standing for election by criminal/civil legal decisions in the country of which the individual is a member.

Deposit

The European Parliamentary Elections Regulations (2004; SI-293) provided that no candidate/list could be validly nominated unless the sum of £5,000 was deposited by the candidate/list or on the candidate/list's behalf at the same time as the delivery of the nomination papers. The same Regulations provided that the deposit would be forfeited unless the candidate/list polled more than 2.5% of the vote in the electoral region concerned (in Northern Ireland the threshold was one-quarter of the quota).

Election expenses

The European Parliamentary Elections Regulations (2004; SI-293) also laid out a maximum amount for the expenses of individual candidates/lists. This was set at £45,000, multiplied by the number of MEPs to be returned for the electoral region in question. For example, the limit for individual candidates/lists in the East Midlands regions was £45,000 x 6 = £270,000.

All parties fielding candidates and all independent candidates were entitled to a single 'freepost' mailshot sent to every UK household. The system was coordinated between the parties and the Royal Mail, with distribution being funded by the government. The total cost to the public of this provision was some £26 million.

The election timetable

A formal timetable was initially established by the European Parliamentary Elections Regulations (2004; SI-293). However, the late introduction of all-postal balloting in four regions necessitated a slightly more advanced timetable in those regions. This timetable was set out in the European Parliamentary and Local Elections (All-Postal) Pilot Order 2004. The two timetables are set out in Box 2.4.

Box 2.4   The formal election timetable

Notice of election: not later than 5 May (30 April for all-postal ballot regions)
Deadline for registration of political parties to field candidates at the election: Wednesday 5 May 2004 (30 April)
Last day for delivery of nomination papers: Thursday 13 May 2004 (11 May in pilot areas)
Last day for voters to change or cancel an existing postal vote or proxy vote appointment: Tuesday 25 May 2004
Last day for new applications to vote by post or proxy: Wednesday 2 June 2004
Polling day: Thursday 10 June 2004, 7 a.m. to 10 p.m.
Declaration of results in England and Wales: Sunday 13 June 2004
Declaration of results in Scotland: Monday 14 June 2004
Declaration of results in Northern Ireland: Monday 14 June 2004

In formal terms, therefore, the campaign could get under way from 30 April in the four postal ballot regions and 5 May in the other regions. Electoral Commission studies had shown that in previous such experiments a majority of postal votes were posted in the two weeks following their arrival. This potential duality was to pose problems for the political parties, since it effectively implied that they had to fight two different campaigns with two different 'peaks'.

Nomination papers for candidates had to be received not later than 4 p.m. on the sixth working day after the last day for the issue of the notice of the election (13 May in areas where conventional elections were taking place, 11 May in pilot areas).[19]

Limitations on publishing opinion poll findings

The European Parliamentary Elections Regulations (2004; SI-293) provided that nobody should publish 'before the close of the poll':

(a)   'any statement relating to the way in which voters have voted at the election where that statement is (or might reasonably be taken to be) based on information given by voters after they have voted or

(b)   any forecast as to the result of the election which is (or might reasonably be taken to be) based on information so given.'

In the 2004 European elections this apparently unambiguous provision was to be tested by a pillar of the media establishment (Peter Riddell of *The Times* – see Chapter 4).

Information campaigns

Despite considerable effort, there was very little visible trace of information activity about the European elections. The Electoral Commission spent £4.5

million on a campaign to encourage turnout including advertising, leaflets in public places, a call centre, a website and a national tour targeting young people. Survey evidence seemed to show that the campaign had had some effect, though the Electoral Commission recognised in its 2004 report that the effects provided a basis to build upon rather than a satisfactory outcome in themselves. The Electoral Commission also contrasted the merits of the 'freepost' rights for candidates in the European elections (see above) with a freepost information booklet distributed to over 5 million London voters for the London Assembly and Mayoral elections. This was reckoned to have been far more effective in raising awareness levels.

The European Movement, once a significant actor in European elections, was almost silent; its membership was only 2,500. However, it did sponsor about 30 hustings meetings in May and June. The most successful, at the Hay-on-Wye Literary Festival, drew an audience of 3,000 but a London gathering in the House of Commons attracted only 40 people. One or two groups gathered money for advertisements and, as the appendix to Chapter 4 recounts, there was some freelance activity on the internet.

The websites of both the Department for Constitutional Affairs and the Electoral Commission were commendably generous with their provision of information to electors and candidates alike. However, the tendency in recent years of favouring web-based information over other means of informing the electorate is almost certainly based on two erroneous assumptions: not everybody is connected to the internet; and not everybody who is connected actively seeks out such information. In Italy, Silvio Berlusconi's government was criticised for having sent out a text message on polling day to everybody with a mobile phone, urging them to vote, but the Berlusconi administration may have had a point. As the appendix to Chapter 4 will discuss, the free provision of maximum information on websites should not preclude the public authorities from exploiting more traditional methods of informing people about their rights.

The various authorities – European, national, regional and local – had together created the complex framework within which the electoral contest was to take place. It is time now to turn to the longer- and shorter-term preparations of the contestants – the political parties.

Notes

1. Seats are allocated in successive rounds. In each round, votes cast for each party are divided by the number of seats the party has already been allocated in the region plus 1. The party with the highest remaining total in the round wins the seat.
2. Of the other peers elected as UK MEPs in 1999, Lord Bethell retired in September 2003 for health reasons (see Appendix 1.2); Lord Stockton was re-selected, but to a low place on the list (see Chapter 3); and Lord Inglewood decided not to stand again on the grounds that 'As I had been elected to remain in the Lords as one

of the elected hereditaries, I thought I ought to turn up more than I could as an MEP' (correspondence with the authors).

3. In August 2004 several newspapers published details of the lax nature of the rules and regulations to which British MPs in the House of Commons were subject. It listed a number of individual MPs and detailed extensively the claims they had made. British MEPs could be forgiven for wondering why this information had not been available before June 2004 or why no British newspaper thought to compare practice in the European Parliament with practice in the House of Commons. See, for example, 'MPs' cushy land of no receipts' (*Sunday Times*, 22 August) and 'Backbench MPs claim £118,000 a year for expenses' (*Guardian*, 23 August). A comparative table of MPs' and MEPs' allowances is given in Corbett et al. (2003a, p. 53).

4. Following his actions, Martin was expelled from the Austrian Social Democrat Party. His actions had, however, generated considerable publicity. He stood and was returned as an independent MEP in the June elections.

5. This attempt was also described critically in the British press: for example, 'MEPs vote for an even longer gravy train with a salary rise to £73,000' (*Guardian*, 5 June 2003).

6. Christine Crawley (Ireland) and Anita Pollack (Australia) were elected as UK MEPs in 1984 and 1999 respectively. The latter has been used in countless Brussels pub charity quizzes! The provisions on who may stand are, curiously, more liberal than those who may vote.

7. An Independent Commission on Proportional Representation, designed to explore the UK's diverse experience of the six new electoral systems established since 1997, was set up under the Constitution Unit. Its March 2004 report covered, among other things, the impact on political activity of the list system used for the European Parliament elections (<www.electoralcommission.gov.uk>).

8. See House of Commons Library Standard Note SN/PC/3127, *The Electoral Commission* (2004f), for an account of its establishment and role.

9. Spanish newspapers reported that the Spanish government was considering bringing a case before the European Court of Justice, calling for the British electoral law to be declared null and void.

10. House of Commons Library Standard Note SN/PC/2051, *Measures to Address Low Turnout* (2003b), gives a succinct summary of the various steps taken and of evaluations of these.

11. A list of all of the schemes, accompanied by an overall evaluation, is set out in House of Commons Library Standard Note SN/PC/2882, *All-Postal Voting* (2004a).

12. See House of Commons Library Standard Note SN/PC/2922, *Referendums for Regional Assemblies* (2004g), for background information on the planned referendums.

13. See House of Commons Library Standard Note SN/PC/2882, *All-Postal Voting* (2004a), p. 13. A comparison is made of turnout figures in four local authorities that piloted all-postal ballots in 2003 and again in 2004. The percentage point change from 2003 to 2004 was, variously −3.1, −7.1, −6.99 and −7.39.

14. In budgetary terms, the Department for Constitutional Affairs set aside £57 million for funding the elections, of which £34.6 million was earmarked for payments to Regional and Local Returning Officers in England and Wales. The Scotland Office allocated £6.8 million for election administration, and the Electoral Office for Northern Ireland £1.5 million. In addition, the DCA allocated a further £13.2 million to meet the extra costs of all-postal ballots in England.

15. These provisions were set out variously in the European Parliament Elections Act (2002) and the European Parliamentary Elections Regulations (2004; SI-293).

16. However, complaints were received in relation to the Conservative Party's description on the ballot paper as 'Putting Britain First', it being argued that this was a campaign slogan rather than a name.

17. Additionally, the Electoral Commission's December 2004 report found that 14% of voters had reported difficulties in filling in the ballot papers (22% in London).

18. The size of the ballot papers did slow down the process of verification (whereby the Local Returning Officer verifies the number of ballot papers issued against the number of ballot papers in each box) – this is a distinct and different process from the count itself.

19. A problem was caused by a prospective candidate in the North West who turned 21 between nomination day and polling day. There was uncertainty over the correct approach to take.

3
Preparations

Getting ready

Before any election campaign, the contestants have to prepare for the contest. Teams are assembled, candidates selected, strategies devised, issues identified, tactics discussed. European elections are no different. But if, as argued in Chapter 1, European elections are second-order national elections, then a number of additional considerations have to be taken into account.

One is the combination of fixed-cycle European elections and variable-cycle General Elections; the strategies and tactics of domestic political parties – which call the shots – necessarily differ depending on the interplay between national and European electoral cycles. A second, linked, consideration lies in the sort of restraints that such an interplay, when combined with the restraints imposed by the framework described in Chapter 2, can create; for example, limitations on overall expenditure, given that a General Election was in the offing within the same twelve-month period. A third concerns the allocation of scarce resources – activists, money, energy; parties must decide how much they are prepared to invest and how and where (and why).

A fourth consideration, linked to the first, concerns a party's basic approach to the electoral contest. Should a party adopt a positive approach and aim to maximise its support? Or should it seek to minimise potentially negative results? Last and not least, political parties have to decide on their basic attitude towards the European election campaign. Do they fight on their record in Europe? Do they fight on their record with regard to Europe? Do they fight 'Europe'? Do they concentrate on their own and their opponent's domestic political records? Do they worry about the results? Or do they use the campaign as a sort of laboratory, a 'dry run' for more consequential electoral contests? Each party found a different combination of answers.

1999–2004

Between the European elections in 1999 and 2004 much had altered in the British political scene. The Conservative leadership had passed from William Hague to Iain Duncan Smith and on to Michael Howard, and the party chairmanship from Michael Ancram to David Davis to Theresa May and on to the duo of Lord Saatchi and Liam Fox. 32 Smith Square, in its last days as the party's headquarters, saw no obvious Conservative recovery. In the 1999 and 2001 contests the Conservatives pursued the theme 'In Europe, not run by Europe', but the party strategists belatedly concluded that they had given too much salience to an issue that was not of primary concern to the great bulk of voters. Iain Duncan Smith and Michael Howard were certainly as Eurosceptic as William Hague but they both tried to move on to other themes.

The Labour Party, which had fared so ill in the 1999 European elections, dropping from 62 seats to 29, seemed to recover effortlessly two years later and produced in the June 2001 General Election a virtual repeat of its 1997 triumph (see Table 3.1). Labour won the election with 412 seats, just six down from its total in 1997 but still the second highest number of seats gained by one party since the war. The Conservatives won 166 seats, an increase of just one seat. The Liberal Democrats won 52, their highest total since 1929. Only 29 seats changed hands, the lowest number since October 1974. The Conservatives made nine gains, including five from Labour, but lost eight seats – seven of them to the Liberal Democrats. All of the Conservative gains were seats that the party had lost in 1997. The Ulster Unionists lost five seats in Northern Ireland – half of their total from 1997 – three to the Democratic Unionists and two to Sinn Féin. The total number of votes cast was 26.4 million, the lowest figure since 1945. Labour won with 10.7 million votes, the lowest number polled by a winning party since 1929 and fewer than the party's total in the 1979 and 1992 General Elections – which the party had lost! Nationally, there was little change in the share of vote for the major parties.

It was thus back to square one for the Conservatives (for them, 2001 was no equivalent to Labour's potentially encouraging performance in 1987), but there were several moments in the 1999–2004 period when Labour nevertheless gave the impression of being a tiring government. The millennium celebrations were adjudged to have been mishandled. Peter Mandelson was forced to resign a second time. Later on, two rising figures, Stephen Byers (forced out over the issue of rail safety) and Alan Milburn (who unexpectedly resigned to spend more time with his family), also left the Cabinet and the consequences of a botched attempt to abolish the office of Lord Chancellor rumbled on. The rivalry between Tony Blair and Gordon Brown was a recurrent source of speculation and comment.

Table 3.1   The 1997 and 2001 United Kingdom General Election results
(1997 results are in italics; not all results are shown)

	Votes	%	MPs
Conservative	8,357,615	31.7	166
	9,600,943	*30.7*	*165*
Labour	10,724,953	40.7	412
	13,518,167	*43.2*	*418*
Liberal Democrats	4,814,321	18.3	52
	5,242,947	*16.8*	*46*
SNP	464,314	1.8	5
	621,550	*2.0*	*6*
UKIP	390,563	1.5	
	105,722	*0.3*	
Referendum Party	*811,849*	*2.6*	
Ulster Unionist	216,839	0.8	6
	258,349	*0.8*	*10*
Plaid Cymru	195,893	0.7	4
	161,030	*0.5*	*4*
Democratic Unionist	181,999	0.7	5
	107,348	*0.3*	*2*
Sinn Féin	175,933	0.7	4
	126,921	*0.4*	*2*
SDLP	169,865	0.6	3
	190,814	*0.6*	*3*
Green	166,477	0.6	
	63,991	*0.2*	
Total votes cast	26,367,383		659
	31,286,284		*659*
Turnout		59.4	
		71.4	

Source: Butler and Kavanagh (1997; 2002)

Iraq

In December 2000 George W. Bush was finally confirmed as the winner
in a very closely fought American presidential election (a result some still
dispute). It therefore fell to him, rather than to Al Gore, to cope with the most
extraordinary and cataclysmic event of the 1999–2004 period – al-Qaeda's
11 September 2001 assault on the World Trade Center in New York and the
Pentagon in Washington. The US administration's subsequent swift invasion
of Afghanistan was followed by a sustained fixation on terrorism, focused
particularly on Saddam Hussein's dictatorship in Iraq and his defiance of
numerous Security Council Resolutions. Tony Blair led his government in
firm support of the United States' goal of overthrowing Saddam Hussein.
The Labour government published an intelligence dossier on 24 September

2002, claiming the existence of Iraqi weapons of mass destruction (WMD) that were capable of being launched within 45 minutes.

Delicate international negotiations culminated in a unanimous UN Security Council Resolution on 8 November 2002 demanding Hussein's compliance with UN resolutions in granting complete access to UN arms inspectors. In early 2003, the US and the UK brought pressure to bear by massing forces around Iraq. The media speculated that in meteorological terms there was only a small window of opportunity available to launch an invasion. France, Germany and Russia refused to support immediate military action, arguing that the weapons inspectors should be given more time. Tony Blair, sensing the risk of unilateral US action and fearing the damage that this would do to the international community, urged his Continental European counterparts to try and negotiate a second UN Security Council resolution. Although his position was nuanced, French President Jacques Chirac appeared to refuse, arguing that the military invasion of Iraq was a fait accompli and that a second Security Resolution would merely legitimise an illegal act.

It was a cardinal moment in the United Kingdom's relations with the European Union. The Prime Minister, Tony Blair, opted for the 'special relationship' with the US over any ambitions he might have had of forging a new relationship with the Franco-German axis and the broader Europe. The US and the UK, together with a few European countries – notably, Italy and Spain – would go it alone. In a celebrated piece of parliamentary oratory, on 3 February 2003 Tony Blair came before the House of Commons to argue the case for war. There was, he argued, an imminent threat from WMD. In the ensuing vote, 139 Labour backbenchers joined with the Liberal Democrats in voting against the war, and the government had to rely on Conservative support to win the key Commons division. An estimated 1 million (some estimates were as high as 2 million) people marched through London on 15 February, protesting against any war. On 20 March hostilities began. Within three weeks Hussein was toppled.

But the victory proved somewhat hollow. In Baghdad and elsewhere resistance fighters and suicide bombers played havoc with the coalition's attempts at reconstruction, and an attritional form of guerrilla war set in, with regular loss of human life among the coalition's forces and among the inhabitants. There was increasingly frequent talk of parallels with Vietnam.

Meanwhile, on 29 May 2003 on an early morning radio news programme, Andrew Gilligan, a BBC journalist, reported allegations from a 'government expert' that Downing Street had 'sexed up' the dossier that gave justification for the war. Mr Gilligan's story was vociferously disputed by the government's chief spokesman, Alistair Campbell. The Foreign Affairs Committee of the House of Commons led a parliamentary inquiry. Dr David Kelly, the weapons expert who, it ultimately transpired, had been the source of Mr Gilligan's story, was interrogated robustly by the parliamentary committee. On 18 July 2003 Dr Kelly's body was discovered and it was later established that he had committed suicide. Tony Blair set up a judicial inquiry into the circumstances surrounding Dr Kelly's death, presided over by Lord Hutton. The inquiry heard public evidence from everyone concerned, including Mr Campbell and Mr Gilligan, and in January 2004 published a report that cleared the government and condemned the BBC in terms that led to the resignation of the Corporation's Chairman and its Director General.

Up to and beyond the June 2004 election the credibility of the government was at stake. Had Tony Blair led the country into an unnecessary and illegal war? Many in the Labour Party and the ethnic community were deeply disillusioned. The ethnic vote, for which the Labour Party was a natural repository, was now largely floating loose (a 15 March 2004 *Guardian*/ICM poll showed that Labour's British Muslim vote had fallen by half since the 2001 General Election because of the UK's role in the Iraq War). The 1 million people who had marched through London on 15 February 2003 to oppose the war still had votes to cast 15 months later and the Labour and Conservative parties were apprehensive. The Liberal Democrats, on the other hand, could now expect to reap the benefits of their principled stand against military action.

From its 1997 victory onwards, Labour support held up well in the polls. Figure 3.1 shows levels of support for the three parties in the period 1999–2004.

Apart from a brief blip during the September 2000 fuel blockade, the party stayed comfortably ahead until 2003 and even when the Conservatives came level, Labour retained a position which, granted the bias in the electoral system, would ensure a comfortable parliamentary majority. The Conservatives and the Liberal Democrats made advances in local council elections but Labour kept control of every big city except Liverpool and Sheffield (which the Liberal Democrats ran).[1] Labour did not lose a parliamentary by-election until Brent East in September 2003 – and then it was to the Liberal Democrats. Despite their setback in the 1999 European election, Labour had little reason to feel threatened by the Conservatives.

The economy continued in good health. In successive budgets Gordon Brown could boast of low inflation, falling unemployment and continued growth. Though the Conservatives complained of his 'stealth taxes' and taunted him for the failure of the increased expenditure to yield tangibly improved services, the Chancellor could find money to spend on health and education and the police. Such a record of sustained investment, coupled with robust 'fundamentals' in the economy, gave Mr Brown and the Labour government a very strong suit.

The immigration issue, on the other hand, caused continual trouble for the government. The press trumpeted horror stories of the smuggling of foreigners and the abuse of the benefits systems by asylum seekers. In April 2004 immigration minister Beverly Hughes was forced to resign after it was revealed that the Home Office had failed to implement proper checks on Eastern

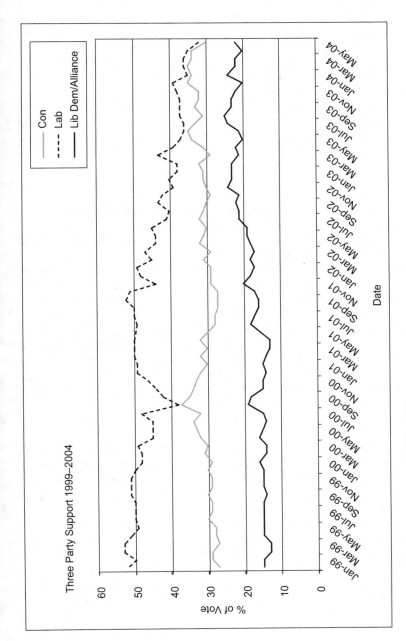

Figure 3.1 Three-party support, 1999–2004

Source: Authors' compilation.

European immigration applications. She was the first ministerial casualty since Michael Howard's appointment to the Conservative party leadership.

The handling of the foot-and-mouth epidemic of 2001 and the abortive attempts to ban fox hunting contributed to a significant rural revolt, culminating in a large London demonstration in September 2002.

The government's efforts at constitutional change aroused little enthusiasm. As seen in Chapter 1, nothing came of the Jenkins Report on electoral reform. The removal of hereditary peers did not make it any easier to get legislation through the House of Lords and the abrupt attempt to abolish the Lord Chancellor proved something of a fiasco. Devolution to Scotland and Wales, however, was acknowledged to be at least a partial success.

Party preparations

Candidate selection for the major parties was mostly completed more than a year in advance. In general terms the process ran more smoothly in 2004 than it had done in 1999, when the parties were adapting themselves to a list system of PR. Indeed, getting candidate selection out of the way early clearly helped.

In 2004 candidates faced a winnowing with the reduction of UK representation from 87 to 78 MEPs (see Chapter 2). If there were no swing, the last elected in nine regions would lose their seat. The nine included four Labour, two Greens, and one each from UKIP, the Conservatives and Plaid Cymru. In terms of gender balance, if no seats were to change hands the selections would mean that (out of 78, not 87, MEPs) the Conservatives would go from three to four women (though Theresa Villiers was likely soon to leave) while Labour would stay at ten. Whether the ratio of women to men would be more or less than three to one would depend on the fate of the two Greens, each lady (Jean Lambert and Caroline Lucas) being endangered by the reduction in seats.

Conservatives

The Conservative selection process (see Table 3.2) ran relatively smoothly. In 1999 the Conservatives had ranked their candidates through party members voting at regional hustings. There was a covert battle between Euroenthusiasts and Eurosceptics in which the enthusiasts were thought to have fared slightly better.

In 2004, eight MEPs ended with a lower place on the list than in 1999, but only three were demoted to a probably losing position (see Table 3.3). One, Robert Goodwill, in Yorkshire, gave up his candidacy, but the others soldiered on. The fate of Lord Stockton (down from third to fifth on the South West list) and Roy Perry (down from second to sixth in the South West) may have been partly due to their pro-European stance, but factional fighting and purely personal considerations may also have come into the decisions. (In April 2003 Roy Perry had come close to being elected as European Ombudsman, losing out narrowly to Greek Nikiforos Diamandouros.)

Table 3.2 Party selection procedures for the 2004 European Parliament elections

Party	Selection Process
Conservative	**1999, 2004:** Meetings of party members at regional level choose from approved list of candidates. Candidate selection and ordering depends on members' votes. No formal 'gender balance mechanism', but this must be 'borne in mind' by electors
Labour	**1999:** Candidate nominations made through constituency parties. Final list and its ordering decided by 'Board of Order' composed of national and regional officials/members. Requirement for one woman on each shortlist **2004:** Regional membership ballot. Requirement for one woman on each shortlist
Liberal Democrats	**1999:** 'Zipping' of candidates, with a male candidate being followed on the list by a female candidate and vice versa **2004:** One of the top three on each list must be of a different sex
UKIP	**1999, 2004:** Candidates chosen and ordered by regional meetings
Greens	**1999, 2004:** regional selection by postal PR ballot
SNP	**1999, 2004:** Candidate shortlist drawn up by regional selection boards. Selection and ordering by membership ballot. No formal mechanisms on gender balance
Plaid Cymru	**1999, 2004:** Candidate shortlist drawn up by an all-Wales selection board. Selection and ordering by membership ballot. Candidates selected from gender-balanced shortlist
Respect	**2004:** Candidates chosen at regional meetings but ordered by party executive

Table 3.3 Incumbent Conservative and Labour MEPs' experience of reselection in 2004

Region	**Conservative**			**Labour**		
	MEPs in 1999	Seeking Reselection	Placed lower on list	MEPs in 1999	Seeking Reselection	Placed lower on list
Eastern	4	4[a]	1	2	1	0
East Midlands	3	2[b]	0	2	1	0
London	4	3[c]	1	4	2	0
North East	1	1	0	3	2	0
North West	5	4	1	4	4	1
South East	5	5	2	2	2	0
South West	4	4	2	1	1	0
Y & H	3	3[d]	2	3	3	1
Wales	1	1	0	2	2	0
Scotland	2	2	0	3	3	1

[a] B. Khanbhai, though reselected, was later taken off the list.
[b] W. Newton Dunn switched parties in 2000 and stood first on the Liberal Democrat list.
[c] R. Balfe (Labour 1999) switched parties in 2003 and was placed fifth on the Conservative list.
[d] R. Goodwill, though selected, withdrew on being placed fourth on the list.

Source: Authors' compilation.

There was certainly no concerted purge of Euro-enthusiasts. One or two complaints were heard of Conservative hustings being packed by groups from farming or ethnic communities or from particular constituencies. There were also a few murmurs about prejudicial leaflets or press comment. But no one could argue that fair play was not in general observed.[2] Three of the five Conservative retirements were entirely voluntary. As will be seen in Chapter 4, Bashir Khanbhai was taken off the Eastern list at the last moment, following allegations about his expense claims while an MEP. Theresa Villiers topped the London list, even though she had been selected for a safe Commons seat (see Chapter 1) and was expected to leave the European Parliament within a year or so when the next General Election came.

There was reassurance for the Conservative Party's Euro-enthusiasts and for the centre-left of the party more generally. When, once the dust had settled, the party's Euro-enthusiasts came to tot up the list of candidates likely to be elected, they found that the balance stayed in their favour. Moreover, their calculations showed that, if more Conservative MEPs were elected, their majority would grow ...

As Chapter 1 described, both Edward McMillan-Scott and his successor as leader of the British Conservatives in the European Parliament, Jonathan Evans, managed to maintain a reasonable degree of coherence within the delegation, notwithstanding a wide range of strongly held views on the issue of European integration and several political developments (the Convention, the draft Constitution and various strong pronouncements by the domestic party leadership) which could have triggered off polemics and hence discord, if not scission.

It was because of this relative coherence that Mr Evans was able, with Mr Howard's support, to maintain the EPP-ED Malaga Agreement intact, thus granting the Conservative MEPs most of the benefits of belonging to a large group without any ideological obligations on the European integration issue. This pragmatic approach was in great contrast to the period of Iain Duncan Smith's leadership, when threats were made to break away altogether from the EPP Group, though the so-called 'H-block' of Eurosceptic Conservative MEPs continued to militate in favour of a more detached stance.

Moreover, in the autumn of 2003 reports of a sort heard sporadically throughout the 1999–2004 period resurfaced that the Conservative MEPs, with the support of Lady Thatcher, were seeking to break away altogether from the EPP and to form a new political group ('New Europe') in the Parliament. Talks were reported to have been held with fellow Eurosceptics in Poland, the Czech Republic, Slovakia, Estonia and Portugal. Iain Duncan Smith was said to have flagged up his party's intentions in his July 2003 'Prague Declaration', and called for a pan-Continental alliance to 'sweep away' the 'Old Europe' vision of an EU super-state. Mr Duncan Smith's intentions did not meet with universal approval, particularly not among the more Euro-enthusiastic Tory MEPs.

Michael Howard, himself a Eurosceptic, set a new tone and direction, seeking out alliances with fellow European politicians on the right (French Prime Minister Jean-Pierre Raffarin and, more cheekily, Spain's José-Maria Aznar and Italy's Silvio Berlusconi – both supposedly Blair allies), but quietly stepping back from the proposal to withdraw from the Malaga Agreement.

Mr Howard's policy position on European issues was set out in a 13 February 2004 set-piece speech to the Konrad Adenauer Stiftung in Berlin.[3] It seemed to follow on from Mr Duncan Smith's Prague speech, with its emphasis on a new departure ('a new deal'), but under Mr Howard the Conservatives were no longer seeking to 'sweep away' the Old Europe. Rather, the new Conservative vision was of a 'flexible Europe' which would build on existing Treaty provisions for 'enhanced cooperation' to enable those countries that wished to do so to forge ahead with the integration process. It would step back from the euro and the Constitution (which it opposed and on which it would organise a referendum). It would seek to negotiate to restore national control over British fishing grounds[4] and over international development and aid funding. It would maintain the special relationship with the US and wanted NATO to remain the cornerstone of European defence.

A measure of Mr Howard's success came in late April 2004, when the *Daily Express* announced that it was abandoning seven years of support for Labour in favour of the Conservative Party.

Together, Mr Howard and Mr Evans managed somehow to maintain cohesion and unity in the run-up to the June elections, and even turned it to their advantage. By April 2004 there was considerable speculation about the results of the forthcoming European elections within the European Parliament. The leadership of the EPP-ED Group had clear ambitions to remain the largest grouping within the European Parliament. This would give it patronage powers, not only within the Parliament, but also an influential say over the choice of the future President of the European Commission (see Chapter 1). Animated debate boiled on within the group, with 'purists', seeking greater ideological coherence, lined up against 'pragmatists', determined to show flexibility if it would win the group the majority it needed to maintain its patronage powers. The pragmatists had the upper hand, and thus Mr Howard and Mr Evans effectively found themselves in a sellers' market. An amendment to the Group Statutes was adopted, granting allied members (such as the British Tories) most of the benefits of membership but very few obligations. This degree of flexibility so infuriated many of the purists that they began actively to seek alliance with Graham Watson's embryonic centrist grouping ...

Even the two men's critics admired this achievement, but there was some apprehension as to what sort of new balance the selection procedure and the 2004 elections would throw up: could the balancing act be continued?

Although Tony Blair's fabled popularity had waned and the issue of trust (both in his judgement and about what he said) was clearly there to be exploited, Michael Howard's chances of capitalising on Tony Blair's problems were restricted by a number of considerations.

First, the Conservatives would be fighting the European elections from a high base – with 36 MEPs they had the second largest national delegation in the European Parliament – whilst the overall number of MEPs was to be reduced. This meant that the Tories would have to improve significantly on their 1999 performance just to maintain the same number of MEPs.

Second, the combining of elections and the decision to hold all-postal ballots in four regions was expected to increase turnout, and this in turn was expected to help Labour disproportionately (see Chapter 1).

Third, as with Labour, a strategic decision had been taken that the party should not unveil its new policies until after the election. It was too early, and the element of surprise would be lost. Inevitably, since this meant the parties could not fight with new, positive policy elements, they would have to concentrate on negative campaigning.

Fourth, this would be Michael Howard's first test at the polls since his appointment as leader. He would naturally be eager to prove himself on the national stage. Such was their place in the electoral cycle that the European elections could naturally serve as a springboard for the General Election largely expected to be held in the spring of 2005. Just as naturally, therefore, Mr Howard would be eager to avoid a disaster.

When Michael Howard took over the leadership, the party's election planning was at a very rudimentary stage. It had already been agreed that a major plank of the envisaged campaign strategy would be to call for a referendum on the draft European Constitution – 'Let the People Decide'. But the manifesto had yet to be drafted and the campaign team yet to be established. Michael Howard's duumvirate at Central Office had allocated strategy to Liam Fox and campaigning to Maurice Saatchi but the leader and his chief of staff, Stephen Sherbourne, were intimately involved, together with Rachel Whetstone and George Bridges in his office. Steve Hilton played a more peripheral strategic role.

Michael Howard was careful, through regular briefings, to keep on board the Europhile 'big beasts of the jungle', (Lord) Leon Brittan, (Lord) Geoffrey Howe, (Lord) Douglas Hurd, and (Lord) Michael Heseltine, and he was at pains to clear all initiatives with the Shadow Cabinet. Jonathan Evans, leader of the Conservative MEPs, was in regular contact and played a key role in the elaborate process of drafting the manifesto (see below).

David Canzini was head of field operations in Central Office, and James Temple-Smithson ran the European part of Central Office operations.

Although the official slogan for the Conservative campaign was to be 'Let Down by Labour', until mid-April the general expectation was that the campaign would focus on the demand for a referendum. There was a quiet but tangible air of confidence in the leader's office about the party's chances, based on its perceived tactical strengths – and Labour's perceived tactical weaknesses;

calling for a referendum was surely more populist than maintaining that one was not necessary. The sense of tactical advantage was further strengthened by the party's measured Eurosceptical stance. Opposition to the Constitutional Treaty was allied to a policy of 'renegotiating' the UK's relationship to the EU's Common Fisheries Policy.

Some party insiders have suggested that this generalised confidence led the leadership into a false sense of security. Whether through nonchalance or inattentiveness, there was clearly a lack of contingency planning. In particular, when in April 2004 Tony Blair conceded a referendum on the future Constitutional Treaty, the Conservatives seemed to be unable to adjust. 'There was no Plan B', several MEPs later complained. Instead, the party soldiered on with its carefully prepared manifesto (though it did not need to worry about the EPP's manifesto from which, under the terms of the Malaga Agreement, it was completely detached) and an elaborately planned campaign 'grid'.

The party decided to concentrate a large part of its efforts on the local elections. Party activists talked of regaining a toehold in the large cities where the party's council representation had dwindled to almost nothing. Some dreamt of becoming the largest party in Birmingham, and of Steven Norris toppling Ken Livingstone in the London Mayoral elections. The party's old hands, looking back in particular to the unsatisfactory 1999 European election campaign, had been unconvinced of the value of a centralised campaign. Party strategists therefore decided to integrate the local and European campaigns and to eschew daily national press conferences in favour of a more decentralised campaign, moving the leader around the regions to carefully orchestrated events. After the party's campaign launch the leader would move to Manchester and then quickly on to Scotland and Wales.

If Labour had shot the Conservatives' fox on the Constitutional Treaty, the issue of the Conservative MEPs' relationship with the EPP Group within the European Parliament was, in the end, the dog that didn't bark. There was to be no public or media interest in an issue which had so exercised MEPs and the party hierarchy. But it was nevertheless an issue which the leadership – in Westminster and Strasbourg – *had* to resolve in a way which would leave no chinks through which the opposition or the media might develop a breach. As seen above, insiders were openly admiring of the way in which Michael Howard and Jonathan Evans had quietly resolved and defused the issue. It was one of those political achievements where the only reward was the absence of any penalty.

Labour

With a couple of exceptions, Labour managed its selection procedure smoothly. The party's procedure was kind to its sitting MEPs; the three retirements were entirely voluntary and only three MEPs were placed lower on the list than in 1999, and all were still in winnable positions, though the reduction in seats put David Bowe (number three in Yorkshire) and Bill Miller (number three in Scotland) in some jeopardy. Only three candidates for seats that had been won in 1999 were newcomers. All MEPs had to secure renomination from constituency parties – but none had any difficulty in doing so.

The unpleasantness that Labour had feared might erupt could not be entirely avoided in Yorkshire and Humber, where there was a struggle between the two incumbent male MEPs to avoid the vulnerable third place on the list (one of the first two winnable positions effectively being reserved for the female incumbent, Linda McAvan). In the end, though, the ballot was decisive (Linda McAvan, 2,610; Richard Corbett, 2,243; David Bowe, 903).

Worse for the party, in Scotland a protracted and unpleasant row (described in the *Sunday Herald* as a 'dangerous mixture of politics and personal animosity' – 4 April 2004) broke out and was to become an issue in the election campaign itself. The row, which involved the party's senior MEP, David Martin (Lothian-based, first elected in 1984 and a Vice-President of the Parliament since 1989), and Bill Miller (Glasgow-based, first elected in 1994, and the European Parliamentary Labour Party's Whip), was triggered off by allegedly preferential treatment accorded to Mr Miller during the selection procedure.[5] It turned nastier just before the campaign itself, when anonymous allegations were made to the party about David Martin's use of expenses to fund his constituency office. Most of Mr Martin's colleagues spoke in his support and bemoaned the anonymous accusations, but Mr Miller – condemned to fight for the third place – made critical remarks which the Martin camp took badly.[6] The initial allegations were handed over to a nonplussed EP secretariat to examine. Just as Mr Martin had been cleared, further allegations and 'documentary evidence' were produced.

Labour Party managers were in a quandary. The closing date for nominations was Thursday 13 May, and it was clear that the European Parliament's authorities would not be able to examine all of the fresh material by then. On Tuesday 11 May, a party spokesman announced that an agreement had been reached with Mr Martin, whereby he would be allowed to remain as a candidate, but with an independent assessor brought in to examine his accounts. Mr Martin had agreed to stand down immediately if the investigator found anything wrong. Mr Martin declared himself confident that no wrongdoing would be found.

Although the affair died down and Mr Martin was later to be elected,[7] he could nevertheless claim that the affair had done him considerable damage. For example, when the outgoing EPLP considered who it might recommend as a potential candidate for the Presidency of the Parliament, David Martin could not put himself forward for the vote. (The EPLP instead gave its backing to Terry Wynn.) This was frustrating for a man who had done creditable battle as the Socialist Group's candidate against Pat Cox in 2002. The affair also left questions unanswered about the way such allegations were managed.

Ironically, the affair would also do damage to the Conservatives. By the time the election campaign got under way, the Scottish public had become well-versed in the issue of MEPs' allowances and journalists were on the lookout for similar stories.[8]

The Labour Party had had an unhappy campaign in 1999 but rallied quickly and took great comfort from its continued success in 2001. The party changed its organisation; instead of a rotating chairman chosen by seniority from the National Executive, they followed the Conservative example of a Chair appointed from the senior rank of MPs. But rotation continued; Charles Clarke (June 2001), was followed by John Reid (October 2002) and then by Ian MacCartney (May 2003).

In 2002 the party moved from Millbank Tower to a more central location in Old Queen Street 200 yards from Parliament. David Triesman took over as General Secretary but in December 2003 he moved over to the Lords as a Government Whip and was replaced by Matthew Carter.

Labour's strategic thinking was almost entirely focused on the next General Election, which it seemed increasingly likely would be called in the spring of 2005. As seen above, the European elections would be the Conservative leader's first national electoral outing. His honeymoon period was now over, and all he had to show for it were a few punches landed in Prime Minister's Question Time. There had been no body blows, no potential knockouts. He had made no progress in the polls, and seemed unable to get the most out of the limited pool of talent at his disposal. Nevertheless, Michael Howard's supporters saw him as being on a roll, and it was clear that the Tories would be seeking to use what was expected to be a strong performance in the European and local elections to build a platform from which a viable pre-General Election campaign could be launched.

Despite bullish language from Charles Kennedy, Labour knew that the Conservatives had most to fear from the Liberal Democrats and that the only General Election threat to Labour would come from the Conservatives. It was therefore decided to go for a simple strategic goal: undermine Michael Howard by stressing his negatives, and by so doing rob his leadership of momentum and deflate Conservative activists' delicate morale. Having changed leader three times since 2001, the Conservatives would have to stay with Michael Howard at least until after the next General Election. This 'negative campaigning' was largely inspired by recent American (Democrat) practice; if you can nail the man, you have no need to embark on a policy debate. It loaned itself well to a campaign where resources would be scarce. It should also be said that Mr Howard, famously branded by fellow Tory Ann Widdecombe as having 'something of the night' about him, was considered a good candidate for the treatment. Labour would measure the success of its strategy not by the number of Labour MEPs returned but by the lack of perceived overall success for Michael Howard and the Conservatives.

This was not to say that Labour did not have positive policy themes to fight on but, as with the Conservatives, it was generally felt that it was too early to break and the atmosphere was in any case wrong; 'Why sow seed in stony ground?' asked one insider.

While there can be little doubt that the Labour government was sincere in its desire to encourage greater turnout in elections, it is equally clear that Labour stood to gain more from greater turnout and combined elections than most other parties.

Ken Livingstone, now safely back in Tony Blair's big tent, was expected to hold off the Conservative challenge in the London Mayoral election, so that it would be impossible for the Tories or the pundits to paint the June elections as a complete disaster. Moreover, as seen above, the Conservatives had performed strongly in the 1999 European elections, so that the onus was more on them to retain their wins than on mid-term Labour to make spectacular gains. Even so, if all postal ballots and combined elections could raise turnout levels, then Labour might do better than was generally expected.

The third year of the parliamentary cycle has tended to be bad for incumbent governments and therefore considerable effort was expended on the local elections. In March a new National Communications Centre had been set up in Gosforth (Newcastle-upon-Tyne). For the local elections the party focused on 169 key wards – just six in Leeds – and had bombarded them with campaign calls from one if its three call centres. The centre had produced literature that could be customised so that it appeared to be entirely local. There had been a concerted effort to devolve campaigning and campaigning responsibility to the regions, though this was to result in scant media coverage.

There had been several months' discussion on how to coordinate the different campaigns. Inevitably, the European elections were seen as a sub-section of a broader and longer campaign. (It was striking how, by May 2004, the expected losses in the European elections had already been 'written off', and how high activists' morale was reported to be.) A tactical decision was taken to play to the party's strengths. In London, for example, the campaign was almost exclusively about the Mayoral election. The four all-postal ballot regions were also singled out for special attention. The overall tactic was to concentrate on strengths and to downplay and discount the rest.

Labour was potentially vulnerable on Europe as an issue and so, from the beginning, energies were focused on reducing the damage potential, rather than making a positive case. A short, general manifesto had been produced at EU-level by the Party of European Socialists, under the chairmanship of its outgoing President, Robin Cook, and with Denis MacShane representing the Labour Party in the drafting process. The manifesto gave five key commitments: boosting Europe's growth, fighting poverty and creating jobs; bringing the EU closer to its citizens; managing migration and pursuing social integration; building a more secure, sustainable, peaceful and just world; and promoting Europe as an area of democracy and equality. The document's provisions were so general that it seemed it could contain no hostages to fortune. At national level Labour decided to forgo a manifesto altogether, preferring a more innocuous policy document.

In early 2004 Tony Blair took two important decisions with major implications for the European election campaign. The first was taken after the tragic 11 March 2004 Madrid bombings led to a change of government in Spain. Until then, it had been broadly assumed that the inter-governmental talks on the draft Constitutional Treaty would remain blocked indefinitely, but the new Spanish government made it plain that a deal could be done and, as Chapter 1 described, Irish Prime Minister Bertie Ahern decided to launch serious discussions with the more intransigent member state governments with a view to brokering solutions. Mr Blair's first decision concerned how he and his government would react to this new situation.

The government had launched its campaign in favour of a draft Constitution back in September 2003, with its position set out in a White Paper. The critical reactions demonstrated by a broad swathe of the media towards the White Paper then must surely have tempted Mr Blair to be grateful for the blockage caused by the Poles and the Spanish in December. Once that blockage was resolved, Mr Blair was left with an awkward choice. If the negotiations succeeded, there was a strong probability he would have to defend the draft Constitution during the European election campaign. But such a prospect could probably only be stopped by Mr Blair giving instructions for his own government to block the talks.

Mr Blair's first decision, taken in early April, was to cast any such temptations to the wind and to instruct his government to negotiate with a view to reaching agreement within the timetable set out by the Irish government.

Mr Blair reportedly agonised far more over a second, related decision. Back in September 2003, the government had argued that the draft Constitutional Treaty was more a cleaning-up exercise than a radical fresh constitutional departure, and hence did not require popular approval through a referendum. Government colleagues, Labour MPs and MEPs rallied to this position though, once both the Conservatives and the Liberal Democrats had embraced the referendum cause, Labour activists reportedly felt increasingly exposed. As late as 1 April former Labour leader and arch-loyalist Neil Kinnock had written to the *Guardian* to argue that 'Drawing attention to (the Constitution's details) is not "downplaying" the treaty or participating in an "elitist plot". It is recognising the facts. They don't add up to a case for a referendum in the UK.'

Health Secretary John Reid was reportedly the first of a number of high-ranking government colleagues (including Gordon Brown, Jack Straw and John Prescott) to argue to Mr Blair that the government could not escape granting a referendum for a simple reason; referendums were no longer a constitutional rarity. If the government could agree to referendums on devolution, then how could it deny one on the Constitutional Treaty? In mid-April the Prime Minister holidayed in the Bahamas. According to press reports, his reflections on the issue included three additional considerations.

One was the more effective style of Michael Howard and the Tory leader's clear strategic goal of winning well in June. The other was, reportedly, a telephone conversation with the proprietor of the *Sun* and *Times* newspapers, Rupert Murdoch. The third was tied up with the behaviour of the House of Lords. The Prime Minister's advisers had pointed out that if the House of Lords tabled an amendment to the expected ratification Bill then there would be insufficient time to invoke the Parliament Act before the expected spring 2005 General Election. That, inevitably, would turn the General Election into a referendum by proxy.

The momentous decision to opt for a referendum leaked out over the weekend of 17–18 April, as Mr Blair returned via Washington. Inevitably, he had to endure many 'U-turn' headlines (a *Financial Times* editorial spoke about 'Blair's reverse gear' – 20 April) and privately party loyalists were swift to express anger and frustration over the way the decision had been taken and the announcement handled. Mr Blair also lost face when Tory pressure forced him to make an announcement personally to the House on 20 April, and Michael Howard was not slow to push home his advantage.

But even as this ritual humiliation was meted out, party strategists recognised the astuteness of the move. The referendum could not be held until at least late autumn 2005, safely after the next General Election, and the Conservatives' position would enable Mr Blair to turn it into an 'in or out of Europe' issue. 'This was', said one Tory insider, 'political triangulation on a grand scale.' Overnight Mr Blair had shot the Tory fox and, in doing so, had probably staved off at least some of the worst in the European elections. Said a Brussels official: 'It's a strategically brilliant move if you are concerned with British politics through 2005 but arguably strategically disastrous if you are concerned with Britain's long-term position in Europe' (*Guardian*, 20 April). The European elections would no longer be 'a referendum on having a referendum'. However, unlike the Tories, the reversal had no consequences for Labour's already prepared electoral strategy ...

At an organisational level, the European elections would be treated as a first test for the General Election machine; the equivalent of taking a car for a spin after a winter spent on bricks in the garage. With the new party secretary general, Matt Carter, in place, it was time to dust down and overhaul Labour's much-vaunted campaign machinery and to road-test techniques.

Under David Triesman the 'Attack' team had been run down to two people. The revered campaigning database Excalibur had been abandoned, and had to be revived, though some of its work was now done by LexisNexis and other search engines. The databases on Conservative candidates and activists needed to be brought up to date. There was, then, a grid, with day-by-day good stories and telegenic happenings planned with the Prime Minister and other Labour stars (whether the media would notice them was another matter).

The election team consisted of Douglas Alexander, Minister for Cabinet Office, Chancellor Gordon Brown, Philip Gould (the party's strategic pollster),

Deputy Prime Minister John Prescott and the Party Chairman, Ian MacCartney. Tony Blair and Jack Straw were both integral parts of the campaign team, but regular affairs of state restricted their ability to participate. There were daily strategy meetings at 16 Old Queen Street. Peter Mandelson was a regular attender. Gary Titley, EPLP leader, attended these when he could. Douglas Alexander was absent in mid campaign on paternity leave but returned before the end of the campaign. Others who attended included David Hill, Matt Carter, Pat McFadden, Peter Coleman, Spencer Livermore and Ed Owen, standing in for Jack Straw, who was theoretically in charge of the campaign. Tony Blair was consulted and informed, with Sally Morgan as the facilitator. Below this level, Matt Doyle was responsible for media; Alicia Kennedy for field operations; Patrick Loughran for 'Attack' and political research.

The postal voting would impose its own imperatives on campaigning. Postal ballots were due to go out on 26–28 May, and it was thought that most of those who would vote would do so within the following two weeks. It meant that the party's strategy would have to peak early, and perhaps peak again later. The launch of the party's campaign was set at 10 May. The plan was to go straight for Michael Howard's political jugular vein.

In 1994, a senior Labour politician involved in the Labour Party's Euro-manifesto drafting exercise declared that the manifesto was there 'because it was there' (Butler and Westlake, 1995, p. 134). Ten years on, Labour had taken this trend to its logical conclusion – there was no manifesto. The first draft of Labour's electoral 'consultation document' was largely drafted by Ed Owen, Jack Straw's political adviser. This draft, which emerged towards the end of April, had drawn on the work of the party's policy commission, *Britain in the World*, and the discussions in the national policy forum in March, which had involved Europe, among other subjects. A consultative paper approved by the policy commission went out to MEPs and other stakeholders, asking them, basically, to indicate what seemed to matter. Gary Titley, the EPLP leader, was closely involved, smoothing inevitable tension between the European and domestic wings of the party. There was an issue over where the emphasis should be placed. Naturally, the party's MEPs wanted more stress to be put on their activities and achievements and the role of the European Parliament more generally.

However, at the end of the day the electoral document had to be a 'prism of national politics' and the party had to avoid giving hostages to fortune. The document had also to be a morale booster but – a big difference from a general election manifesto – it was impossible to be too specific about policy intentions.

Liberal Democrats

The Liberal Democrats chose their candidates by postal ballot, though no longer with the 'zipping' system that had ensured gender balance in 1999. There were no major incidents and, unlike Labour and the Conservatives, there was no apprehension, and nor were the three sitting Liberal Democrat MEPs to be affected by the reduction in overall numbers.

As seen in Chapter 1, two of the ten Liberal Democrats elected in 1999 were selected in 2003 to stand for Westminster seats held by Liberal Democrats. One, Nick Clegg, gave up his East Midlands candidacy to be replaced at the head of the ticket by the veteran MEP, Bill Newton Dunn, who had switched from the Conservatives soon after the 1999 election. But Chris Huhne, although prospective candidate for Eastleigh, still headed the South East list.

The Liberal Democrats, in contrast to 1999, did not formally insist on alternate regions having male or female candidates in the lead position, but they still achieved a gender balance since their ten MEPs standing again at the head of their tickets (Chris Huhne and Emma Nicholson at one and two in the South East) included five men and five women. Since all occupied the party's most winnable list positions, the incumbents could be satisfied but, as with the Conservatives and Labour, this meant that there was very little space for newcomers.

The European elections of 1999 served the Liberal Democrats well. Thanks to proportional representation they jumped from two MEPs to ten, which greatly helped their organisation at home as well as in Brussels.

The Liberal Democrats acquired a new leader immediately after the 1999 election and, under the amiable Charles Kennedy, the party consolidated its position as a significant player in local government and in Parliament. It shared power with Labour in the new Executives in Scotland and Wales. The previous Liberal Democrat leader, Paddy Ashdown, had developed a close friendship with Tony Blair. Their closeness owed something at least to the commonly held belief, prior to 1997, that an apparently in-built Conservative majority could only be overcome by an organic alliance of the centre and the centre-left.

Under the genial but determined influence of Roy Jenkins, the two party leaders had discussed the perspective of a permanent centre-left coalition elected by proportional representation. The 1997 General Election result showed that Labour was still able to win a working majority alone, but both Labour and the Liberal Democrats continued half-heartedly to cooperate. Occasionally, Mr Blair made a significant gesture; the decision to introduce PR for the 1999 European elections was one such. But the 2001 General Election result – a virtual repeat of 1997 – made it plain both to Mr Blair and to Mr Kennedy that the old Ashdown–Jenkins–Blair vision of an organic Lab-Lib coalition was unnecessary.

While the Labour government quietly dropped its language about a 'Third Way', Charles Kennedy rapidly distanced his party from Labour's embrace, letting the joint constitutional committees which the 1997 Labour government had created fall into abeyance, and seeking distance on salient policy issues. Mr Kennedy was equally careful to steer his party away from the temptation to go left of Labour. As the Conservative Party failed to revive its fortunes so Mr Kennedy's Liberal Democrats increasingly spoke about a 'three-party system' or even about the possibility ultimately of usurping the Conservatives' role as main opposition party. Given the Chancellor's investment programme, the issue could not be about expenditure. Rather, it was an issue of delivery, and by the 2002 party conference Mr Kennedy had been able to get adopted a set of proposals that set out a coherent Liberal Democrat alternative, with an emphasis on decentralisation for health and education and a commitment to increased consumer choice.

The outbreak of hostilities in Iraq in 2003 gave Charles Kennedy an issue on which he could take a clear stand, arguing that the country had gone to war on a 'flawed prospectus', and distance his party from both Labour and the Conservatives. Opinion polls showed that the party's principled stand was proving popular with ethnic voters who had floated away from Labour over the war issue. Mr Kennedy held his party together effectively, most notably in preserving a united front against the war in Iraq and in favour of joining the euro.

In March 2004 Mr Kennedy cried off from the budget debate and Prime Minister's Questions because of a 'violent stomach bug'. Westminster watchers recalled that he had also missed an important June 2003 parliamentary debate on the euro on health grounds, and there was therefore some press speculation about his state of health. A restored Mr Kennedy later poured scorn on the idea.[9]

The party had consistently called for a referendum on the future draft European Constitution, but it had also consistently called for a 'Yes' vote in that referendum. With the exception of some Eurosceptical pronouncements made by the party's treasury spokesman, Vince Cable, in early April 2004, Europe remained dormant as a potentially divisive issue. The party machine worked smoothly, with Lord Razzall as Head of the Campaigns Unit and Lord Rennard as Chief Executive and election strategist. The veteran Sir Menzies Campbell, who became Deputy Leader in 2003, provided sage strategic advice and added gravitas to the party's image.

The party flourished in local elections; it had 2,609 councillors and 20 councils in 1999 and still had 2,624 councillors and 28 councils in 2003. The 2001 General Election saw the Liberal Democrat vote increase from 17% to 18% and its representation up from 46 MPs to 52; it at last had a presence in every region of Britain. The party's poll rating stayed above 20%.

In the 1999 European election the party received 12.7% of the Great Britain vote and won ten European seats. Their tally was increased to eleven in November 2000 by the defection of Bill Newton Dunn. With the number of seats being reduced to 75 (78) it was clear that there would be pressure on all of the parties. However, the Liberal Democrats did not win the last seat in any of the regions which were to lose an MEP, and with their poll rating holding firm and their popular critical stance on the invasion of Iraq, they could hope to win more seats, rather than less, in 2004. They therefore decided to concentrate their fire on the three regions where gains were most likely.

The November annual congress of the European Liberal Democrat and Reform Party, held in Amsterdam, had adopted a pan-EU manifesto for the European elections. As with the PSE manifesto, the ELDR manifesto consisted more of general policy priorities than specific policies to be implemented. Major planks included reforming the MEPs' expenses system, better access to EU documents, creating a genuine single transport market, strengthening EU climate change initiatives, deregulation of agricultural policy, and a new strategic partnership with the US.

The Liberal Democrat national manifesto was far more European than in the past; 'the best European manifesto we've had', as one MEP put it. A 'pre-manifesto', *Common Problems, Shared Solutions* had been published in September 2003. The climate of Euroscepticism had made the draftsmen more rigorous. The primary draftsman was Richard Grayson, an internationalist, but not pro-European. The main aim had been to reach agreement between the Liberal Democrat MPs and the MEPs. The manifesto sought to head off accusations that the party was too 'soft' on Europe. As Mr Kennedy wrote in the introduction:

> We are not supine in our attitude towards Europe. We are committed to Britain maintaining a national veto on fundamental constitutional issues – the right of the House of Commons to decide if British troops are ever sent into military conflict, budgetary and taxation matters, and regulations over pay and social security.

UK Independence Party

UKIP's unexpected success in electing three MEPs in 1999 gave the party a boost. Despite the disaffection of their founder, Alan Sked, and the disappearance of their first Strasbourg Leader, Michael Holmes, UKIP was encouraged to think of running 300 candidates in the 2001 General Election; rank and file enthusiasm pushed that figure up to 428. They were less successful than Sir James Goldsmith's Referendum Party had been in 1997; they only averaged 2.1% of the vote and only six saved their deposits; the highest vote was 7.8% in Bexhill for their most prominent figure, the MEP Nigel Farage. But the members kept up hope. By January 2003 they numbered 9,000 and a year later 17,000.

Max Clifford, the publicist, was recruited late in 2003 and he worked hard to improve the image of the party in the national media. Robert Kilroy-Silk, the former Labour MP turned chat show presenter, who had been dismissed by the BBC in January 2004 for publishing an anti-Arab article, was recruited by the Earl of Bradford. He only came publicly on the scene in May, well after the election had started – the other candidates in the East Midlands would subsequently have to agree to his being jumped to the head of the ticket.

Other celebrities lent their names to the cause, including three Dukes (Devonshire, Rutland and Somerset) and four Conservative peers, led by Lord Pearson. Joan Collins, Sir Patrick Moore and later Geoff Boycott joined in. In addition to four former MPs who stood as candidates, others announced their support, including Jonathan Aitken and Teresa Gorman. The party was intent on shedding any extremist aspects of its image.

The party's activities were masterminded by the three MEPs, Nigel Farage, Jeffrey Titford and Graham Booth, together with Roger Knapman, the UKIP Leader and a former Conservative Westminster Whip, and aided by David Lott as chief organiser. Paul Sykes, a Yorkshire millionaire, and Alan Bown, a Kent bookmaker, contributed massively to party funds – although there were substantial contributions from the rank and file. The party entered the European elections on a remarkably solid base.

Thus, the party got significant help from Dick Morris, an erstwhile campaign adviser to Bill Clinton whom Roger Knapman had met on a cruise. At a gathering in Torquay in January 2004 he had enthused the 80 or so key figures by emphasising their strategy based on a simple well-publicised 'NO'.

The party's strategy, as advised by Dick Morris and Max Clifford, could be summed up in that one word: 'NO'. The message was clear and unequivocal and unique; UKIP was the only party (apart from the BNP) to advocate complete withdrawal from the European Union. The party's advertising campaign was also cleverly nuanced: by saying 'NO to European Union', rather than *the* European Union, the party subliminally sent out a message that Union was an ongoing process rather than an end state. Mr Clifford's first intervention was to promote Elizabeth Winkfield, an 83-year-old UKIP member from Devon, as 'the lady in tweed' ready to go to jail rather than pay her council tax. He led Nigel Farage on a tour around newspaper offices where 'they put out the word that the party was on the way up and had no links to the BNP or the racists' (*The Times*, 3 June 2004). Mr Morris designed a six-month strategy to raise the party's profile. The first stage was to move from cramped London offices to more spacious offices in Birmingham. The next step was to prioritise billboard advertising with the simple 'Just Say No' slogan. Mr Clifford had planned a classic drip, drip, revelation of supporters. The charismatic Mr Kilroy-Silk's recruitment was a bonus.

The party's avowed aim was to increase its Strasbourg representation from three to ten members, and it entered the campaign quietly confident that it had prepared well.

The Greens

In 1999, the British Green Party had won a significant toehold of two MEPs, Jean Lambert and Dr Caroline Lucas. In an ideal world, the party would have been seeking to build on this performance by winning further seats. In reality, they were painfully aware that both Jean Lambert in London and Dr Lucas in the South East had been the last to be returned in their respective regions.

Since both regions were to lose a seat under the Nice Treaty adjustments (see Chapter 2), both Green MEPs were under threat.

Thus the June 2004 elections were crucial for the Greens and the party had been anticipating them for some years. An experienced Executive had been led by Penny Kemp, but in 2002/03 a new Chair had allowed reserves to be spent on a burst of activity to set the Party up for the election year, without raising additional funds to fight the European Election itself.

Mike Woodin was the well established Principal Male Speaker, having taken over from Darren Johnson, and was matched by Caroline Lucas, probably the best known of all the Green politicians whose work as an MEP had earned her much media attention. The Elections Coordinator, Geoff Forse, was in the fifth and final year of his term of office, assisted by the longstanding paid election agent Chris Rose. Danny Bates was the Policy Coordinator, who together with Penny Kemp wrote the manifesto, and he also convened the Political Committee whose telephone conferences were instrumental in the political positioning of the party.

Spencer Fitzgibbon, the External Communications Coordinator, managed the Press Office with a team of part-time staff and volunteers. The new post of Publications Coordinator was filled by the young and energetic Matt Wootton. Together these two embarked upon what became known as the 'rebranding' exercise. Tony Cooper as Administration Coordinator supervised the expansion of the office and Chris Keen was Campaigns Coordinator.

Hugo Charlton became Chair of the Executive in the Autumn of 2003 and therefore led the team. He had been the party's Law Officer for seven years before becoming the Home Affairs Speaker in 1998, and thus knew the party machine intimately. Initiating a discussion on election themes and the party image, Mr Fitzgibbon's idea of a 'progress' theme was developed by Mr Charlton's addition of the word 'real' to distinguish the party from the conventional neo-liberal economic notion of progress. This was seized upon by Matt Wootton and taken to his Publications Committee, which included the young designer Jim Killock, where a whole new look and 'brand image' around the theme of 'real progress' was built up and launched on a slightly stunned party but an appreciative public. ('Real progress', declared a 9 March 2004 *Guardian* editorial, quite simply.)

Mike Woodin convened a brainstorming session including most of the above, and also Jean Lambert, the London MEP, who had won reselection after a strong challenge from Paul Ingram, an ex-Oxford councillor who went on to be the London Campaign Manager. At this session the themes of the campaign were decided, namely 'peace & justice', concentrating on Iraq, 'safe food' and 'globalisation and economics'. Having established the party's direction, Mike Woodin was shortly afterwards diagnosed with severe cancer and was too ill to contribute further. His loss was a major blow.

The party firmly positioned itself to the left of Labour, and resisted the blandishments of the new left-wing party Respect. In fact the grassroots of the party were firmly opposed to any sort of alliance, not least because of the distrust of many experienced Green activists of the Socialist Workers Party. However it posed a serious threat, in that it could cost both the MEPs their seats. Although discussions were held, it would have been constitutionally difficult to come to an arrangement, and George Galloway's insistence on standing a candidate against the well-respected anti-war campaigner Caroline Lucas unless the Greens stood down in another regional constituency was seen as unacceptable.

Despite what was called their 'progressive scepticism' about Europe, the Greens knew that it was through their work in the European Parliament that they had gained most credibility. In London, where Assembly Members Darren Johnson, Jenny Jones (the Deputy Mayor) and Noel Lynch had also played a crucial role in raising the party's profile, it was felt the electorate was more sympathetic to Europe and the London Party was concerned to retain Jean Lambert's seat and see off the threat from Mr Galloway. Although outspoken against the euro and consistently Eurosceptic, the Greens agreed to a Europe-wide manifesto.

Whilst the party publicly claimed that it was hoping for six seats, it was more privately concerned about holding on to its two existing seats. To do so, it would need to do better in both regions than it had done in 1999. This was by no means evident.

The British National Party

The British National Party (BNP) was formed in 1982 by John Tyndall. It spent much of the next decade in the shadow of the larger National Front (NF). When the Front split, the BNP became the main far-right organisation in Britain. It first came to national attention in 1993, winning a council by-election in the Tower Hamlets ward of Millwall, but during the 1990s the party lost momentum. Nick Griffin, a Cambridge graduate and former NF chairman, became leader in 1999. In the 1999 European elections its candidates won some 100,000 votes – far from enough to win a seat. In 2002 the BNP won three council seats in Burnley, averaging 28% of the vote. In Oldham, the party came second in four of the five wards it contested and took an average of 27%. Across the country, the BNP averaged 16% in the wards it contested. In May 2003 the BNP trebled its number of seats in the local elections.

A number of European developments encouraged the BNP to raise its ambitions. Under the provisions of the Nice Treaty (see Chapter 1), European political parties could hope to receive European funding, and these provisions were expected to be implemented after the 2004 European elections. The 1 May 2004 enlargement would bring into the Union several member states where far-right parties were expected to do well in the European elections, and among the existing 15 there were several countries with a strong far right. The 2002 French Presidential elections raised right-wing extremism to new levels of respectability when incumbent President Jacques Chirac was obliged to fight off French Front National leader Jean-Marie Le Pen in the second round.

Buoyed by consistent levels of strong support in the North West, the BNP had hopes of winning one Euro-seat in the 2004 elections. This would enable the party to form an alliance with fellow far-right Continental European parties (most notably the French Front National) and hence to benefit from European funding. In April 2003 Jean-Marie Le Pen made a supposedly secret but much-reported visit to the BNP in Manchester, and talks about the future alliance were said to be top of the agenda. The BNP's simple strategy was therefore to play to its strengths, aiming for gains in the local elections and for one MEP in the European elections. It would, however, put up a full slate of candidates in all regions in order to benefit from political broadcasts.

British mainstream political parties were acutely aware of the BNP phenomenon. In February 2004 there were media reports of an impending BNP breakthrough ('BNP ready to gain toehold in EU', *Guardian*, 4 February 2004). These coincided with polling research by the Joseph Rowntree Charitable Trust in the Oldham, Burnley and Calderdale areas which showed that some voters considered the BNP to be a mainstream, democratic political group. The BBC reported that representatives from the three major parties, including a member of Michael Howard's Shadow Cabinet, former Senior Ministers and Shadow Ministers, met at least twice to discuss how to deal with the phenomenon. These meetings were said to have led to a visit by Mr Howard to Burnley on 19 February where, stressing his own family's experience in the Holocaust, he described the BNP as 'a stain on our democratic way of life'. He warned of the danger of the BNP winning a Euro-seat: 'Imagine the shame of this great nation if Britain sends a member of the BNP to Brussels.' The BNP professed itself flattered by the attention: 'It shows how worried they are', said a BNP press spokesman.

Respect

Respect was launched as a party on 25 January 2004, only 20 weeks before the June elections. George Galloway regretted not having started after the 18 March 2003 vote against the Iraq War (he was in fact expelled from the Labour Party on 23 October 2003).

Respect (an acronym for Respect, Equality, Socialism, Peace, Environment, Community, Trade Unionism) was essentially a left-wing coalition protest against New Labour and 'Blairism'. But its main focus was opposition to the Iraq War and the subsequent occupation. It was a coalition with three main elements – the Socialist Workers Party, Muslims and the old left. It tried in vain to draw the Greens into an electoral pact. It had a distant relation with the more Trotskyist Scottish Socialist Party and did not fight in Scotland (it had unsuccessfully sought a similar understanding with the protest and anti-Iraq parties in Wales). In its early stages, Respect escaped the traditional factionalism of the left. The hard left did not insist on its nostrums – a common wage, open borders and republicanism. The moderates in the party relied on numbers to resist a hard-left takeover. It was estimated that only 2,000 of the first 7,000 members were traditional hard-left.

The short ballot paper label for its candidates was Respect, the Unity Coalition (George Galloway), basically on the grounds that George Galloway was the only nationally known figure in the Coalition and that his name would help protesters in placing their vote.

Respect was not large enough to have a full structure of constituency branches but it was set up with an executive answerable to an annual conference.

The Liberal Party

The Liberal Party was set up in 1989 by those Liberals who refused to merge with the then Social Democratic Party to form today's Liberal Democrat Party. The party was led by Michael Meadowcroft, a former Leeds MP (1983–87). The party's strength lay in pockets in Yorkshire and Merseyside. For the 1999 European elections the party put up 43 candidates in five regions and ran on an idiosyncratic platform. In 2004 it put up nine candidates in the North West region alone, headed by its leader and Liverpool City Councillor, Steve Radford. The Party supports 'traditional Liberal values' but, for the 2004 European elections, it opted to focus on a single element of its policy platform – opposition to the euro. Its tactics illustrated well the way the regional list system combined with all-postal balloting could give rise to new techniques. In particular, the party registered its distinctive 'No euro!' logo in such a way that it would appear on all of the ballot papers. The party also incorporated elements of its website address in the party description appearing on the ballot paper.

Scotland

Scottish National Party

Since 1999 the SNP had had two MEPs: Ian Hudghton (who was first elected in 1994), and Sir Neil MacCormick (first elected in 1999). The party had had at least one MEP returned since the first direct elections to the European Parliament in 1979, when Winnie Ewing won the Highlands and Islands seat (which she held until 1999). The SNP's views on Europe were basically supportive:

> The SNP supports the EU as a confederation that collectively exercises certain sovereign rights pooled by states, but in which each state retains its own residual sovereignty in respect of constitutional, fiscal and other matters of national importance. On this understanding, the SNP supports the development of a European constitution while flatly rejecting any idea of a centralised European super-state.

Since the mid-1980s, the formerly Eurosceptical SNP had increasingly called for Scottish independence within Europe, so that the confederation it envisaged would include a Scottish state. With the advent of the Scottish Parliament, the SNP further emphasised its calls for an independent Scotland in Europe, arguing that the establishment of a separate Scottish executive warranted greater attention in Brussels. The SNP would not settle for regional status. Rather, the party believes that, under the terms of the Nice Treaty, an independent Scotland would be entitled to seven votes in the EU's Council of Ministers and would have the right to nominate a European Commissioner.

Another strong plank in the SNP's policy platform concerned the Common Fisheries Policy, where the party argued strongly that the 2002 reforms and the Convention position had undermined the Policy's previous founding principle of relative stability. The SNP therefore argued that it would not support the new European Constitution unless control over fisheries was repatriated and the Common Fisheries Policy abandoned.

Beyond policy issues, the 2004 European elections were seen as an existential test for the SNP. In 2000 its charismatic and longstanding leader, Alex Salmond, had stood down unexpectedly and his place was taken by the more business-like John Swinney. The challenge facing the party and Mr Swinney was how it should position itself in a post-devolution landscape. As a *Guardian* editorial (23 June 2004) put it:

> The SNP had a good 1990s, steadily increasing its share of the Scottish vote and boosting its toll of seats at Westminster and Strasbourg on a tide of rising national confidence as the Tory years came to an end. Devolution, though, has made the going tougher for the advocates of independence in both Scotland and Wales, precisely as it was intended to do, and the SNP has struggled to find a role – and to maintain its unity – in the new political conditions brought about by Edinburgh rule.

The party's problems were compounded by financial woes, themselves in part caused by declining membership and the party's failure to attract donations. The 2004 European elections were portrayed by the leadership as a moment when these trends would be reversed.

Scottish Socialist Party

The charismatic Tommy Sheridan had, thanks to PR, won a seat in the first Scottish Parliament election in 1999. The SSP contested every seat in Scotland in 2001 and averaged 3.35, saving 10 of its 72 deposits. In the 2003 Scottish Parliament elections it won 6.7% of the regional list vote and managed to elect an MSP in seven of the eight Scottish regions. Mr Sheridan's SSP was largely portrayed by the Scottish media as a growing force.

The SSP was anti-war and pro-environment and on these grounds was given a free run by George Galloway's Respect coalition. The SSP was very critical of the European Union, which it saw as a neo-liberal club without proper democratic accountability.

All of the parties in Scotland risked suffering from overcrowding of the electoral marketplace, with no less than ten parties submitting full slates. Nor could the SSP count on the anti-war vote alone, since this was a stance it shared with the SNP, the Liberal Democrats and the Greens.

Wales

Plaid Cymru

Plaid won its first European seats with the election of Jill Evans and Eurig Wyn in 1999. Mr Wyn decided not to stand again in 2004, but Mrs Evans topped the list. Plaid's basic policy platform was that Wales should be accorded recognition as an independent state in Europe: 'The Party of Wales's aspiration is for our country to achieve the status of member state within the European Union. However, we recognise that such a momentous change would have to be subject to the approval of the people in a referendum.' The party was strongly pro-euro, arguing that the structure of the Welsh economy was more like that of the European mainland than that of southern England. The party was also pro-Constitution, arguing strongly for a more open and democratic Union.

As with the SNP in Scotland, devolution had brought existential challenges for Plaid, which had had similar difficulties in positioning itself in a post-devolution political landscape. Back in 1999 the party had been on a roll, capitalising on Labour's disarray following bitter wrangling over the party leadership in Wales. But once the charismatic Rhodri Morgan had assumed the leadership a surer grip was exercised, and he was at pains to put 'clear red water' between Westminster and Cardiff. Plaid's own charismatic leader, Dafydd Wigley, stood down in 2000. His successor, Ieuan Wyn Jones, was left with the task of repositioning the party. He bounced spectacularly out of and back into the leadership in the summer of 2003, following the loss of five Assembly seats, falling from 17 to 12, but by 2004 the leadership had stabilised (with Jill Evans as Vice-President). With the force of the independence argument waning, Plaid's main task was to appeal beyond its core Welsh-speaking vote.

Forward Wales

Former Labour Welsh Secretary Ron Davies headed a list of four candidates for a relatively new party in Wales, Forward Wales. The party aimed at a vacuum it believed had been left by Labour's move to the right. Ron Davies declared that 'New Labour has sold out its past and is frightened of the future. Wales needs a new political force that puts Wales first and stands up to London. Every vote for Forward Wales builds up that force.' Founded by John Marek in November 2003, the party's primary focus was on the local elections, but as an anti-war, Green and nationalist party it hoped to nibble into the support of both Labour and Plaid Cymru. Its chances of success were potentially undermined by the failure of Welsh anti-war parties to reach an understanding with Respect similar to the one that had been brokered with the SSP in Scotland. As a result, the anti-war vote risked being badly split.

As in Scotland, there was a general problem of crowding, with ten parties putting up full slates of candidates for Wales.

Northern Ireland

The political landscape of Northern Ireland had changed since the 1999 European elections. In 1999, Ian Paisley topped the poll for the three Northern Ireland seats, with 28.4%, with the SDLP candidate John Hume closely behind on 28.1%. Ulster Unionist Jim Nicholson, remained in third place on 17.6%, with Sinn Féin at fourth on 17.3%. The 2003 Northern Ireland assembly elections produced a more polarised result than the same elections had done in 1998. The four main parties squeezed the vote from the smaller parties. The DUP and Sinn Féin both succeeded in increasing their share of Assembly seats, while the more moderate parties – the Ulster Unionists and the SDLP – failed to retain their support.

The review of the Belfast Agreement belatedly got under way in February 2004 and the parties once again polarised into two main camps: the Alliance Party and the DUP, who wished to see fundamental reform to the Good Friday Agreement, and Sinn Féin and the SDLP, who would have been content with a progress report and no major changes. As seen in Chapter 1, in the first two months of 2004, the SDLP leader, John Hume, and the DUP leader, Ian Paisley, both announced their intentions to stand down as MEPs at the 2004 European elections. The Revd Paisley, 77, cited his commitment to domestic Northern Ireland politics. Mr Hume, 67, stood down through ill health. Between them, they had accumulated almost 50 years' presence in the European Parliament.

Unlike the rest of the United Kingdom, the Northern Ireland region uses the single transferable vote (STV) system in European elections, whereby votes are cast by putting a '1' in the column next to the voter's preferred candidate, a '2' beside their second favourite candidate, and so on, until they no longer wish to express a preference. With the parties fielding only one candidate each, clearly voters can, and do, express preferences for several parties. A simple quota is established to determine which candidates are elected on the basis of first preferences. To decide which of the remaining candidates are elected, the surplus votes beyond the quota are transferred, so that second preferences come into play. In 1999, all three MEPs were returned on the basis of first-preference votes cast.

Democratic Unionist

Jim Allister QC, an active Northern Ireland politician since the 1980s, was selected as the DUP candidate. His strategy for the elections would be three-dimensional: first, European issues; second, constitutional issues; and, third, 'the increasing necessity to face down Sinn Féin'. Mr Allister was implacably opposed to the EU constitution, to the single currency, and to a common foreign and defence policy.

SDLP

Martin Morgan, 36, and Belfast's Mayor since June 2003, would replace Mr Hume as the SDLP's candidate. If trends in the 2003 Assembly elections continued, the SDLP was in danger of losing its seat to Sinn Féin. The SDLP favoured the euro, EU enlargement, CAP reform and an all-Ireland position on the Common Fisheries Policy. The SDLP sat with the Group of the Party of European Socialists in the European Parliament.

Sinn Féin

Bairbre de Brún, a member of the Assembly for the constituency of West Belfast since June 1998, would be bidding for Sinn Féin's first ever seat in the European Parliament. On European issues, Sinn Féin opposed any dilution of unanimity in justice and home affairs decisions and favoured enlargement and CAP reform (by introducing a new income subsidy strand). On fisheries, Sinn Féin called for the reassertion of the principle of sovereignty over territorial waters.

Ulster Unionist Party

Incumbent MEP and UUP leader Jim Nicholson remained as the party's candidate. The UUP lost support in the 2003 Assembly Elections and Mr Nicholson had faced some internal dissent. The party's policies on Europe mirrored those of the British Conservatives, with whom Mr Nicholson sat as an allied member of the EPP-ED Group: opposition to the draft Constitutional Treaty, to the euro and to a common defence policy.

Others

A number of smaller and one-issue parties decided to contest one or several regions in the 2004 European elections. These, which are set out in Box 3.1, fell into a few distinct categories: English regionalism; the interests of older people (mirroring demographic trends, a growing phenomenon in several EU member states); the countryside; the environment; and Christian values. This proliferation demonstrated a particular aspect about PR based on regions.

Beneath the main story about the major parties contesting the elections in order to win seats and representation in the Strasbourg Parliament, there was an important sub-text, chiefly regional, about delivering messages and winning support, but not necessarily seats.

Box 3.1   Other registered parties contesting the 2004 European elections

English Democrats Party (contested London, South East, Eastern, Yorkshire & Humberside, North West)
Prolife Party (contested South East, Eastern, North West)
Christian Peoples Alliance (contested London, South East)
The Countryside Party (contested South West, North West)
The Senior Citizens Party (contested South East)
The Peace Party (contested South East)
Operation Christian Vote (contested Scotland)
Socialist Environmental Alliance (contested Northern Ireland)
Alliance for Green Socialism (contested Yorkshire & Humberside)
Christian Democratic Party (contested Wales)
Scottish Wind Watch (contested Scotland)

Independents and micro-parties

With the exception of Wales, every region threw up at least one independent candidate (see Table 3.4) or a micro-party (fielding just one candidate). Despite this relative proliferation, only one of the independent candidates was in any way well known. Martin Bell, a former BBC journalist, had made his name in the 1997 General Election as an anti-sleaze candidate, successfully standing against Neil Hamilton in Tatton. Mr Bell was unable to find similar success in the 2001 General Election in Brentwood and seemed thereafter

Table 3.4   Independents and micro-parties

Name	Region	Label
Martin Bell	Eastern	Independent
Robert Ellis	Yorkshire & Humberside	Independent
John Gilliland	Northern Ireland	Independent
Shadmyraine Halliday	East Midlands	Independent
Neil Herron	North East	Independent
Barry Hodgson	West Midlands	The Pensioners Party
Jim Naisbitt	Eastern	Independent
Ronald Neal	North West	Independent
Christopher Prior	London	The Peoples Party for Better Government
Philip Rhodes	South East	Independent
Dick Rodgers	West Midlands	The Common Good
Russell Rogers	East Midlands	Independent
Fergus Tait	Scotland	Independent

to have retired from political life. But in 2003 he was persuaded to stand in the 2004 European elections by an invitation from the *Eastern Daily Press*, which had noted that none of the major parties' candidates came from the Eastern region they hoped to represent (Mr Bell came from Suffolk). Arguably, Mr Bell's greatest success came before the election campaign began when, following an investigation carried out by the *Eastern Daily Press*, it seemed that a Conservative MEP, Bashir Khanbhai, had given a fictitious home address within the region (see Chapter 4).

Absent friends …

There were a few notable absences from the 2004 campaign. The Pro-Euro Conservative Party, which had been formed by two breakaway Conservative MEPs in 1999 and had then run a full slate of candidates, made no reappearance in 2004 (most of its members formally joined the Liberal Democrats). At the other end of the scale, the Referendum Party, which had seemed such a looming presence in 1997, was also absent, though its erstwhile supporters could argue that its main aims had been achieved. The Natural Law Party, extolling the virtues of the Maharishi Mahesh Yogi's philosophy on eternal laws, had fielded full slates of candidates in the 1994 and 1999 European elections. Its full-page advertisements and political broadcasts, typically featuring Yogic fliers, had brought colour to the 1994 and 1999 campaigns but would be entirely absent in 2004.

The campaign approaches …

Though not visible as a phenomenon at the time, it is clear that a number of issues were converging in the run-up to the European elections campaign. One of these was the question of trust; there was a general decline in levels of trust about the political process, but this combined with specific doubts arising out of the Iraq invasion and the WMD affair about the trustworthiness of the Prime Minister and the Labour government.

A second was increased apprehensiveness about frontiers and immigration. This was not necessarily xenophobia, though perhaps was closely related to it.[10] The apprehension was derived from concern about terrorism, post-9/11, but also from such episodes as the Sangatte refugee centre, the deaths of illegal workers and from concerns about the effects on employment of the May 2004 enlargement.

A third was concerns about the single currency and, behind and below these, concerns about the draft European Constitution. Euroscepticism and patriotism combined with distrust about such seemingly elitist and arguably alien constructions as the euro and the European Convention. The European integration process, it was argued, seemed never to stop. Nearly all the popular British press continued to publish 'horror stories' about the European Union.

As the European election campaign was about to begin, all of these themes came together in a swirl of concern and apprehension. The theme of distrust was encouraged still further when, as was seen above, the government insisted at short notice on imposing all-postal ballots in four regions for the European elections. In retrospect, this combination provided fertile terrain for simple, attractive and negative messages ...

Appendix 3.1: A summary of the main contents of the parties' manifestos/policy documents (based on 2004 campaign leaflets and documentaries)

Liam Spender

Conservative party

Putting Britain First

'The European Union is failing many of its people. European business is over-regulated and over-taxed, thanks in large part to the European Union.'

Summary:
The document features a Union Jack on nearly every page. Opposition to the European Union Constitution proposals form the main part of the text. There is a box on specific threats posed by the Constitution on areas such as Regulation, Finance, and so on. Conservative policy was that not all European countries needed to move in the same direction: 'live and let live, flourish and let flourish'. Continued opposition to the euro and tax harmonisation.

Labour has let people down through its determination to be involved in all that the EU does; the Liberal Democrats would do a worse job since they are: 'Brussels' yes men'. The Conservative approach is based on strong national parliaments and 'enhanced co-operation' allowing others to integrate more closely when some do not. The European Parliament should gain the right to repeal legislation, and the national parliaments to propose legislation. Conservatives would make referendums on all future 'significant constitutional changes' in treaties compulsory.

Conservatives would introduce a new Commissioner for Budgetary Control and make further institutional changes to reduce corruption. Neil Kinnock blamed for not introducing sufficient reforms more quickly. Conservatives pledge to cut 25% of all existing regulations and to introduce 'sunset clauses' for all new ones.

Conservatives would introduce environmental directives quicker and with more simple guidance. The Common Fisheries Policy would be scrapped in current form and control repatriated. Conservatives would also retain controls over borders and state that: 'our objective is a fully-fledged transatlantic market place by 2015.' Conservatives say that the EU Constitution allows the EU to take Britain's UN Security Council seat.

The European Parliament should meet only at a single seat and have the power to dismiss individual Commissioners for misconduct. MEPs' expenses should be made more transparent and all MEPs' salaries should be taxed at the same rate as their constituents.

Labour

Britain is Working – Don't Let the Tories Wreck it Again

'The 1.9 million new jobs created since 1997 have been helped by Britain's EU membership. We have come too far to put this jobs record at risk with the Conservatives.'

Summary:
Most of the document is focused on how Labour's UK achievements stand in stark contrast to how the Conservatives governed. Labour says the EU must become more relevant by becoming more open and improve its accountability to national parliaments. The document stresses the Conservatives' proposed withdrawals from Common Foreign and Security policy; Common Fisheries Policy and EU Development Aid Coordination.

Labour supports the Lisbon Agenda and its aim to improve European competitiveness, so that it should become the most competitive world economy by 2010. Labour promises a more open Europe to reduce costs to consumers and provide new markets for UK businesses. A progress review on the five economic tests is promised for the 2005 budget.

Labour says it is working hard to end the 'gold plating' of regulations and directives issued by the Commission by civil servants in Whitehall in order to ensure better regulation of the Single Market. Labour also notes the importance of EU membership in ensuring a loud voice for British interests at the WTO trade talks.

Labour notes the benefits created for workers through signing up to the European Social Chapter. Labour promises further work to reduce UK car prices; increase compensation for passengers 'bumped off' flights and more rights for internet shoppers.

On asylum and immigration, the document pledges to continue collective bargaining on environmental and trade issues, and to retain NATO 'as the cornerstone of our collective defence'. Labour is happy to maintain contributions to the EU aid scheme, since 'the Tory policy [of withdrawal] would require the agreement of the 24 other EU member states'. Labour promises on the constitution that: 'if an agreement is reached between the 25 member states, and after the British parliament has debated the issue, then it should be the British people who decide in a referendum'.

Environmental improvements since 1997, such as cleaner water and exceeding Kyoto emissions reduction targets, are emphasised, with promises to work to include aviation emissions in the carbon dioxide emissions trading scheme and to reform the CFP. The manifesto's conclusion is that: 'Tories would leave Britain isolated and weak.' Furthermore, Conservative policies would 'betray our national interest by putting British trade, British jobs and British prosperity at risk'.

Liberal Democrats

Making Europe Work for You

Summary:
The Liberal Democrats' manifesto takes the form of a newsletter detailing the achievements and pledges of the party's MEPs and likely MEPs. 'Liberal Democrat members of the European Parliament are a growing and successful force.' Andrew Duff is described as a 'leading Federalist' who represented the UK on the Constitutional Convention; Sarah Ludford as a woman who fought for the plane spotters detained by the Greek government in 2001.

'Graham Watson piloted the European Arrest Warrant through Parliament and helped to frame other legislation boosting EU measures against terrorism.' Fiona Hall's role as Senior Research Assistant to Alan Beith is highlighted, along with Nick Clegg's role as Trade and Industry spokesman. Bill Newton Dunn gets much coverage. Chris Huhne has 'put a "sunset clause" into EU regulations for the first time, so that powers given to the EU Commission will be removed if they are abused or do not have the desired effect'. Liz Lynne's work to reduce age discrimination by making it illegal for job applications to be refused on grounds of age is mentioned.

Two pages on what Europe has achieved for the UK: 'European Unity is good for Britain.' Bolstering trade, jobs, environmental protection laws, terrorism, and peace throughout the World. Reform of the EU would also be good: institutional reform and a greater scrutiny role for MEPs; consistent enforcement to spread the pain of EU laws; stronger measures on fraud; better Westminster scrutiny of EU legislation; a single seat for the Parliament.

More detail added to the bare bones of these reforms: plans for US–EU cooperation to alleviate global poverty and to kick-start agreement on the environmental protection protocols.

UK Independence Party

Say NO to European Union: Vote UK Independence Party

Summary:
The manifesto is two sides of A4 designed to express the general principles of the party. Party was founded in 1993 and describes itself as 'the only moderate, democratic party to advocate withdrawal from the European Union'. Claims a membership of 20,000. The promised referendum will be accompanied with

a flood of expensive propaganda from the Commission, 'as it has flooded every country due to hold an EU related referendum in the past'. The EU costs Britain £1.8 million/day – enough for 100 new hospitals every year.

The letter from leader Roger Knapman states that 'on June 10th, I ask you to lend us your vote'. In order to prevent the EU from developing any further, UKIP argues that since Britain is the world's fourth largest economy and the Commission itself admits that British jobs and trade would not be harmed by withdrawal, the UK may as well withdraw. The manifesto takes a paragraph from Labour's 1983 General Election manifesto, which advocates withdrawal from the EU. 'A vote for UKIP is the only way to say NO.'

On other documents published on the UKIP website, one – entitled *Freedom from the European Union* – claims that the EU ensures that 'from our taxes directly to Brussels, £30 million pounds a day' is spent ensuring continued membership. On crime UKIP claims that the number of recorded crimes has risen from 2.4 per 1,000 of the population in 1900 to 9.4 per 1,000 in 1954 to 94 per 1,000 in 2004. 'A UKIP government would do whatever necessary to reduce the levels of crime and criminality to the levels of the 1950s.'

In a document entitled *Freedom from Overcrowding*, UKIP says 'the UK is already full up', with higher population densities than France or Germany. Withdrawal from the EU would mean that no asylum claim would be entertained unless the UK was the first port of call; no asylum claims will be entertained from 'multiparty democracies since these will be deemed, like the UK, to be politically tolerant of varying points of view'. No asylum claims from countries with UN/UK peacekeepers present. 'No more "economic migration" except in very special circumstances.' And 'unsuccessful applicants will be returned to their country of origin'.

The document *Freedom from Bureaucratic Politicians* would see a UKIP government passing legislation to allow referenda 'at all levels of local government on issues of concern to local residents when the required number of signatures has been collected on a petition'. Bans on special advisers, targets, withdrawal from the 'jurisdiction of the European courts' and an 'aim for a steady long-term reduction in the proportion of our money taken in taxes'.

The document *Freedom from Political Correctness* pledges a UKIP government to ending 'Political Correctness' via a restructuring of the law 'to ensure that free speech once again would come to mean just that'.

Green Party

Real Progress: The Future is Green

Summary:
Caroline Lucas claims that 'there is a vacuum in British political life today' and she promotes the Greens as the perfect substitute for that. Voting Green

means helping to elect politicians who care about present-day needs as well as our future. Green policy is to press the EU into working the US into the Kyoto Protocol and to 'contract' CO_2 emissions to a low level and to have all countries converge on a level of low CO_2 emissions proportionate to population size. Targets for zero waste in the UK to end dumps and shut down incinerators. Greens favour the EU introducing a Tobin Tax to minimise speculation and provide funds for 'economic justice'.

Green Party policy is to renationalise and reintegrate the railway network; introduction of road and car-park pricing to reduce usage and an end to hidden aviation subsidies; an EU-wide tax on aviation fuel and subsidies to make rail cheaper than air. Scrapping VAT on energy efficient buildings and building modifications. Opposition to GATS (and all other WTO measures) and increased public sector spending. On Defence spending: 'Greens reject both options, preferring a Europe that leads by example, with an effective, largely non-military security based on trust and co-operation.' This means 'building OSCE; withdrawal from and dissolution of NATO; closure of all US bases on European soil.' The Greens want to ban the £400 million annual subsidy spent on arms production by the UK.

The EU itself should sign the European Convention on Human Rights. Greens favour bans on live animal transportation; fur imports; GM modifications of animals; primate testing; battery egg production, transportation and sale. Conclusion: 'If you live in the South East or London, voting Green will ensure that Green MEPs get re-elected for your region. But regardless of where you live, your Green vote will help more Greens get elected to the European Parliament.'

Plaid Cymru

Plaid Cymru, The Party of Wales: Fighting Hard for Wales

Summary:
'Our MEPs were at the heart of new legislation on workers' rights, food safety and standards, CAP reform, keeping Wales GM free, better food labelling, the promotion of Welsh produce as a quality product, and bolstering Europe's stance on the position of minority languages.' Enlargement has meant some states with half the population of Wales gaining full-member status and, in some cases, more MEPs. PC supports the Tobin Tax.

Emphasis on PC Council's ability to spend Objective One funding better than Labour councils. PC MEPs scored equal first place (of 685 MEPs) assessed on 100% backing for all environmental regulations. PC continues to work to make Welsh an official Community language with its own legal framework along with the other languages spoken but not recognised within the EU.

Scottish National Party

Vote for Scotland: SNP

Summary:
'If even tiny Malta can sit at the top table then why shouldn't Scotland?' Scotland's real problem is not the EU, just lack of representation within the Union. London is not committed to proper, fair representation of the Scottish interest. 'Until Scotland is independent, our nation cannot take part in decision-making at the very heart of the EU.' An independent Scotland would have 14 MEPs.

'We have seen far too many of our great, national industries destroyed. We cannot sit back and watch another one – fishing – go the same way.' SNP wants an EU as a 'confederation of sovereign states'. Apparently, 'for more than 30 years, London government ministers have betrayed our fishermen'. SNP has the only record of consistent defence of fishermen. Scotland has had her oil reserves bled from it by England. Scotland's 30-year-long record of low economic growth can be reversed if Scotland joins the euro, regardless of whether the UK does. The SNP favours the Scandinavian economic model. 'Other small independent nations have made lasting contributions to building peace by influencing the work of the EU and other international forums. This is the vision we share for Scotland.'

Respect

A Referendum on Blair

Summary:
'The European elections will be the first national poll since two million people marched in the biggest demonstration ever seen in this country against war and racism, and in defence of democracy and civil liberties ... Tony Blair wants us to forget that he took us to war on a lie.' The EU is fundamentally anti-democratic, as evinced by the euro. 'Health and education are faced with privatization and deregulation.' Tony Blair wants to drive the EU farther down this path. The EU's 'Fortress Europe' immigration and asylum policy 'promotes racist ideas and strengthens the far right'.

The EU Constitution is setting in stone the neo-liberal consensus behind the management of the Union. Respect wants a referendum before ratification. Respect's antidote is withdrawal from Iraq; ending privatisation; free education and health systems; minimum wage at the European decency threshold [£7.40 per hour]; scrapping the 'Fortress Europe' policy.

Scottish Socialist Party

Another Europe is Possible

'Since 2001, the SSP has been the most active anti-war party in Scotland. From Day One we opposed the reckless and deceitful "war on terror".'

Summary:
Each of the six SSP MSPs donated half of their salary to the party, in order to live on the same amount as a skilled Scottish worker. 10 June is the first time the voters have their chance to pass judgement on the Iraq War. The wealth of the 1,000 people on the *Sunday Times* 'Rich List' has doubled since 2000 and now stands at £200 billion (the entire African aid budget taken care of for the next 200 years). The SSP wants 'a Europe of the peoples rather than a Europe of the multinational corporations and the big nation states'. The SSP wants internationalist socialism: cancel all Third World debt and deliver justice for the Palestinian people.

'Forced unity from above will not unite the peoples of Europe, but will fertilise the soil for conflict and resentment to proliferate like poisonous mushrooms in a dank forest.' According to the SSP, all new entrants to the EU are required to join the euro: 'the EU was never intended as a force for social progress. Its entire construction is designed to protect the political and economic elites of Europe from the pressures of ordinary people.' The SSP wants the Commission to be 'downgraded to the status of an administrative back-up unit, confined to implementing decisions and providing information'; wants the CFP scrapped and Glasgow to be given Objective One status. The SSP pledged to transparent accountancy for MEPs' expenses and to preparing monthly public reports.

The SSP wants a minimum wage of £7.50 per hour across the EU and a minimum pension of £200 per week. 60% top rates of corporate and personal income tax; the Tobin Tax on all cross-border financial transactions; removal of all nuclear weapons from European soil and dissolution of NATO; cancellation of all Third World debts owed to Europe; absolute guarantee of trade union membership and right to strike.

British National Party

The British National Party: Building a Future for British Children

Summary:
Britain's EU membership costs the taxpayer £2 million an hour or £48 million a day. The BNP wishes to see 'withdrawal from the bureaucratic EU and the rebuilding of Britain's trading and family ties to the Commonwealth'.

Brussels proposes to undo 1,000 years of British independence with a federal super-state.

On crime, which 'is out of control! Time for "zero tolerance"!' The BNP remembers that 'Britain used to be a peaceful country where crime was rare, where old ladies and children could walk the streets at night, without fear of mugging or rape. People could leave their doors unlocked without fear of burglary.' The failure of the police to do their jobs properly is all due 'to politically correct politicians, and the judges and the courts have got to apply stricter sentences'. The BNP demands the restoration of capital punishment for paedophiles, terrorists and premeditated murderers with DNA evidence. Corporal punishment for petty crimes: 'it's cheaper and far more effective than sending them on holidays'.

On asylum, the BNP policy is based on the view that 'hundreds of thousands of so-called "asylum seekers" come to Britain and are immediately given free homes and full benefits – paid for by British taxpayers. This is at a time when our schools are short of teachers and our hospitals are short of beds, while our pensioners freeze in winter.' Asylum seekers are directly responsible for increases in hospital waiting lists and the population growth that requires 5 million new homes on green-belt land. White Britons heading for minority status in own country inside 60 years: £4 billion a year is spent on immigrants. The BNP wants illegal and criminal immigrants to be deported, and a ban on all future asylum seekers.

Notes

1. The Liberal Democrats also ran Hull for a brief period before it returned to Labour control.
2. However, there was a great deal of *sotto voce* criticism from party insiders about the mechanism. Said one national politician: 'The identity and ranking of the Conservative MEP candidates in the North West was carried out by no more than 500 people.' A senior official spoke about 'absurd procedures' and 'perverse results', and the authors were assured – off the record, naturally – that several Tory hustings had been 'stuffed' with supporters.
3. It should be noted that the speech had been carefully cleared with all of the 'big beasts'.
4. It seems that this policy plank had not been entirely thought through. Logically, a Conservative government could only have renegotiated the Common Fisheries Policy if the other 24 member states were in agreement to open such negotiations – a remote possibility. The only other way of achieving the same end would have been unilateral withdrawal – just as unlikely a possibility.
5. See 'Labour hit by candidates row', *Scotland on Sunday*, 27 October 2003.
6. Quoted in 'Labour MEPs fail to back Martin', *Sunday Herald*, 4 April 2004.
7. In the event, Labour's performance held up well. Bill Miller failed to get re-elected, but it was because of the reduction in the overall number of seats from eight to seven and not because the Labour vote fell significantly.
8. The following is a selection of the press and media coverage during the 'affair': 'With friends like these' (*Sunday Herald*, 4 April); 'Blow to Martin's hope of top EU

job' (*Herald*, 23 April); 'Probe continues for "cleared" MEP' (BBC News, 6 May); 'Attempt to clear MEP over expenses is stifled' (*The Scotsman*, 6 May); 'Expenses inquiry deal keeps Martin as Euro candidate' (*The Scotsman*, 12 May).

9. For example, 'Leadership shadow over Chatshow Charlie' (*Gaurdian*, 27 March 2004) and 'In sickness and in health' (*The Economist*, 27 March 2004).

10. Though, as Chapter 6 examines, there is some academic evidence that UKIP and BNP support is fungible (perhaps even some Conservative support) and that racism in the British population has been quietly on the rise.

4
Campaign

The off?

In David Hare's *The Absence of War* (1993), George Jones, the fictitious leader of the opposition, only realises a snap General Election has been called when a Special Branch security guard suddenly appears in his House of Commons office – the Prime Minister, it becomes clear, has pulled a fast one. The choice of the General Election date is an important weapon in a British Prime Minister's armoury, but there can be no element of surprise with the fixed cycle of European elections. In such circumstances, political parties, like athletes in a track event, may seek advantage by breaking early (perhaps with the publication of their manifesto) or by holding back until the last lap, but the only real surprises can come from policy issues, electoral tactics or external events.

When does a European election campaign start? To some extent the timetable, as Chapter 2 described, is set by rules and regulations. But when does the campaigning proper get under way? The simple answer is that it starts when the main actors, the political parties, want it to. There is, however, an important caveat. In a General Election – a first-order national election – government stops, Parliament rises, and the media's full gaze is concentrated on the election campaign. In a European election, on the other hand, government decidedly does not stop, Parliament does not rise and the media's gaze is, at best, divided.

Moreover, in 2004 – ostensibly for the very best of motives (that is, to encourage turnout) – the media's attention was further divided between several second-order contests, including local elections and the London Mayoral elections.

The beginning of the June 2004 European election campaign in the UK was like a smudged line and, in the absence of the thrill of 'the off', it was difficult to foster a thrill in the ensuing chase. Moreover, because there were three simultaneous elections, there was no clear-cut campaign for the European

Parliament elections in particular – the smudged line continued. To the extent that the media's attention and the public's imagination would be caught, it was by odd highlights. There was no continuum, no sustained argument and certainly very little sense of a distinctive campaign.

Describing a non-campaign

In a warm May and a warmer June the European and local elections did not often provide the lead stories (see the chronology in Appendix 4.1). These came from the continuance of suicide bombings and gun-battles in Iraq and Saudi Arabia; allegations of abuse of Iraqi prisoners by American and British troops; the sacking of the *Daily Mirror*'s editor; a Glasgow factory explosion; the gory death of hostages in Iraq; the 5 June passing away of former US President Ronald Reagan; the 4–8 June D-Day commemoration ceremonies, including an assemblage of all the Western Heads of State on the Normandy beaches; football's forthcoming European Cup in Portugal; Manchester United's victory in the FA Cup; England's cricket triumphs in the Test matches with New Zealand; and even Venus's passage in front of the sun. At another level, there were the United Nations Security Council discussions about the 30 June handover of power in Baghdad.

Some of these stories had political implications. Hopefulness over the handover of power may, in the end, have done something to defuse Iraq as a political issue. The St George's crosses flown everywhere in anticipation of a strong performance by the English team in the European football championship may subliminally have underscored the UK Independence Party's patriotic/nationalist theme. The good economic figures coming out (despite the election purdah on government announcements) may have helped Labour. So too may the prominence given to Mr Blair and the Queen in Normandy on 6 June. But equally the scares over oil prices and interest rates, as well as over threatened Tube strikes, may have worked for the Conservatives. But these were underlying political currents that would have flowed in any case; they certainly had nothing to do with the European election campaign.

These observations lead to an underlying question. In a study which is supposedly about the evolution of an election battle, how can such a non-event – the absence of a distinct and specific campaign – be described? Traditionally, the campaign chapters of the Nuffield Studies, whether of a UK or a European election, mix chronological and thematic analyses. But such an approach would be inappropriate for the June 2004 European elections. In chronological terms, the sense of a European election campaign was very rarely apparent. The ghastly hostage crises in Iraq and, on a happier note, the European football championship finals in Portugal, were among the many powerful distractions that helped to keep the European election campaign out of the public consciousness.

There were no major policy debates and very few visible policy differences. Clearly, all of the major parties were keeping their policy powder dry for the autumn conference season and the expected spring 2005 General Election and, as Chapter 3 described, the two major parties opted by default for negative campaign techniques as a way of seeking tactical advantage.

Deprived of the oxygen of major policy differences and of charismatic political figures, the media rooted around for 'public interest' stories. Thus, to the extent that a European election campaign was visible, it tended to focus on fraud, then on the issue of postal ballots, and then on the UK Independence Party, particularly following the sudden appearance of Robert Kilroy-Silk.

Political journalists detected a clear but skewed pattern to party leaders' activities, with concentration on the four postal-ballot regions before the end of May, further undermining any impression of a cumulative campaign.

Worse, there were other campaigns under way at the same time. The absence of any energetic countermanding campaign – a repeat of the situation described in Chapter 1 with regard to the euro and the Convention – offered more Eurosceptic campaigners with an almost free run. With the benefit of hindsight, perhaps, all these considerations left the June 2004 field ominously clear for a party led by a charismatic, media-savvy, distinctly anti-European newcomer.

Paradoxically, therefore, the analysis contained in this chapter comes with a proviso; it focuses on a number of thematic issues, but that does not mean that those issues necessarily enjoyed a particularly high profile during the campaign period.

Launches

All parties found difficulty in securing attention from the media. The only sure way seemed to be a summons to the 'launch' of a manifesto or a campaign, with many opting for both (hence the confusing proliferation set out in Table 4.1). Such launches would hopefully guarantee a minute or two in the national news bulletins and a paragraph or two, at least in the broadsheet press. But with three sets of elections being held, there were many launches. The parties tried to find photogenic venues and to assemble their leading figures to give weight to the pictures. Another tried-and-tested method of generating at least some press interest was to launch a party's campaign through the presentation of campaign posters, though in the case of the Conservatives this almost backfired, as some television reports panned their cameras to show how Mr Howard was obliged to present his posters to a large, empty and echoing room, with only a small phalanx of television cameras and press photographers for company. Some parties had separate launches for a local government manifesto or for a London, or a Welsh, or a Scottish manifesto. The newest parties put out their manifestos early – Respect on 15

March and UKIP on 16 April. The Conservatives launched as early as 28 April, whilst the Greens waited till 19 May and the SNP till 21 May.

Table 4.1   Dates of the parties' campaign/manifesto launches[a]

Date	Location	Party	Elections
15 March	London	Respect	European
24 March	Brussels	Greens (pan-European)	European
16 April	London	UK Independence Party	European
17 April	Sutton Coldfield	UK Independence Party	Manifesto
24 April	Brussels	Party of European Socialists	European manifesto and campaign
26 April	London	Liberal Democrats	London
29 April	Manchester	Conservatives	European
29 April	Edinburgh	Conservatives	European
29 April	Cardiff	Conservatives	European
29 April	Zaventum (Brussels)	European Liberal Democrat and Reform Party (ELDR)	European campaign
30 April	Cardiff	Plaid Cymru	European
4 May	Birmingham	Conservatives	Local government
4 May	Leeds	Labour	Local government
5 May	London	Liberal Democrats	European
6 May	London	Conservative	London
6 May	London	Labour	London
10 May	London	Labour	European
10 May	Rhondda	Plaid Cymru	Local government
11 May	London	Greens	London
11 May	London	Liberal Democrats	London
12 May	London	UK Independence Party	European
12 May	Manchester	Greens	Local government
13 May	Edinburgh	Scottish Liberal Democrats	European
13 May	London	UK Independence Party	London
14 May	London	Respect	London
14 May	Glasgow	Scottish Labour	European
17 May	London	Conservatives	London
18 May	Caerphilly	Plaid Cymru	European (again)
19 May	Rhondda	Welsh Labour	European and Local
19 May	London	Greens	European
20 May	Cardiff	Welsh Liberal Democrats	European
20 May	London	Respect (again)	European
21 May	Edinburgh	Scottish National Party	European

[a] Respect did not contest the local elections.

Labour, the Greens and the Liberal Democrats also participated in pan-European party manifesto launches. As Chapter 1 described, these new pan-European political parties might, as they become better resourced, figure more prominently in future European election campaigns. In the run-up to the 2004 European elections they were invisible.

All campaign managers later lamented that the most carefully prepared events or press conferences drew very small audiences and very little coverage. Coordinated days on 'health' or 'education' or 'the environment' or 'fisheries', with spokesmen and candidates across the country instructed to get themselves publicised in the appropriate context, earned frustratingly small notice – frequently none.

Significantly, the BBC only launched its election website, with all its serious campaign coverage, on 17 May, unthinkably late by General Election standards.

The near campaign was generally recognised by the media as having first got under way on 28 April, when Michael Howard pre-launched the Conservatives' campaign with a 'Let Down by Labour' slogan; 'I want to lead a government that won't let you down', he declared, leading inevitably and deliberately to echoes of the famously successful Saatchi campaign of 1979 – 'Labour Isn't Working'. A world-weary *Times* predicted the next day that voters could look forward to a year-long General Election campaign.

Mr Howard's campaign was properly launched the next day in Manchester. In his speech 'A Live and Let Live Europe', Mr Howard called for a more flexible Europe and promised to put Britain first. Mr Howard, accompanied by a cheerful Jonathan Evans, the leader of the British Conservatives in the European Parliament, was relaxed and upbeat. With Mr Blair taking heavy fire (see below), it seemed that Mr Howard could be optimistic.

True to the Conservatives' pre-established plan for a 'three nations campaign' launch, Mr Howard went the same day to Murrayfield, Edinburgh, to deliver a similar set-piece speech, and from there to Cardiff. A 'Putting Britain First' battle bus would then take the energetic Mr Howard to launches in all of the British regions, ending in Leicester on 12 May. His extensive schedule would also take him to Gibraltar on 17 May. But it was in Murrayfield, on its very first day, that Mr Howard's campaign was badly derailed.

In that morning's BBC Radio 4 *Today* programme Mr Struan Stevenson, a sitting Tory MEP and Chairman of the European Parliament's Fisheries Committee, was named as one of those MEPs who engaged in the practice of signing the register in Strasbourg on a Friday morning, thus benefiting from a per diem payment, before flying out (see Chapter 2 for an account of this practice). Mr Stevenson admitted to the practice but angrily defended himself; he was doing nothing wrong and his party wanted the system reformed – indeed, the manifesto's insistence that 'reimbursement of MEPs' expenses must be fully transparent' was considered one of the party's stronger suits.

By prior arrangement, Mr Stevenson, one of the Tories' two Scottish MEPs, sat on the podium with Mr Howard at the Murrayfield launch. In the exchanges following the leader's speech, the journalists (already sensitised to allegations of malpractice by an earlier row involving Labour's David Martin – see Chapter 3) repeatedly questioned Mr Howard and Mr Stevenson about the latter's behaviour. The first question was whether Mr Howard found it acceptable that Mr Stevenson should sit with him, given the former's acknowledgement of the alleged 'malpractice'. Mr Howard repeated the party's commitment to changing the system and refused to disown Mr Stevenson, but as he fielded repeated questions on the issue he became visibly angry and frustrated. 'Miffed', as the *Daily Telegraph* put it, 'he most certainly was.' In the end, he refused to answer any more questions on the issue.

Inevitably, it was the 'incident' of the allegations and Mr Howard's irritation, rather than his party's campaign launch, that made the evening news bulletins. It was as though a shiny new car had driven out of the salesroom and straight into a muddy puddle. After Murrayfield and Cardiff, the 'grid' dictated that Mr Howard should tour the regions, so there were no immediate possibilities for him to recreate the more assertive impression he had been able to give in Manchester.

The Liberal Democrats launched their campaign at their Cowley Street, London, headquarters on 5 May. 'These are extraordinary times for Europe and for Britain's position within Europe', declared Mr Kennedy. 'Yet at one and the same time, Britain finds itself inadequately engaged at the heart of Europe.' He described Mr Blair's referendum decision as smacking 'more of political expediency than political principle'. Iraq had done much damage. Mr Kennedy was accompanied by Deputy Leader Menzies Campbell, London Mayoral candidate Simon Hughes, and the Leader of the Liberal Democrats in the European Parliament, Diana Wallis, who duly spoke about the work of the Liberal Democrat MEPs and the European Parliament.

In the ensuing question-and-answer session Mr Kennedy said he wanted Iraq to be one of the main issues of the election. This led *The Times* to publish a cartoon of Mr Kennedy at the podium with the party's manifesto slogan 'Making Europe Work for You' behind him and the words 'Making Iraq work for us' on his lips.

On 10 May Mr Blair launched the Labour Party's European elections campaign at Canary Wharf, London. The basic question, he argued, was whether Britain wanted to be at the heart of Europe or not. That morning's newspapers had carried full page advertisements setting out in stylised CV form Mr Howard's past political 'achievements'. Mr Blair defended the advertisement. It was not, he argued,

> a personal attack, it certainly is a political attack, and we are certainly entitled to point out that he was the minister who told the British people that the poll-tax was a good idea; that when he was Home Secretary the numbers of asylum seekers went up and he cut the numbers of police; and that he was a member and a leading supporter of the previous government.

By implication, Mr Howard was not to be trusted on matters European.

This personal and negative approach was noted by a critical media: 'Dud Labour launch', said the *Guardian* – 'If you cannot be positive about Europe in a European election, when can you be?' A number of Labour MPs and MEPs were openly critical. In an interview on the BBC Radio 4 *Today* programme, Glenys Kinnock, probably Labour's best-known MEP, complained that Mr Blair had 'wasted an opportunity for us to get a positive message across'. Labour MEPs were privately incensed. Although the EPLP's leader, Gary Titley, was present at the Canary Wharf launch, it was noted that Mr Blair had not mentioned the European Parliament or the Labour MEPs once ...

On 19 May the England and Wales Green Party launched its campaign at London's Royal Horticultural Halls Conference Centre. On the podium were Dr Caroline Lucas, one of the Party's principal speakers; Jean Lambert, a former party principal speaker; Professor John Whitelegg, a candidate in the North West and party spokesperson on sustainable development; and David Taylor, a candidate in the South West and party spokesperson on agriculture.

Whatever private misgivings they might have had, the party took a very upbeat approach. Declared Mr Taylor:

Our vote has been going up and we're in a strong position for serious gains. In 1999 we had near-misses in Eastern, North West, South West and Yorkshire. In all those regions we're now stronger, with more members (two) and more councillors ... This year we will keep taking votes off Labour and we'll attract votes from the other parties too because we're offering the policies the public wants.

By the time of the UK Independence Party launch in London on 12 May, Robert Kilroy-Silk was already being described by the BBC as the party's 'star candidate', though his arrival was still so recent that there was no sign of the 'star' in the party's accompanying political broadcast, screened in the evening (see below). A charismatic communicator, already well known to the media, and with more than a faint whiff of political danger about him, Mr Kilroy-Silk immediately began to overshadow the party's leader and its sitting MEPs. Indeed, in the BBC's web report the next day, entitled 'Kilroy opens UKIP election push', he was virtually the only UK Independence Party figure mentioned.

Sound-bites obligingly tumbled from his lips and were duly reported. He turned on 'the politicians'; 'they lied to us then and they are lying to us now'. He denounced the 'Metropolitan political elite': 'They are not listening to us. They are not taking account of what we want. They are not representing our interests.' He railed against the bureaucracy and corruption of the EU. He loved the Spanish, Dutch and Danish, but he did 'not want to be governed by them. I want to be governed by my own people.' 'I want my grandchildren', he continued, 'to grow up in a country called Britain – I don't want my grandchildren to grow up in a country called Europe.'

Whatever his political views, Mr Kilroy-Silk clearly knew how to tickle the media's fancy. But he was also adept at using the media to talk to a public constituency which he claimed to know well; the quarter of a million people who, he claimed, had been through his television studio: 'They want their country back and this campaign is about doing that.' Mr Kilroy-Silk's media skills combined powerfully with a simple 'NO' message, echoed by 1,800 billboards posted throughout the country. In a matter of days, the UKIP/ Kilroy-Silk combination had become *the* phenomenon of the elections.

Among the smaller party launches, Plaid Cymru wittily illustrated their argument about relative European representation when nine 'footballers' in Latvian shirts and four in Welsh jerseys walked down the Cardiff Millennium Stadium. Wales and Latvia have similar sized populations, but the number of Welsh MEPs had been cut to four, whilst Latvia would have nine.

Campaign coordination

In 2004 the main parties, with unhappy memories of 1999, did not follow the General Election custom of daily press conferences in central London. In previous European elections they had at times had to pack the hall with party people to prevent the audience seeming risible.

By doing away with the traditional daily national press conferences, the parties risked unknowingly doing away with important coordination mechanisms. Under the tried-and-tested method, the parties would traditionally hold their strategic coordination meetings early in the morning, before the obligatory press conferences. Even in the absence of daily national press conferences, Labour continued with this procedure simply because it had no choice – affairs of state obliged the party's ministers and officials to meet early if they wished to meet at all. The Liberal Democrats made an attempt to continue with the traditional method three or four times a week, though only the two main television news channels and one or two broadsheet reporters attended.

The Conservatives, on the other hand, had deliberately eschewed a centralised approach in favour of a series of regional events, with the party leader ferried hither and thence by the 'Putting Britain First' battle bus. By force of circumstances, the daily centralised strategy meetings fell into abeyance, and this was to have potentially awkward consequences for the party leader when it became clear that the UK Independence Party was on a roll and beginning to attract Conservative voters. More than any of the other party leaders, Mr Howard had to perform a difficult balancing act, keeping both the passionate Eurosceptics and the passionate Europhiles within his party satisfied through regular information and consultation. But the balancing act became extremely difficult when the leader was on an intensive regional tour, with no daily coordination mechanisms to keep everybody on message and with an obligation to respond rapidly to the imminent UKIP threat. As that threat loomed larger, the pressure on the leader and on the leader's office to respond grew.

Party leaders' activities

Michael Howard was assiduous in travelling the country and his regional appearances drew some coverage in the local media, though activists were disappointed that there was not more coverage (on the regional media, see below). Charles Kennedy made just three set-piece speeches throughout the campaign period, one of them in Brussels, but he had deliberately eschewed set-piece occasions in favour of press statements at local and regional events. He at first concentrated on the North East and the North West, where the party was most likely to win seats, and he was also supportive of the London Mayoral campaign of Simon Hughes. Tony Blair, ever busy with affairs of state, could only appear at occasional media functions – Table 4.2 sets out the main party leaders' attendance at set-piece occasions.[1] Members of his entourage argued that he had made efforts to speak on European issues, but the table shows clearly that he made only one set-piece speech in the European election context, and then he concentrated largely on the issue of Michael Howard's record in domestic politics. This apparent absence encouraged the Conservatives to describe him as the 'invisible man' of the election campaign, additionally pointing out that Mr Blair was absent from the party's final political broadcast and much of its electoral material.

Table 4.2   The main party leaders' set-piece speeches during the campaign

Leader	Date	Location	Topic/occasion
Charles Kennedy	26 April	London	Manifesto/campaign launch
Tony Blair	27 April	London	Climate change address; announcement of review of immigration system
Michael Howard	28 April	Manchester	European manifesto launch
	28 April	Cardiff	European manifesto launch
	28 April	Murrayfield	European manifesto launch
Charles Kennedy	30 April	Brussels	European Liberal Democrat and Reform Party Congress
Tony Blair	2 May	Cardiff	National Association of Head Teachers annual conference
Michael Howard	4 May	Birmingham	Local elections campaign
Charles Kennedy	5 May	London	European manifesto launch
Tony Blair	10 May	London	European campaign launch
Tony Blair	14 May	Coventry	Jaguar assembly plant
Michael Howard	17 May	Gibraltar	European election campaign
Tony Blair	20 May	London	National alcohol strategy
Michael Howard	20 May	Sedgefield	Burdens of government regulations
Michael Howard	1 June	Southampton	European election campaign
Michael Howard	7 June	Bristol	European election campaign

Candidates and the campaign

This study has relied on the replies of some 30 MEPs and candidates to a confidential questionnaire and will here draw on their often astringent comments. It was striking how much overlap there was in the responses. Almost all candidates seemed to have spent their time in the same ways and to have suffered the same frustrations with headquarters and with voters as well as with the Royal Mail. There was, moreover, surprising cross-party agreement on the issues that had mattered.

All the established parties, mindful of the abysmal turnout in 1999, focused on their heartlands and on getting their own people to vote; known supporters were bombarded with phone calls and e-mails. Only UK Independence Party respondents seemed able to regard the whole electorate as their target: 'the polls show 54% want us out of Europe, so they are all possible for us ...'.

All parties claimed to have regionalised their campaigns, but all took advantage of the economies of centralised printing and there was appreciable variation in the degree to which their localised appeals were well focused. Said one central official: 'we talked about regionalisation, but it was the most centralised campaign I've ever known'. Only the Liberal Democrats seem to have made a comprehensive effort to tie the European efforts into their Westminster campaign in marginal seats, with leaflets focused on individual constituencies.

Almost all candidates professed to have started full-time campaigning early in May though two respondents admitted waiting till the last fortnight before beginning their campaign activities. For most of the respondents full-time campaigning meant canvassing on the doorstep and by telephone, walkabouts in shopping centres or occasional hustings meetings. The Conservatives deployed their 'Putting Britain First' battle bus to tour the country, while Respect sent a campaign bus up and down the Mile End Road in their East End target area.

There were grumbles in all parties about the failure of council candidates to cooperate with the European campaign. And there were still more grouses about the inactivity of most Westminster MPs. Some candidates felt that the European elections had been hermetically sealed off from the local elections, as though implying that somehow they mattered less.

UK Independence Party candidates were uniformly enthusiastic about the way the campaign had been conducted, with its simple 'NO' message, and with the unexpected bonus publicity drawn in by Robert Kilroy-Silk. Candidates from other parties complained, to take one example, that 'The media neglected the election except for boosting UKIP.'

Almost all candidates reported, wistfully or enthusiastically, the antagonism to Europe manifest on the doorstep. A Labour MEP discovered fears of 'an Armada sailing up the Thames'. A Conservative candidate spoke of 'the water torture of Euroscepticism'. But there was surprisingly little reference to the topical issue of the Constitutional Treaty. Asylum and immigration loomed much larger. Some said that Iraq was the main issue while others claimed in surprise that it had never been mentioned. Mr Blair was unpopular on the doorstep and, complained more than one Labour candidate, inactive in the campaign. The word 'trust' was much heard, but several candidates reported that initial disillusionment with Mr Blair and the government seemed to have developed into a generally low regard for politics and politicians.

Labour candidates varied in their opinions. One thought simply that 'We never tried.' Another acknowledged that 'It was an opinion poll on the government ... and we didn't do well.' A third, presciently, declared that 'It was Dieppe, not D-Day.'

Conservative candidates' opinions also varied. 'We tried but it didn't impact', said one candidate. 'We had no simple message', said another. But another candidate felt that 'We got our people out but they voted UKIP.' And another declared that 'We were targeting the wrong enemy.' This analysis was reinforced by one acerbic candidate:

> With the economy bowling along well, there were few signs of people feeling 'let down by Labour' so that their natural conclusion from it might be 'don't vote Tory'. Above all, such a slogan was irrelevant in those many parts of the South West where Labour simply doesn't figure at all: the Lib Dems are the Tory 'enemy'.

The profusion of parties and candidates in Scotland and Wales led one candidate to declare that 'Voters got confused by all the minor parties.' In Scotland, it was pointed out, there were four parties opposed to the Iraq War.

There was a tendency to look back cynically on the campaign – 'Campaign? What campaign?' more than one candidate wrote – and there was a lot of criticism of headquarters' activity or inactivity.

With from three to ten candidates in each region, there was a mixture of praise and complaint about the energy shown by those lower down the ticket. Some really worked as a team with a shared electronic diary. Some were 'disaffected because of their place on the ticket'. One MEP complained that less than half his regional colleagues could drive, while he spent four to five hours a day behind the wheel.

Candidates from all parties were indignant about the Royal Mail, which often failed to deliver the freepost addresses before the postal vote forms.

London

There were other contests in London; one for the Mayorship and a second for the London Assembly. The contest that drew most attention was Ken Livingstone's attempt to secure re-election as Mayor of London. There had been much controversy over Ken Livingstone being readmitted to Labour Party membership a mere three years after being expelled for his 2000 action in standing (and winning) against the party's official candidate; however, the resentment that his behaviour had caused was conquered by the tactical advantage of a solid Labour vote in London. Mr Livingstone had won considerable credit for his political courage in pushing through plans for a congestion charge in central London. This scheme, which was, on the whole, successfully implemented, was the focus of international interest and admiration.

Though Mr Livingstone started as a clear frontrunner, facing him was a range of strong candidates. Chief among these was former Conservative minister and former London opponent, Stephen Norris. But Mr Norris's colourful reputation and a controversial directorship of a rail maintenance company, Jarvis, together with the Conservative Party's generally poor performance in national opinion polls combined to take the edge off his challenge.

The Liberal Democrats also put up a relatively major figure in the form of Simon Hughes, and there was some media speculation about whether a strong performance by Mr Hughes could lead to an alternative power base within the party (he having been the main challenger to Charles Kennedy in the party's 1999 leadership election). Mr Hughes launched a campaign plan for a safer, easier and cleaner London in Tower Hamlets, followed by tours of London's streets in an open-topped bus.

The Greens also had high hopes of their candidate, Darren Johnson, an experienced and well-known London local politician, and a senior politician within the Green Party since the early 1990s. Mr Johnson, leader of the Green Party Group in the London Assembly, set out a twelve-point action plan for a 'quality London'.

The UK Independence Party put up boxing promotor and local man, Frank Maloney. A well-known figure, Mr Maloney had helped guide Lennox Lewis to the world heavyweight championship, and it was hoped his ten-point plan on crime and sport would chime with the electorate's concerns.

The potential dark horse of the campaign was the British National Party. Their candidate for Mayor, Julian Leppart, was never likely to make much impact. A 26 May interview on BBC London radio's John Gaunt show, where Mr Leppart proposed to solve London's congestion problems by expelling all asylum seekers from the capital, demonstrated the lack of a thought-through campaign platform. But the BNP had high hopes of making an impact in the Assembly elections, particularly if, as seemed likely, turnout was low. The BNP threat brought all of the other Mayoral candidates together with ethnic vote operations such as 'Operation Black Vote' and media operations such as 'Celebrities Against Racism' in a concerted effort to raise turnout. These efforts were intensified following a 9 June *Evening Standard* YouGov poll which predicted both low turnout and a strong BNP performance. Fears were compounded by a Joseph Rowntree Trust publication which warned that the BNP was successfully shaking off its image as a party of extremists and was being identified in peoples' minds with local issues.

From the outset, London candidates for the European Parliament and for the local elections complained of their efforts being totally submerged by the Livingstone–Norris battle. As the Norris challenge faltered, it became increasingly clear that Labour was set to emerge from the June elections with at least one triumph. Helpfully, on election eve Ken Livingstone pleaded with voters not to ditch Mr Blair and he persuaded the militant railwaymen's Labour leader, Bob Crow, to call off a planned election day Tube strike, winning him further credit in the eyes of London's harrassed commuting community.

The local elections

London aside, the Metropolitan boroughs drew most attention. They all had new ward boundaries and therefore every seat was being contested with the possibility of complete council overturns. The Liberal Democrats had to hold Liverpool, regain Sheffield and perhaps make a breakthrough in Newcastle, while the Conservatives dreamt of becoming the largest party in Birmingham and gaining a toehold in the great cities from which they had been eliminated over the last decade. Travelling around the country in this quiescent contest there was much more evidence of local election activity than of efforts to help people to choose an MEP.

But it was not only 'Europe' that was absent. The local election contests were necessarily regional affairs, with local parties adapting their campaigns to the local opposition and exploiting local issues and personalities to further their cases. To some considerable extent, therefore, the national campaigns were irrelevant. Conservative candidates were painfully aware of this detachment of the local from the national and the European. Said one: 'It gave our "supporters" the option of doing the right thing by voting Conservative in the locals and then voting UKIP in the Europeans.'

Postal voting

Local council nominations only closed on 11 May, and in the four all-postal regions there was an obligation to get the ballot papers to the Royal Mail by 1 June. By 28 May it had become plain that this was not going to happen. Some printers had not been able to keep to the promised schedule and some errors had been made in the printing. There were vociferous protests from both Conservatives and Liberal Democrats and some of the trouble was blamed on the government for its insistence on the inclusion of the North West region, despite the warnings from the Electoral Commission. However, on 2 June it was announced that all ballot papers had reached the Royal Mail by dawn, even though in a few cases council workers had to stay up all night to meet the deadline. But by then the constant stream of negative headlines (see Table 4.3) had done lasting damage.

Table 4.3   The postal ballot saga, as seen through a selection of headlines

Date	Newspaper	Headline
27 May	Daily Telegraph	All-postal ballot plans 'turning into shambles'
	Guardian	Delays threaten postal voting
28 May	Daily Mail	Postal vote chaos could see election scrapped
29 May	The Times	Postal vote chaos puts poll at risk
	Guardian	Postal vote chaos could put back election date
	Mail on Sunday	Government 'dithering' caused postal vote fiasco
	Sunday Times	Post vote chaos as deadline looms
31 May	Daily Mail	Postal vote experiment 'hours from disaster'
	Independent	Printers have 24 hours to avert postal voting fiasco
1 June	Guardian	Race to meet postal ballot deadline
2 June	The Times	Postal ballot still running late despite desperate rush
3 June	The Times	Postal ballot system facing big overhaul
	Daily Telegraph	Postal vote farrago

The ongoing controversy certainly served to publicise the elections but it also brought dire warnings of the complications of postal voting and of the possibilities for fraud and confusion. Charles Kennedy announced that his party would consider launching legal challenges. More than one candidate pointed out that the witness requirement introduced by a House of Lords' amendment (see Chapter 2) had caused many problems. On 8 June there were even reports of street brawls over a missing sack of postal ballots in the Small Heath area of Birmingham.

Episodes and themes

Mr Khanbhai's address

In mid-April the *Eastern Daily Press* reported that Bashir Khanbhai, elected in 1999 as a Conservative MEP for the Eastern region, had given a fictitious constituency address in Wroxham ('57 Peninsula Cottages'). It was alleged that he was claiming travel expenses from Heathrow to Wroxham, though he actually lived almost 200 miles away in Sevenoaks, Kent. Mr Khanbhai, an Oxford-educated millionaire pharmacist, had made much of the fact that he was the region's only MEP who actually lived in it, and it was this that had led to the *Eastern Daily News* investigation. Questioned, he claimed that the address was a way of collecting post, since a friend owned the complex of cottages and would hold his mail for him. The story led independent Martin Bell to stand (see Chapter 3).

Tipped off by local party activists, Tory Central Office held an internal investigation into the allegations and decided that Mr Khanbhai should be deselected. However, on 20 April and after an appeal, Mr Khanbhai was reinstated on the list. Said Mr Howard, 'There was an investigation and at the end of the investigation the conclusion was reached that what had happened was an inadvertent error. As far as I'm concerned, that's it.' But the local media's interest, fanned by Martin Bell's candidature, intensified.

In Cambridge, on 7 May, Michael Howard gave his unequivocal personal support to Mr Khanbhai. With Mr Khanbhai alongside him on the platform, and asked whether he gave his 'full backing', Mr Howard replied 'Yes.'

Then, on 12 May, the Conservative Party's press office released a statement:

> The Board of the Conservative Party has removed Bashir Khanbhai MEP from the Party's list of candidates for the Eastern region in the European elections on 10 June.
>
> In the light of new information about his travel allowance claims sent to the Conservative Party by Mr Khanbhai on Monday, 10 May, John Taylor CBE, Chairman of the Board's Committee on Candidates, will be referring a number of issues to the European Parliament authorities for further investigation.

Mr Khanbhai furiously protested his innocence, alleging that he been a victim of local racial prejudice. He argued that the announcement had deliberately been made too late for him to be able to stand as an independent, and these allegations were reported in the national (*Observer*, 16 May) and Muslim (*The Muslim News*, 23 May) press.[2]

Denis MacShane and the PES manifesto

In Brussels, on 24 April, Denis MacShane had signed, as Minister for Europe, the pan-European manifesto of the Party of European Socialists, which included demands for a common European policy on immigration and asylum. The Conservatives belatedly noticed this and demanded to know if the minister was expressing the government's position.

On 9 June John Prescott, standing in for Tony Blair at Prime Minister's Questions, had to deny that the manifesto represented government policy. When pressed by Michael Ancram, standing in for Michael Howard, John Prescott teased the Conservatives over their own strange position on Europe and Michael Howard's unrealistic demands. He quoted a pro-UKIP Tory peer, Lord Willoughby, who said that renegotiating the EU Treaties was like ordering lobster thermidor at McDonald's: 'It would be nice but it is not on the menu.'

This episode nevertheless demonstrated a fresh development in British politics; calls for a reduction in political asylum seekers (as opposed to illegal immigrants) had become acceptable mainstream party politics. The scene had been set by Tony Blair at his party's Canary Wharf launch, when he pointed out that when Michael Howard 'was Home Secretary the numbers of asylum seekers went up'. There was a time when a Labour government could have presented such a statistic as a humane achievement. To argue that higher numbers of asylum seekers were a political failure was grist to the BNP mill.

As Chapter 1 described, immigration and asylum, subliminally linked to the far more sinister issue of terrorism, had become major political issues. Paradoxically, this development had occurred in a country in which large swathes of urban terrain had become genuinely multicultural. Said one candidate: 'I was amazed how ignorant and xenophobic voters have become.' The challenge for Michael Howard, himself the son of immigrants, was how to keep the party's faithful sweet whilst warding off racists. An example of this, another sort of balancing act, came with a 24 May Birmingham speech in which he argued passionately for a British multicultural society. But he also called for immigrants to 'speak and read English', and it was that demand which made the next day's headlines.

Roger Helmer's Euroscepticism...

On 8 June Roger Helmer, who led the Conservative ticket in the East Midlands and was hard-pressed by the Robert Kilroy-Silk bandwagon, went too far in expressing Euroscepticism; he called for Britain to seek associate membership of the European Union and described the rise of the UK Independence Party as

> an historic development, a seismic change, a wake-up call. The party leadership has been trying to bridge the gap between the old dinosaurs – Clarke and Heseltine – and the vast majority of the members and activists. But in the effort to keep a few distinguished Europhiles onside, we are letting party activists and the public slip away.

The reaction was swift and he was forced to clarify his remarks, saying: 'People should vote Conservative on June 10. I do not support withdrawal from the European Union. I am advocating a more open and flexible relationship for Britain.'

But his remarks had provoked the Europhiles. David Curry, who had recently resigned from the Shadow Cabinet, said that Michael Howard should confront the Eurosceptics rather than seek their votes. Ian Taylor argued that the party leadership had played into UKIP's hands by giving the impression that Britain was continuously under threat from Europe. Mr Howard, who had maintained his difficult balancing act for so long, wobbled badly on the high wire.

Mr Howard and the UK Independence Party

As the UK Independence Party bandwagon continued to gather pace, largely at the expense of the Conservatives, two questions dogged Mr Howard: should he do something, and, if so, what? He received passionate but contradictory advice. Eurosceptics argued that he was allowing the UK Independence Party to steal Conservative ground. Euroenthusiasts warned him not to succumb to the Euro-sceptic temptation. The 'Helmer episode' meanwhile showed that many Tory candidates were badly rattled.

On 30 May a 14-page briefing paper on the UK Independence Party, drafted by Conservative Research and Development, was leaked to *The Times* and the *Daily Telegraph*. Tory candidates had been sent the dossier the previous week, after the first opinion poll evidence showing that support for UKIP was rising. The paper argued that, as a minor party, UKIP stood no chance of delivering any change in Europe but, under a section headed 'Cranks in the Ranks', the paper argued that 'A vote for UKIP is a vote for the little Englanders.' It went on: 'The UK Independence Party claims to be a home for Euro-sceptics but in reality it is full of cranks and political gadflies.' The paper further alleged that UKIP had links to figures such as controversial historian David Irving. The next day's editions of *The Times* and the *Daily Telegraph* sported glaring headlines, the latter declaring 'Howard rages at UKIP "gadflies"'.

Whether or not the leak was deliberate (the *Daily Telegraph* reported that the leak had been 'authorised' by Mr Howard), many Conservative candidates were bemused, if not alarmed. As *The Times* reported, details of UKIP MEPs' voting records were of little use on the doorstep. Some candidates secretly felt that UKIP should be congratulated for helping to extract the promise of a referendum from Mr Blair. But perhaps worst of all, old party hands warned that Conservative voters were intent on splitting their tickets, voting UKIP for the European elections as a strong gesture, and Conservative in the local elections, where some sort of power was at stake. To criticise UKIP, and by implication UKIP voters, as being 'cranks and political gadflies' was to insult the Conservative Party's own.

Notwithstanding these reservations, on 1 June Michael Howard went on the attack. Naming the rival party just once in his speech to party activists in Southampton, Mr Howard said that its MEPs had abdicated their responsibilities:

> At one extreme there are the candidates from the UK Independence Party. They represent a party that wants to pull out of the European Union altogether. They have frequently failed to vote in the European Parliament on issues that are vital to Britain.

This was of little use in pacifying Mr Howard's own Eurosceptics. Sir Teddy Taylor acknowledged that Howard 'was taking a stronger line but he may be persuaded to go further – he knows what is happening in public opinion'. Behind the scenes, an argument ensued. The leader of the Conservative MEPs, Jonathan Evans, was furious at having been kept out of the loop – this was a simple consequence of the absence of any central coordination mechanism.

But he also disagreed with the tactics. More Euro-enthusiastic party grandees were also unhappy with the leader's clumsy attempt to discredit the UKIP threat.

Labour made the most of it. On 4 June Jack Straw attacked Michael Howard for causing 'panic and chaos' over Europe. Mr Howard was paying the electoral price for

> encouraging an ideological opposition to the EU which for years was a minority and now forms the mainstream of today's Conservative party ... [UKIP is] Michael Howard's Militant Tendency. Ten days before polling day the big issue is Michael Howard and UKIP. It takes serious political skill – by which I mean error – to have got the Tory Party into that strategy.

A large part of the Conservatives' problem was the absence of a 'Plan B'.[3] As Chapter 3 described, the Tories believed that they would be able to make political capital out of Mr Blair's refusal to countenance a referendum on the expected Constitutional Treaty. As Chapter 6 considers, the logical inconsistencies of their strong 'renegotiation' line on the Common Fisheries Policy was soon unravelled by the media, yet this was the only other distinctive Eurosceptical part of their overall policy platform. That they had no contingency plan for dealing with Mr Blair's U-turn was perhaps understandable (one MEP likened it to 'having your prize marrow stolen the night before the village fete'), but the party had less excuse for underestimating the UKIP threat. The omens – about backing from millionaire Paul Sykes, about help from Max Clifford and Dick Morris, and others – had been apparent from the early spring.[4]

Mr Blair's demise?

The chronology of headlines in Table 4.4 illustrates the way in which Mr Blair's perceived fortunes changed over the campaign period. To paraphrase Mark Twain, early reports of the Prime Minister's impending demise were clearly exaggerated. A number of significant anniversaries (the seventh anniversary of Mr Blair's 1997 victory on 1 May; the twenty-fifth anniversary of Margaret Thatcher's 1979 victory on 4 May; and the tenth anniversary of John Smith's death on 12 May) encouraged a sense of political mortality, and the newspapers constantly speculated about whether and when Mr Blair would call it a day. An offhand comment by former Labour leader Neil Kinnock in late April prompted Mr Blair to let it be known indirectly that he intended to serve a full third term.

The endlessly recycled stories of a Blair–Brown split and a possible leadership challenge flared up inevitably as the campaign advanced. On 9 May John Prescott and Gordon Brown were seen talking in a Loch Fyne oyster bar car park. Ominous conspiracy theory headlines appeared on 16 May when

Prescott confirmed the talks. But these were rapidly followed by reassuring headlines about the Blair–Brown relationship.

At another level, on 19 May Mr Blair was reminded of a Prime Minister's vulnerability when a protest group, Fathers for Justice, managed to infiltrate the Strangers' Gallery in the House of Commons, allowing one of the protesters, with an extraordinarily accurate throw, to hit Mr Blair squarely between the shoulders with a condom full of purple-dyed flour.

An autumn indiscretion from Melvyn Bragg, a close family friend of the Blair family, made it clear that Mr Blair had at some stage during the campaign undergone a moment of doubt. It was a tribute to his political toughness that there was no outward sign of this. By mid-May, and despite further polls indicating that Gordon Brown would be a more popular Labour leader than Mr Blair, the Prime Minister seemed to have come through the worst. A Commons intervention over Iraq by Mr Howard enabled him to fight back. The headlines dried up, leading *Times* journalist Peter Riddell to write 'Blair bounces back but there's still trouble ahead'.

Table 4.4 Changing perceptions of Mr Blair's fortunes, as seen through the headlines

Date	Newspaper	Headline
21 April	*Financial Times* (editorial)	Lost leader
28 April	*Financial Times*	Blair steels himself as storm clouds gather on Iraq and Europe strategy
29 April	*The Times*	I'll go on and on – Blair vows to serve third term
30 April	*Daily Telegraph*	Blair is staring poll defeat in the face
1 May	*Guardian*	Brown allies plan campaign
2 May	*Observer*	'Blair to go' rumours shake Labour
4 May	*Daily Telegraph*	Loss of trust shows Blair's fall from grace
9 May	*Mail on Sunday*	Dump Blair ... or lose
11 May	*Guardian*	Blair: I will quit if I become electoral liability
13 May	*Guardian*	Pressure grows for Blair to go
15 May	*The Times*	Race to seize Blair's crown is under way, says Prescott
	Financial Times	Blair on the ropes
16 May	*Sunday Telegraph*	Blair told to go now
17 May	*Daily Telegraph*	Blair fights to silence doubters
18 May	*Daily Telegraph*	Blair: I'll stay until job is done

The BNP

The BNP began the campaign period on something of a roll, particularly in the North West, where one candidate declared that the BNP had been 'the main threat until late May/early June'. In late April French Front National leader Jean-Marie Le Pen made a high-profile visit to Manchester and later confidently predicted that he would soon be leader of a new grouping within the EP, bringing together MEPs notably from the French Front National, the Belgian Vlams Blok and the British BNP. There was a flurry of interest when a BNP broadcast had passages cut and Channel 5 refused to run another with suggestions that white girls were being 'groomed' for underage sex with Asian men (*The Times*, 25 May).[5] The BNP's high expectations galvanised opposition across the cultural spectrum: the Rt. Revd Doctor John Sentamu, Bishop of Birmingham, issued a full-page advertisement in the local press with the slogan 'For god's sake Birmingham use your vote!', whilst the Muslim Council of Britain issued an open letter to the Islamic Community urging Muslims to turn out and vote to counter the threat from the far right. By mid-campaign the BNP had largely faded from view.

Broadcasts

Table 4.5 gives the dates of the various party political broadcasts during the campaign period. Very few of these concentrated on a European theme or touched on European issues. Both the Conservatives and Labour consolidated their negative campaign themes ('Let Down by Labour? Putting Britain First – Vote Conservative' and 'Britain is Working: Don't Let the Conservatives

Table 4.5 Election broadcasts during the campaign period[a]

Party	BBC1	BBC2	ITV1
Conservative	7 May (6.55 p.m.)	7 May (5.55 p.m.)	–
Labour	10 May (6.55 p.m.)	10 May (5.55 p.m.)	–
Liberal Democrats	11 May (6.55 p.m.)	11 May (5.55 p.m.)	–
UKIP	12 May (6.55 p.m.)	12 May (5.55 p.m.)	–
Greens	13 May (6.55 p.m.)	13 May (6.55 p.m.)	–
Christian People's Alliance	–	–	14 May (6 p.m.)
Respect	–	–	17 May (6 p.m.)
UKIP (repeat)	–	–	18 May (6 p.m.)
Greens (repeat)	–	–	19 May (6 p.m.)
Liberal Democrats	20 May (6.55 p.m.)	20 May (5.55 p.m.)	–
Labour	21 May (6.55 p.m.)	21 May (5.55 p.m.)	–
Conservative	23 May (6.55 p.m.)	23 May (5.55 p.m.)	–
Liberal Democrats	26 May (6.55 p.m.)	26 May (11.15 p.m.)	–
Labour	27 May (6.55 p.m.)	27 May (11.20 p.m.)	–
Respect	27 May (11.30 p.m.)	27 May (5.55 p.m.)	–
British National Party	28 May (11.30 p.m.)	28 May (5.55 p.m.)	–
Conservative	28 May (6.55 p.m.)	28 May (11.20 p.m.)	–
Greens	1 June (6.55 p.m.)	1 June (5.55 p.m.)	–
UKIP	2 June (6.55 p.m.)	2 June (5.55 p.m.)	–
Liberal Democrats	4 June (6.55 p.m.)	4 June (5.55 p.m.)	–
Labour	7 June (6.55 p.m.)	7 June (5.55 p.m.)	–
Conservative	8 June (6.55 p.m.)	8 June (5.55 p.m.)	–

[a] Broadcast times are shown in parentheses.

Wreck it Again – Vote Labour' respectively). The Greens' broadcast was a notable exception, emphasising European environmental issues and the benefits of working together across national boundaries. Another notable exception was the UK Independence Party's broadcasts, though these set out to make their case through mockery.

Of the two main parties, the Conservatives covered European issues in two broadcasts, though in the context of a negative campaign, but Europe wasn't mentioned at all in Labour's broadcasts. In thumbnail sketch style, the themes of the two party's broadcasts were as follows:

- Con I: stealth taxes, bureaucracy in the public sector, education, police/crime, NHS/bureaucracy, pensioners/poverty; Con II: PES Group manifesto (tax, immigration, welfare, UN Security Council); Con III: tax (66 increases under Labour), choice/education/health; Con IV: tax and wasted opportunities, the cost of the European Parliament.
- Lab I: unemployment, negative equity and the poll tax under previous Tory regimes; Lab II: Michael Howard's CV; Lab III: Mr Howard again; Lab IV: Mr Howard yet again.
- Lib Dem I: new PAYE council tax proposal; Lib Dem II: Britain's and Lib Dems' active membership of the EU, peace dividend, the EU and the environment.

Again, there was no clear impression of a distinct contest for elections to the European Parliament, and no clear campaign themes.

Opinion polls

After 2001 the political polling industry changed radically. Three national newspapers continued to publish regular monthly polls. But the *Daily Telegraph* switched in 2002 from its longstanding link with Gallup to Peter Kellner's innovative YouGov. *The Times* switched from MORI to Andrew Cooper's Populus. Only the *Guardian* stayed with Nick Sparrow's ICM. MORI (which alone continued with face-to-face polling) and NOP provided one-off studies for newspaper and broadcast specials, and both recorded monthly polls on their websites.

The coverage of opinion polls normally focuses on the question 'How would you vote if there was a general election tomorrow?' The methods of the pollsters varied. ICM continued with their well-trusted telephone surveys weighted on the basis of evidence about past voting. Populus followed methods very similar to ICM. YouGov used the internet to draw opinions from a weighted panel. Some used unprompted open-ended questions; others used prompted questions, reminding respondents of the party names, including, importantly, the Liberal Democrats. There were slightly different approaches to the headlines on the findings; it was not always clear whether percentages were based on what their whole sample said or referring to those 'likely' or 'certain' to vote.

The polls with their different methods found results that at times varied somewhat, but the general picture over the three years before the European contest was of a continued but declining Labour lead; the Conservatives seeming to have hit a ceiling around 34%; and the Liberal Democrats were almost always above 20% and on a higher plateau than they had achieved at any time since they were founded in 1989.

Figure 3.1 (p. 81) shows three-party support in the polls, 1999–2004. Tables 4.6 and 4.7 show the findings during the campaign period. There was no significant departure from the long-term trend of Westminster voting intentions. But when asked about the European elections there was a sharp falling off in support for the major parties, as Table 4.8 shows.

Table 4.6   Regular monthly polls, 2003 to April 2004

	Conservatives (%)			Labour (%)			Lib Dems (%)		
	Top	*Lowest*	*Av.*	*Top*	*Lowest*	*Av.*	*Top*	*Lowest*	*Av.*
YouGov	40	31	35	41	30	36	30	18	22
ICM	35	29	32	43	35	38	28	20	22
Populus	35	29	33	41	34	36	26	18	23

Table 4.7   Polls, April–June 2004

Poll	Pub. date	Interview date	Con (%)	Lab (%)	Lib Dems (%)	UKIP (%)	Other (%)
ICM *Guardian*	20 April	16–18 April	33	38	22	n/a	8
MORI	22 April	15–19 April	34	36	22	4	8
YouGov/*D. Tel.*	30 April	27–29 April	39	35	19	n/a	7
Populus/*Times*	13 May	7–9 May	36	32	22	n/a	10
YouGov/*D. Tel.*	24 May	20–22 May	36	33	19	4	8
ICM/*Guardian*	26 May	20–23 May	34	39	20	n/a	7
YouGov/*D. Tel.*	29 May	25–27 May	34	33	19	4	8
MORI	4 June	27 May–1 June	34	35	18	4	10
YouGov/*D. Tel.*	7 June	4–6 June	26	24	15	19	11
Populus/*Times*	8 June	4–6 June	29	31	22	5	13
ICM/*Guardian*	15 June	11–13 June	31	34	22	n/a	13

Questions about voting intentions for the European Parliament were oddly lacking. Populus only asked about this once in early June. ICM did not ask it at all except in their post mortem survey. Only YouGov pursued the matter – and with far-reaching consequences. Their poll published on 24 May revealed that the UK Independence Party, on 14%, was a far more serious competitor than had been realised. On 7 June that figure jumped to 19% (or 21% among those most likely to vote). The Liberal Democrats came fourth in both surveys. On 8 June Populus put UKIP on only 9%.

Table 4.8   Contrast in General Election and European Parliament election voting intentions

		Con (%)	Lab (%)	Lib Dems (%)	UKIP (%)	Other (%)
24 May	Gen. El.	36	33	18	4	8
YouGov/*D. Tel.*	Eur. Parl.	28	27	15	14	13
	Difference	−8	−6	−3	+10	+5
8 June	Gen. El.	29	31	12	5	12
Populus/*Times*	Eur. Parl.	17	24	22	9	5
	Difference	−12	−7	+10	+3	−7

YouGov had prepared the parties for an upset. On 7 June the headline writers of the *Standard* had suggested that YouGov was predicting a 51%–49% race for the London Mayor, although the 'certain to vote' figures were actually 55%–45%; the article did make clear that if turnout rose Ken Livingstone would win reasonably comfortably. In a YouGov exit poll for Sky television, released at the close of the London voting on 10 June, those figures had moved to 54%–46%. Ken Livingstone actually won 55%–45%.

In another exit poll (on a 7,491 sample), which was held back till all European voting was over at 9 p.m. on Sunday 13 June, YouGov suggested that the UK Independence Party would get 20% nationally while the Conservatives and Labour would each get 22% and the Liberal Democrats 14%.

It was a difficult election to forecast and no one got it absolutely right. Although YouGov was 4% out for UKIP and 5% out for the Conservatives, on 14 June YouGov declared itself to have been the most accurate pollster.

One reason for YouGov overestimating the UK Independence Party vote and for Populus and others underestimating it seemed to lie in how far question-wording gave a prompt; some polls mentioned UKIP by name along with the three main parties, while some only detected UKIP supporters by asking what they meant by 'other'. YouGov's high estimate of UKIP could also have been partly due to the fact that volunteers for YouGov's panel are by definition attracted to novelty and UKIP certainly seemed a novelty. There seems to be no substance in the suggestion that UKIP successfully packed YouGov's panel with its own volunteers. But many critics argued that YouGov's high estimation of UKIP support had given significant momentum to the party's campaign. Barry Sheerman and other MPs suggested that internet polling should be investigated and at Prime Minister's Questions on 16 May Tony Blair approved the idea of a cross-party approach to the problems of political polling.

Polls on issues and personalities also had their message. Every poll showed that the proposed European constitution was unpopular, suggesting that it would be defeated in a referendum by margins ranging from 57%–28% (ICM, June 2004) to 60%–33% (Populus, May 2004). The numbers favouring complete withdrawal from the EU were much less extreme.

Views on leaders were unfavourable. The negative rating (30% satisfied, 61% dissatisfied; that is, –31%) for Tony Blair was much worse than that for Michael Howard (30% satisfied, 31% dissatisfied; that is, –1%). Charles Kennedy was better perceived (36% satisfied, 28% dissatisfied; that is, +12%) (MORI, May 2004). But when it came to issues, Labour led the Conservatives as the party best to handle health, education and social services. Only on Europe and law and order were the Conservatives preferred.

An interesting, if small, row developed at the end of the campaign when *The Times* published a Populus poll on 8 June, 48 hours before election day, which reported what people in all-postal areas said about how they had voted. An Electoral Commission official pointed out that this violated the ban on exit polls being published before the booths had closed (see Chapter 2). The idea that knowledge of how Britain had voted on Thursday would sway the preferences of the Continentals who marked their ballots on Sunday was somewhat absurd. The ban also raised questions of freedom of speech. On 10 June Peter Riddell replied robustly in *The Times*'s defence; the matter was allowed to lapse.[6]

The media

The media, like nature, abhors a vacuum. Before the European election, the BBC's Analysis and Research department prepared a *Guide to the European Parliamentary Election 2004*. Its introductory overview concluded with a list of 'stories to look out for'. Both the UK Independence Party and postal balloting were flagged up. But with regard to UKIP the only question was whether it, together with other 'minor parties', would be squeezed out by the reduction in the number of MEPs. With regard to postal ballots, the question was whether they would actually raise turnout ...

Nobody could have predicted how Robert Kilroy-Silk's sudden entry into the fray would seemingly mesmerise the media, and it is a moot point as to whether there ever was such a large-scale crisis in the mechanics of the all-postal balloting regions. But the simple fact was that, as far as the national media were concerned, there were no other 'big' stories about the European elections.

An exhaustive examination of regional press reports tellingly reveals that there was little coverage of the European election campaign. Occasional reports focused on allegations of fraud and malpractice, whether by MEPs or candidates and voters, or 'human interest' stories about local figures. At the same time, regional newspapers such as the *Yorkshire Post* and the *Western*

Mail provided a number of high-quality journalistic analysis pieces. It seems that these and other papers realised that there *was* a story to tell, but it was not so much about the campaign as about the forces underlying it.

The end?

On Thursday 10 June, the BBC reported that the polls had opened for 'Super Thursday'. Britons were reportedly 'heading to the polls' for European, local, London Mayoral and Assembly elections. Curiously, though, 'millions of people across Northern England and the East Midlands' had already cast their votes by postal ballot. For them, the thrill of the chase, if it had ever existed, had been over for as much as two weeks.

The weather was generally dry and relatively warm. Rain, it can safely be assumed, did not keep voters away from the polls.

Michael Howard and his wife, Sandra, went to their local polling station in Lympne, Kent, to cast their votes. Tony Blair posted his vote in from London before heading to Savannah, Georgia, for the G8 summit of world leaders. Liberal Democrat leader Charles Kennedy and his wife Sarah visited a south London polling station to cast their votes.

The front pages of the tabloid newspapers told their own stories: 'Cocktail of drugs can beat arthritis', reported the *Daily Mail*; 'Asylum is six times worse than feared', said the *Daily Express*; 'Twinkle twinkle little star', declared the *Daily Mirror*, reporting on a child murder case; 'My romp with French footie ace', blared the *Daily Star*; 'Hold 'em balls', declared the *Sun*, with an early story on the European football championship. At the broadsheet end of the scale, the impression was generally similar: 'Competition forces Bupa rethink', led the *Financial Times*; and 'Bush: our Middle East mission has just begun', declared the *Guardian*. Clearly, the European elections were not to the forefront of most people's minds. There were three exceptions. The *Independent* ran a front-page polemical piece entitled 'You British, the elections, and your special brand of hatred', whilst *The Times* and the *Daily Telegraph* both ran on the postal ballot theme – 'Postal ballot dirty tricks exposed' and 'Elections cast into doubt by post vote turmoil', respectively.

The 2004 European election in the UK was by some standards a massive operation. There were 672 candidates. About £10 million was spent by the parties. At least 200 million leaflets were printed, if not always distributed. There were 20 nationwide broadcasts. Some events, such as the emergence of Robert Kilroy-Silk, the attack on UKIP by Michael Howard and the row over postal voting, received wide coverage. As the campaign drew to a close, Labour ministers and spokespersons began to talk down the expected results. David Blunkett memorably declared that the Labour Party was headed for 'a kicking'.

Yet for most UK citizens, including party activists, the election was a non-event. Few received more than one piece of literature from each party. Very few attended meetings (one Conservative candidate described his main activity during the campaign as being 'Driving long distances to tiny meetings'). There were no great rallies and hardly any local meetings. Days went by in the provincial press without a single story about the contest. In the bulk of the country there was little canvassing. In so far as there was a campaign, it focused primarily on council elections. National campaigning was negative in tone, concentrating on the defects of the rival party leaders and policies. It was not a month that showed British politics at its best.

What began as a smudge would end as a smudge. The first local election results were due at 11 p.m. on 10 June. The results of the London Mayor and Assembly elections were expected for the early evening of the next day, Friday. The European election results in the UK would not be known until late Sunday evening, with the results for Northern Ireland and parts of Scotland expected only on Monday 14 June. 'Muddy electoral waters', Peter Riddell had presciently written in *The Times* (5 May), 'should allow all parties to claim victory.'

In any case, all involved in the European elections campaign could legitimately ask whether their efforts had been worthwhile. The day after polling day not a single mainstream British newspaper front page mentioned the European elections. It was as if they had never been. And yet ...

Appendix 4.1: Campaign chronology, European elections 2004

15 Mar   Respect launches its European elections campaign.

23 Mar   Regulations for Returning Officers published.

31 Mar   Government succeeds on tuition fee increases: 316–288.

1 Apr   Bill on postal voting areas enacted after ping-pong with Lords.

1 Apr   Beverly Hughes resigns as Immigration Minister over 'dodgy visas' affair.

16 Apr   UKIP launches European elections campaign with a national poster launch.

20 Apr   Blair agrees to referendum on the European Constitution.

21 Apr   Blair says EU membership will remain, regardless of a 'No' vote.

23 Apr   Hoon admits mistakes in treatment of Kelly.

23 Apr   Blunkett to seek new powers to stop terrorist suspects being released on bail.

25 Apr   Le Pen attacked at a press conference with BNP's leader Nick Griffin.

30 Apr   YouGov says 81% thought Blair 'opportunistic' in referendum switch.

30 Apr   51% said they'd vote 'No' in a Constitution referendum if asked tomorrow.

30 Apr   *Daily Mirror* publishes photographs of alleged torture in Iraq.

30 Apr   Plaid Cymru launches its election campaign.

1 May	European Union admits ten new member states.
3 May	Bank Holiday.
3 May	MOD report concludes that the *Daily Mirror* torture photographs are staged.
4 May	Labour launches its local elections campaign: attack on Howard's record.
5 May	Liberal Democrats launch European election campaign.
6 May	MPC raises interest rates by 0.25% to 4.25%.
6 May	John Scarlett named by Number 10 as the next Director General of MI6.
6 May	David Martin investigated for row over expenses claims.
8 May	A new draft of EU Constitution breaches some of Tony Blair's 'red lines'.
10 May	Labour launch poster attacking Howard.
11 May	Robert Kilroy-Silk announced as a UKIP candidate in the European Elections.
11 May	ECOFIN Finance Ministers' meeting held in Brussels.
12 May	Conservatives launch European election campaign.
12 May	Bashir Khanbhai deselected as Con MEP candidate.
14 May	*Daily Mirror* editor Piers Morgan sacked over torture photographs.
15 May	UKIP relaunches campaign.
16 May	Brown and Prescott's 'secret' talks in a restaurant car park.
17 May	Greens launch their European election campaign.
19 May	Purple flour thrown at the PM during PM's Questions.
19 May	West Midlands police launch postal vote fraud investigation in Birmingham.
21 May	European Parliament unveils an election advertisement to promote voting.
21 May	SNP launches its campaign.
22 May	IDS attacked Howard for his stance on the Iraq war.
22 May	Concerns about postal voting system emerge.
24 May	YouGov shows UKIP 18%, Lib Dems 15%, Lab 23%, Cons 31%.
27 May	Cons unveil a poster campaign designed by ordinary voters.
27 May	Labour MP Jim Cunningham (Leicester South) dies.
29 May	C. Leslie says postal ballot fears 'politically motivated'.
31 May	Bank Holiday.
1 Jun	Howard brands UKIP 'extreme'.
1 Jun	Lord Falconer admits midnight deadline for postal votes will be missed for a few.
2 Jun	Lib Dem Oldham Councillor arrested for alleged postal vote fraud.
4 Jun	Jack McConnell chooses to attend the D-Day commemorations.
4 Jun	Rhodri Morgan chooses not to go to the ceremony.
5 Jun	Ronald Reagan dies.

5 Jun	The Queen, Bush, Blair, Chirac, Schroeder and Putin at D-Day commemorations.
7 Jun	Helmer says Britain should seek 'associate membership' of EU.
8 Jun	Three-day G8 economic summit opens at Sea Island, Georgia.
9 Jun	Police investigating hundreds of cases of postal vote fraud.
10 Jun	Local and European elections polling day.
13 Jun	European election results announced.
17 Jun	Three-day summit opens in Brussels to discuss the EU Constitution.

Appendix 4.2: IT and the June 2004 European elections campaign

Liam Spender[7]

The World Wide Web was important to politics in 2004 because individual politicians, political parties, governments and the media all saw websites as important channels of communication and therefore invested considerable energy and resources in developing websites and web-related campaign strategies.

Britain's 79 MEPs were better adapted to the internet than their Westminster cousins, since in September 2004 only four of them had no e-mail address (all newly elected MEPs) and just two had no website (again, newly elected MEPs). Clearly, in the light of the gulf in public knowledge about the EP and its members, MEPs are keen to ease contact with voters, and e-mail addresses and the maintenance of websites are an easy and cost-effective way of facilitating such contacts with at least part of the electorate. A number of MEPs expended considerable effort in creating attractive and dynamic websites, with a few producing regular 'blogs' (tools also to organise 'meet-ups' of supporters and requests for small amounts of money) and others producing downloadable pedagogic material.

Personal websites may also provide a degree of useful autonomy. For example, Roger Helmer MEP (Con, East Midlands) was obliged to apologise for writing a piece calling for Britain to switch to 'associate membership' of the EU, but left the article on his website.[8] Bashir Khanbhai, the Conservative forced to stand down from the Eastern regional list after a row over expenses, used his website to post a long and detailed defence of why he was not guilty of the charge made against him.[9]

In July 2004, a Eurobarometer survey found that 7% of respondents used the 'internet' to discover information about the 2004 elections,[10] but this did not mean that the internet was 93% irrelevant to politics. The importance of television in its infancy lay in the effect it had on political parties' campaigning strategies, rather than its effect on voters. The dawn of the television era prompted parties to coach their leaders toward better performances.[11] The technology that the parties used in 2004 was less important than television in presenting policy, it was still an infant; however, an ability to use the Web was seen by pundits and the public alike as a new, crude measure of politicians' credibility.

The BBC was in the vanguard of the electronic revolution. On the 1997 election campaign it had claimed 10 million visits (Butler and Kavanagh, 1997, p. 215) and in November that year it launched the BBC News Online site.[12] By 2004, BBC News Online had 1.5 million web pages on its servers,[13] and claimed to reach 3.2 million users a week – a quarter of all UK internet users – one of the largest and most popular websites at the time.[14] The comprehensive BBC websites produced since 1997 for each General Election and European election gave voters, journalists and all interested in politics access to information and video news reports about the election campaign and reporters' commentaries.[15] Those BBC websites were one of the signposts by which to judge the beginning of a new election season.

Newspapers soon also offered sprawling and increasingly sophisticated websites with news and analysis. Indeed, the *Guardian* and *The Times* began to offer a facility to view digitised versions of their newspapers as they appeared in print.[16] And as these sites developed, so did tools to exploit them. For example, an invaluable tool in the process of writing this book was LexisNexis, an online archive of most major national and regional newspapers produced within the UK. LexisNexis has effectively eliminated the need to gather and maintain newspaper clippings.[17] All of these online developments enabled those voters with access to the internet to be very much better informed than could previously have been the case.

In 2004 the Web dictated the speed and style of party political campaigning. In 2003, the US Democratic Presidential aspirant Howard Dean showed through a combination of 'blogs' (requesting $50 a time from visitors to the site) that it was possible to raise large sums of money in this way ($25.6 million in Dean's case) in a very short period of time.[18] Mr Dean raised ten and a half times the amount John McCain raised via his website in 2000 and his successful formula was rapidly copied by his American rivals. In Britain, the UK Independence Party was also inspired by Howard Dean's success.

In the 2004 election, all political parties – and the vast majority of independents – running for election had websites. Websites contribute to modern political parties' credibility in the eyes of voters and activists. Jackson in 2003 found that all but 33% of 659 British MPs made use of e-mail as a campaigning tool,[19] while the majority of parties exploited e-mail to ask for help and actively inform supporters of policies throughout the electoral cycle – but usually only during the heat of election campaigns to communicate with voters.[20]

All the political parties' webmasters felt that the Web provided an opportunity to overcome 'unsatisfactory media coverage and to circumvent the media'. The Web also offered a way for the richer political parties to show their broadcasts again and again, and not just within the regulated slots on television, since broadcasts could be streamed directly, or downloaded, from party websites to web surfers' screens. Last but not least, providing material primarily via a website in electronic form can be an effective way of reducing campaign costs. This approach was taken to its logical conclusion by the Labour Party, which decreed that the paper-based versions of its campaign documentation should only be available by post and on request, while remaining freely available for downloading from the website.

An important aspect of parties' websites are extranets (private zones of party websites accessible via passwords known to members) for party activists. Labour, the Conservatives and the Liberal Democrats all possessed such facilities. Labour (<www.labour.org.uk>) allowed members to access campaigning literature, photographs and party logos; to vote online in National Executive Committee (NEC) elections; to donate to the party; to renew membership. Labour's extranet also provided tools for councillors and constituency parties to manage casework as well as an online directory of approved party candidates from which to select Parliamentary candidates. Labour spokesmen were also proud of the web's star role in their *Big Conversation* policy consultation exercise: 'The *Big Conversation* would not have been the project it was without the Internet.'

Labour headquarters played an important role in bringing affordable – if basic – websites to MPs not yet converted to online activity via its Web-in-a-Box facility. In 2004, 66 MPs (16.2% of the 407-strong Parliamentary Party) were using the scheme.[21] Labour launched the second version of this tool in March 2002, which for £211.50 allowed MPs to develop their own website with a domain of <www.mpname.labour.co.uk> and with six megabytes of storage and technical support.[22]

The Conservatives operated an advanced and comprehensive website (<www.conservatives.com>) that provided a means of attracting donors; membership applications; an online shop; and sign-ups for various e-mail newsletters. The Conservative website had two main extranets, one for activists and constituency associations, and another for journalists. Conservatives happily noted that the extranets were secure, since other parties only cited publicly available information – rather than what was available on the extranets. Conservative associations benefited from the extranet as they compiled their shortlists of Prospective Parliamentary Candidates (PPCs) from an online directory. Candidates themselves enjoyed a small amount of free publicity, since each had his or her photograph and biography online.[23]

As with the other parties, some local areas were farther along the information superhighway than others – a senior Conservative campaigner was horrified to discover that one local constituency he visited had no e-mail address. An important theme identified by all the parties was the fact that the most popular parts of their websites were those that allowed users to find out information about their *local* areas – either through postcode searches or maps. So while party websites carried national themes, voters were most concerned about what that meant for their local areas before larger units of government.

The Liberal Democrats' site (<www.libdems.org.uk>) contained the obligatory facilities to join, to donate, or to learn about MPs and PPCs and party policy, as well as downloadable resources for use in campaigning. The Liberal Democrats' site was slightly less polished than those of its larger rivals, which was perhaps only to be expected since the party itself calculated that it had been outspent by a 15:1 ratio on the web by Labour and Conservatives. Liberal Democrats recognised the value of e-mail as a means of pushing out information and alerting activists and interested observers to developments on their website and to resources available on their extranet.

The British National Party (BNP), often scorned or ignored by the media, used its website (<www.bnp.org.uk>) as a dedicated channel for its own publicity. The site offered a variety of campaigning logos and leaflets, and chances for activists to contribute 'think piece' articles about the direction of policy. Since the website was privately owned and operated it fell outside the regulations concerning party election broadcasts, and so the BNP screened several videos and animations that would have been heavily edited if used on television. So, while the BNP's television broadcasts were not carried in full, those same broadcasts were accessible online.[24] Indeed, the BNP perhaps provided the best illustration that the internet was radio-like in the opportunity it offered to target specific sections of the electorate from under the same party political umbrella. The BNP's 'Land and People website'[25] expressed the party's view on land and countryside issues and the solutions that the BNP offered to environmental problems. Perhaps this was an attempt to garner the votes of the discontents of the fox-hunting fraternity, but it nevertheless made the BNP a multi-headed demon in the eyes of the other parties.

The UKIP had a clear idea of the importance of a web strategy to their electoral success. From January 2004 the party began asking voters to: 'lend your support' to the UKIP and told visitors to its website (<www.ukip.org>) that the 'The British love affair with the EU is over – please give £20 towards the divorce.' Senior party figures boasted that their website received 10,000 new hits following their two election broadcasts. So confident was the party that on 7 April it also took the step of registering the names of their top candidates (who were not already MEPs) as internet domain names.[26] Those involved at the UKIP added that the pre-emptive registration of domain names was 'Partly to maintain the discipline of domain names and partly to avoid cyber-squatters cashing in on the UKIP brand name after the election.' This step both prevented others from registering the domains and allowed the UKIP MEPs to set up their websites the day after the count.

The Greens were the only other party to compete nationally. Their web presence was professional, but without the resources for streaming videos or an extranet. Party members could download resources from the public pages of the site (<www.greenparty.org.uk>), just as UKIP activists could. This prevented the circulation of confidential briefings online, but still allowed for some reduction in printing costs and campaign time spent on administration by allowing the use of e-mail to distribute resources.

Respect ran a rather basic website (<www.respectcoalition.org.uk>) that contained campaign artwork; a manifesto; a list of candidates and the option of downloading a membership form along with some audio/video files of addresses by George Galloway and Bob Crow to potential sympathisers. The party developed online membership and donation forms after the European election and continued to offer an archive of press releases and documents issued during the campaign – something that set it apart from other parties. However, Respect lacked an extranet and thus could not fully utilise the medium to communicate with activists.

In other areas of the UK, the nationalist parties had a more uncertain relationship with the web. While the SNP operated a special micro-site (<http://voteforscotland.snp.org>) for the European Elections that allowed users to view variously its election broadcast, resources for schools and press releases, the parent site (<www.snp.org>) was out of date and focused firmly on the 2003 Scottish Parliament elections. Plaid Cymru's website (<www.plaidcymru.org>) did provide much text-based information, but lacked facilities for joining or donating to the party online, or indeed for viewing the party's election broadcasts. The DUP (<www.dup.org.uk>) and UUP (<www.uup.org>) ran extremely sophisticated websites in Northern Ireland, contrasting vividly with the decidedly low-tech Sinn Féin website (<www.sinnfein.org>).

This appendix has offered a brief survey of the developments in technology in the European election of 2004. Britain was ahead of its European partners in the use of the Web and computer technology to mobilise and choreograph election campaigning. British political parties had little choice, with over 74% of the working-age population and 58% of all households possessing internet access. In 2004, technology began to exhibit its great ability to flatten the main parties' oligopolistic grip on media coverage. Websites could create stories about their causes, as the DumpBlair pressure group demonstrated on Iraq, and YouGov's internet polling showed of UKIP.

Political parties have always sought to gain advantages over their rivals in campaigning. Evolving communication techniques and information technology are obvious sources of potential advantages, if only temporary. For example, the SDP, despite its failure to 'break the mould', introduced the idea of computerised membership rolls; the Labour Party used the symbolism of a red rose 'brand', one copied from the corporate world, to signify its break with its 1980s past; the Greens have used new websites to demonstrate the credibility of their policies as potential better alternatives for voters in a way that their relatively limited resources would not otherwise have allowed them to do.

But perhaps above all, the use of the mainstay technologies of the internet in 2004 – the Web and e-mail – showed that political parties could communicate more effectively with their activists and that those activists could have a (small) role in policy development, such as Labour's *Big Conversation*, and with the use of 'blogs' and e-mail newsletters could be kept regularly informed of what was happening at the centre of their party. The future path of technology will create further opportunities for individual members to become much more closely involved in the direction of politics. The main problem that technology poses for parties and individual politicians is that events move more quickly, news cycles become shorter and that standards of proof in debate risk being lowered. Political parties must find a means of using technology to continue to motivate electors to vote and members to work for their platforms. Parties must not only offer auditory sound-bites, but also use computer bytes to remain relevant to modern Britain.

Notes

1. One special adviser to a senior Labour minister remarked that 'I had always believed it would be far easier to manage a European elections campaign once we were in office, but I have now discovered the opposite is the case. Opposition parties can do what they wish and concentrate their fire, but when you're in office you can't just drop the affairs of state. The minister's diary is as full as it always is and I find myself squeezing in an odd European election campaign activity where I can and against resistance, I have to say.'
2. At the time of going to press, Mr Khanbhai's closely argued version of events was still available on the website <www.bashirkhanbhai.co.uk>
3. Mr Blair's U-turn obliged the Conservative Party to pulp a leaflet they had prepared, calling for the government to agree to a referendum, but several Tory candidates assured the authors that their constituents had received copies of the outdated leaflet.
4. An analysis of the Conservative Party's promise to withdraw from the Common Fisheries Policy is given in Chapter 6.
5. Insidiously, the unexpurgated version could be viewed on the BNP's website.
6. A far greater breach of the electoral rules was considered to have occurred in the Netherlands, where the Dutch government released the preliminary results of its Thursday poll, arguing that only the final results could not be revealed before all polling stations throughout the Union had closed. The European Commission was said to be considering legal action.
7. For a general exploration of the effects of new media on representative democracy, see Coleman and Spiller (2003). For Professor Coleman's assessment of the internet's usage in the European elections, see Electoral Commission (2004b, pp. 78–80).
8. Roger Helmer, 'A Seismic Change' (7 June 2004 [cited 7 September 2004]); available from <www.rogerhelmer.com/euroblog6.asp>
9. See the site at <www.bashirkhanbhai.co.uk>
10. The European Commission, 'Post European Elections 2004 Survey' (27 July 2004 [cited 11 August 2004]); available from <http://europa.eu.int/comm/public_opinion/flash/FL162en.pdf>. The poll does not appear to have been weighted to take account of the differing degrees of penetration between member states.

11. Butler and Rose (1960, ch. 4, pp. 94–7); and Butler (1995, ch. 10, pp. 106–7); give full accounts of the importance of television to a General Election campaign. A good account of the use of online campaigning in the 2001 General Election is Coleman (2002); see also Ballinger (2002).

12. BBC News Online, 'About Our Site' (13 August 2004 [cited 13 August 2004]); available from <http://news.bbc.co.uk/1/hi/help/3281815.stm>

13. BBC News Online, 'News Sources' (13 August 2004 [cited 13 August 2004]); available from <http://news.bbc.co.uk/1/hi/help/3281815.stm>

14. BBC News Online, 'Weekly Reach of News Services' (2003 [cited 13 August 2004]); available from <http://news.bbc.co.uk/aboutbbcnews/spl/hi/facts_and_figures/html/default.stm>

15. The BBC 'Vote 2004' website, 'Don't Mention the War' (Brian Wheeler, 4 June 2004 [cited 13 August 2004]); available from <http://news.bbc.co.uk/1/hi/uk_politics/3772357.stm>

16. *Guardian* Electronic Edition (13 August 2004 [cited 13 August 2004]); available from <www.guardian.co.uk/digitaledition/subscribe> and *The Times* Online: Newspaper Edition (13 August 2004 [cited 13 August 2004]); available from <www.timesonline.co.uk/section/0,,169,00.html>. *The Times* service is free, while the *Guardian*'s is more advanced but costs £9.99 a month.

17. LexisNexis is a pay service division of Reed Elsevier Inc., its URL is <www.lexisnexis.com>

18. BBC News Online, 'Dean Tops Democrat Fundraising' (Steve Schifferes, 1 July 2003 [cited 14 August 2004]); available from <http://news.bbc.co.uk/1/hi/world/americas/3035680.stm>; BBC News Online, 'Internet Insurgent Howard Dean' (Kevin Anderson, 1 January 2004 [cited 14 August 2004]); available from <http://news.bbc.co.uk/1/hi/world/americas/3394897.stm>

19. See Jackson (2003, pp. 14–15).

20. See Jackson (2004, p. 1).

21. My own figures, using the list of MPs provided at <www.parliament.uk/directories/hciolists/alms.cfm>. 151 Labour MPs (37.1%) had no website at all; 147 (36.1%) had designed their own websites while the remaining 43 (10.6%) used the EPolitix website tool.

22. Labour Party, 'About Web in a Box 2' (2002 [cited 14 August 2004]); available from <https://www.labour.co.uk/WiabPPT.htm>. An example of a WIAB-2 website is

23. A typical example of such a profile is <www.conservatives.com/people/person.cfm?PersonID=92481>

24. See the British National Party website at <www.bnp.org.uk/audio.html> for examples.

25. The British National Party, 'Land and People' website (16 August 2004 [cited 18 August 2004]); available from <www.bnp.org.uk/landandpeople/index.htm>.

26. The domains were parked at <http://62.128.194.55/> and are presumably the non-finalised list of candidates. The domain <tomwisemep.co.uk> was registered on the 23 April; <piersmerchantmep.co.uk> was registered on 22 April and <robertkilroysilkmep.co.uk> was registered on 6 May. Data extracted from <http://sunny.nic.com/cgi-bin/whois>

5
Outcome

Smudged 'closure'

In elections, as in life, people naturally seek 'closure' – a clear end to an event. But the European election had a protracted finale and the 'smudge' continued. The voting which started with the arrival of postal ballots at the end of May ended with the majority of United Kingdom voters going to the polling booths on Thursday 10 June. For European, as for parliamentary elections, voting goes on from 7 a.m. to 10 p.m.; for local contests the polls normally close at 9 p.m., but on this occasion the hours were standardised to end at 10 p.m. This extension induced a number of local councils, including London, to delay the local elections count until Friday morning. However, the early returns on Thursday night, together with an exit poll in London, made plain the way the wind was blowing. Headlines about Conservative and Labour humiliation and about a UK Independence Party breakthrough appeared in Friday's papers.

But the story could not be completed until the European votes were counted on Sunday night. The ballots had been separated and stacked in advance on Thursday or Friday but the actual tallying by party in each local authority area[1] was only allowed to begin at 6 or 7 p.m. on Sunday. The totals were e-mailed to the regional counting centre for the adding up before the allocation of seats.

The expectation of speedy announcements after 9 p.m. on the Sunday evening was only partially fulfilled. It was not until 9.55 p.m. that London became the first region to report its figures, showing UKIP's first gain; this was followed ten minutes later by the North East with an unexpected gain for the Liberal Democrats. Results from the other regions were spread over four hours with the North West ending at 2.00 a.m. on the Monday morning. For sabbatarian or security reasons Scotland and North Ireland did not count till Monday and, because of the complications of single transferable vote counting, it was only at 8 p.m. that the last announcement came from Belfast.

There were a few minor glitches. In one or two cases Returning Officers, underestimating the turnout, had not recruited enough tellers. But there were no serious problems and there was little scope for recounts. The verification process, checking the number of ballots issued with the number returned, had already been done. And when seats were allocated according to the d'Hondt system for the region, there were no cases where the last person elected was not comfortably ahead of the next challenger.[2] Table 5.1 summarises the outcome.

Table 5.1   European election results, 2004

Party	%	+/–%	Total	1999 seats	Cut to 78	2004 total	+/– after cut
Conservative	26.7	–9.0	4,397,087	36	35	27	–8
Labour	22.6	–5.4	3,718,683	29	25	19	–6
UK Independence Party	16.1	+9.2	2,660,778	3	2	12	+9
Liberal Democrat	14.9	+2.3	2,452,327	10	10	12	+2
Green	6.3	0.0	1,028,283	2	0	2	+2
British National Party	4.9	+3.9	808,201	0	0	0	0
Respect	1.5	+1.5	252,216	0	0	0	0
Scottish National Party	1.4	–1.3	231,505	2	2	2	0
Plaid Cymru	1.0	–0.9	159,888	2	1	1	–1
Scottish Socialist Party	0.4	0.0	61,136	0	0	0	0
Other GB	4.6	+3.7	749,645	0	0	0	0
GB	100.0		16,458,603	84	75	75	0
All NI	3.3		549,277	3	3	3	0
United Kingdom	100.0		17,007,880	87	78	78	–9

Source: Electoral Commission.

Muddled outcome

As *The Times*'s Peter Riddell had predicted, the results in the various elections, and the way in which the announcement of results was staggered, permitted all sides to claim a success of sorts, but underneath the bravado there were some serious messages for the British political establishment.

Allowing for the reduction in UK seats, the Conservatives still lost eight MEPs and Labour lost six, while the Liberal Democrats gained two and, spectacularly, the UK Independence Party gained nine. A revolutionary aspect of the statistics was that, for the first time in the history of party government, the two main contenders secured less than half of the GB vote (Conservatives 26.7%; Labour 22.6%; a total of 49.3%). Compared to 1999 the Conservatives, thanks to the strong UKIP performance, fell more (–9.1%) than Labour (–5.4%). (See Table 5.2.)

By far the most headlined aspect of the result was the breakthrough of the UK Independence Party, which won 16.1% of the vote and jumped from three seats to twelve. The party made a mark in every English region but one. In that one where they failed, the North East, they might have won if Neil Herron, the 'metric martyr', had succumbed to UKIP's blandishments and headed their ticket (he secured 6.2% of the vote as an Independent). UKIP came top of the poll in 21 local authority areas – mostly in the South West (although their record – 37.6% – was in Boston in the East Midlands).

Table 5.2 Vote and turnout by region, 2004[a]

	CON (%)	LAB (%)	LD (%)	UKIP (%)	BNP (%)	GRN (%)	PC/SNP (%)	Other (%)	Turnout (%)	+/– (%)
NE	18.6	34.1	17.8	12.2	6.4	4.8	n/a	6.2	41.0	+21.1
NW	24.2	27.4	15.9	11.7	6.4	5.6	n/a	8.8	41.1	+21.6
Y&H	24.6	26.3	15.6	14.5	8.0	5.7	n/a	5.2	42.3	+22.7
EM	26.4	21.0	12.9	26.1	6.5	5.5	n/a	1.7	43.7	+21.1
Postal vote regions:									42.6	+21.8
EA	30.8	16.2	14.0	19.6	4,3	5.6	n/a	9.4	36.5	+12.3
WM	27.3	23.4	13.8	17.5	7.5	5.2	n/a	5.4	36.3	+15.3
SE	35.2	13.7	15.3	19.5	2.9	7.9	n/a	5.5	36.6	+11.9
SW	31.6	14.5	18.4	22.6	3.0	7.2	n/a	2.9	37.7	+10.1
LO	26.8	24.8	15.3	12.3	4.0	8.4	n/a	8.4	37.3	+14.3
SC	17.8	26.4	13.1	6.7	1.7	6.8	19.7	7.9	30.6	+5.9
WA	19.6	32.9	10.6	10.7	3.0	3.6	17.6	2.0	41.4	+13.3
Non-postal vote regions:									36.3	+11.3
GB	26.7	22.6	14.9	16.1	4.9	6.3	1.3	5.8	38.2	+15.1
NI	n/a	n/a	n/a	n/a	n/a	n/a	n/a	100.0	46.1	–10.9
UK	25.9	21.9	14.4	15.6	4.8	6.1	2.3	13.9	38.5	+14.5

[a] Invalid votes amounted to 1.0% in all-postal regions and 0.7% elsewhere

Source: Electoral Commission.

UKIP seemed to have broken the political mould, although some commentators were quick to point out that their percentage vote almost exactly matched what the Greens had secured in their unexpected but short-lived triumph in the European election of 1989.

Candidates standing for parties other than the seven which actually elected MEPs increased their share of the vote from 9.4% to 10.7%. In one or two regions the English Democrats Party and the Pensioners' Party got near to 2%, but, as Table 5.3 shows, in only four regions was 2% topped.

Apart from Neil Herron, the only outsider to make a dent in the figures was Martin Bell who, as an anti-corruption Independent with 6.2%, won two-thirds of a winning vote in the Eastern region;[3] the Scottish Socialists did almost as well in Scotland. The British National Party won 4.9% of the GB vote, faring best with 8.0% in Yorkshire and 7.5% in the West Midlands. No other party got more than 1.5% of the national vote, although Respect did secure

4.8% in London and (with 20.8%) they actually came top in Tower Hamlets, even though they only scored half a winning vote overall. Ron Davies, once Secretary of State, could only get 1.9% in attempting a Welsh comeback with Forward Wales (and only 5.9% in his old constituency, Caerphilly).

Table 5.3   Largest other votes

Region	% vote	Party
Scotland	5.2	Scottish Socialist Party (SSP)
North West	4.6	Liberal Party
London	2.4	Christian People's Alliance
South West	2.1	Countryside Party

Source: Electoral Commission.

Northern Ireland, as always, presented a very different pattern with its single transferable vote election of three MEPs. At 51.2% it had much the highest turnout in the UK. The DUP (without Ian Paisley standing) increased its lead over the Ulster Unionists while the SDLP (without John Hume standing) fell victim, as expected, to the resurgent Sinn Féin's Bairbre De Brún. The two more extreme parties were confirmed as the dominant forces in the Province (see Table 5.4).[4]

Table 5.4   Northern Ireland result, 2004

Party	Candidate elected	2004 vote (%)	Change 1999–2004 (%)
DUP	J. Allister	32.0	+3.6
UUP	J. Nicholson	16.6	−1.0
Sinn Féin (SF)	B. De Brún	26.3	+9.0
SDLP	M. Morgan	15.9	−12.2
Independent	J. Gilliland	6.6	n/a
Soc Env A	E. McCann	1.2	n/a
Green	L. Whitcroft	0.9	n/a

In Gibraltar, meanwhile, the only surprise was the turnout figure of 56.6% – relatively low by Gibraltarian standards. Michael Howard's flying visit clearly paid off, with the Conservatives taking 8,300 of the 11,700 votes cast. The Greens (1,058) won almost as many votes as Labour (1,127), with the Liberal Democrats not far behind (905). The UK Independence Party (140), like the BNP (105) and Respect (20), made little impression.[5]

The election saw the defeat of ten MEPs who were standing again; four could blame being pushed down the list in the selection process,[6] while six lost through the swing against both Conservative and Labour.[7] All the successful Labour MEPs and all but one of the Conservatives had sat in the 1999–2004 Parliament.

Turnout rose impressively to the highest figure yet recorded in the United Kingdom for a European election. At 38.5% it was above the 36.8% recorded in 1989 and 1994 and hugely different from the 24.0% of 1999. There were two obvious reasons for the increase: postal voting and local elections. Turnout in the four all-postal vote regions was doubled, rising from 20.8% to 42.6%. In the rest of the country the increase was only +11.3%. One of the largest advances was in London where there was a Mayoral battle. And it rose in other areas where local elections were prevalent or universal. In Wales, where everyone faced two contests, turnout rose +13.5% in contrast to +5.9% in Scotland, where voters had only to choose MEPs. Some of the additional turnout can be attributed to the growing skills of the parties in marshalling postal votes under the newly relaxed rules. Rallings and Thrasher (2004a) estimate that 10% of all votes in the seven regions where postal voting was optional were postal votes, more than double the number in the 2001 General Election. But allowing for all special factors, there plainly was a genuinely greater interest shown by voters in 2004. The impact of UKIP must take some credit.

The local elections provided bad news for Labour. They lost 460 seats – almost a quarter of those they were defending. They forfeited Newcastle to the Liberal Democrats while Birmingham slipped further into 'No Overall Control'. They took comfort in holding on to Sheffield and Plymouth and in regaining Stoke as well as remaining the largest party in Birmingham. But all over the country Labour had local setbacks. The Conservatives had triumphs in Swindon, Rossendale and Thurrock; more importantly, they achieved an impressive showing in terms of share of the vote. It was estimated that the results projected nationally (and only half the councils were voting in 2004) would be equivalent to 37% Conservative, 27% Liberal Democrat and 26% Labour. It was the worst Labour percentage for two generations. But Labour apologists could point out that in 2000 William Hague had done better in terms of seats, only to be soundly beaten in the 2001 General Election. Labour could also boast of holding on to the Mayoralty of Greater London by a 10% margin, even if Ken Livingstone, newly readmitted to the Labour Party, was not the most orthodox of Blairites.

Fears that the BNP would make an embarrassing breakthrough were not realised; they only held five seats in their best territories – Burnley, Oldham and Bradford. Of all regions, the BNP were closest to winning a European seat in the West Midlands. A further 24,000 votes would have seen them take the seventh seat.

However, UKIP, thanks to proportional representation, secured two seats in the Greater London Assembly and five councillors elsewhere. The UK Independence Party almost certainly drew some of the BNP's fire.

Labour comfortably won the most votes in Wales, the only region where they increased their share of the vote compared to 1999. Plaid Cymru's share of the vote fell by 12 percentage points from 1999, and they came third behind the Conservatives. UKIP narrowly beat the Liberal Democrats into fourth place. The Green Party polled their lowest regional share of the vote in Wales.

Labour again won more votes than any other party in Scotland. The SNP were second, despite a 7 percentage point fall in their vote relative to 1999. The Conservatives' share of the vote fell by 2 percentage points relative to 1999, their best performance by this measure. Both UKIP and the BNP polled their lowest regional shares of the vote in Scotland. Turnout in Scotland, which did not hold other elections on the same day, was the lowest of the UK regions.

A remarkable 17% of all European votes were given to parties that failed to win any seats. A further 10% or more were 'wasted' as being surplus to the winning vote needed to secure further representation in a particular region. Under proportional representation, we are told, 'every vote counts'. Many, none the less, are still wasted.

There was a notable amount of split-ticket voting. Although Liberal Democrat support in local elections could be projected to a national figure of 27%, they only won 15% in the European contest. Looking at 45 English local authorities that were fully fought at the local level by all three main parties, Rallings and Thrasher (2004a) have calculated that among those who went to the polls, 24.6% chose different parties for MEP and for Councillor. This contrasts with the 11.4% who split their votes in 1997 when the General Election also coincided with local contests.

A poor show

The overall outcome was treated caustically by the press, which dwelt at length on the failure of both the main parties. 'Apathy has been replaced by an even bigger problem: antipathy', John Curtice pointedly observed in the *Independent*. He noted that this, among other things, was the worst Labour result in Scotland since 1918.

Peter Riddell commented that 'Britain is destined to remain a perpetually awkward partner in the European Union. Mr Blair is losing the big battle over Europe' (*The Times*), while William Rees-Mogg observed that 'The Conservatives are again serious contenders for power' (*The Times*). Max Hastings, writing in the *Daily Mail*, saw the result as a message to Labour MPs 'to change leaders quick ... Europe and uncontrolled immigration are the most visible manifestations of Blair's ambitions and failures.'

Lord Tebbit told David Frost that voting for UKIP was voting for Labour to continue in office. Melanie Phillips argued that UKIP's electoral success changed the terms of political debate. 'The vote is a protest by people who for years have felt totally disfranchised ... The European parliamentary elections have buried almost the entire Westminster village under a torrential mudslide. The Conservative cottage, which looked so neat and trim after last week's local elections, has had its roof torn off.'

A *Daily Telegraph* leader argued that Michael Howard should take heart for having shamed the government into having a referendum on the European Constitution. Roy Hattersley observed in the *Guardian* that, since Labour failed to campaign in the elections, it could not hope to win, but called those who sought a change in leadership 'Fantasists'.

An *Independent* leader said that 'These election results leave the Prime Minister with no option but to argue the case for Europe.' Its Political Editor, Steve Richards, wrote that 'Mr Blair's strategy of keeping his head down, hoping to change people's minds by stealth, has failed disastrously.'

With characteristic frankness, Deputy Prime Minister John Prescott recognised that the Labour Party had got a 'thumping'. For the Home Secretary, David Blunkett, it was a 'kicking'. The Deputy Leader of the Opposition, Michael Ancram, drew a stark conclusion: ' I hope that if there is one message Tony Blair takes out of this, it is that he has no mandate to go this week to Brussels and sign up to this wretched constitution.'

Costs

The election cost the taxpayer about £65 million – including £25 million for the Royal Mail's somewhat unreliable delivery of election addresses, £27 million for the routine costs of Returning Officers managing polling stations and the counting of votes, as well as a supplementary £13 million for the extra costs of delivering ballots in the all-postal vote regions. As this study went to press the official party outlays were reported (see Table 6.2). These are analysed in more detail in Chapter 6, but by far the most striking figure was the UK Independence Party's £2.3m – some £600,000 more than Labour.

Characteristics

Table 5.5 gives some basic details about the backgrounds of the successfully elected candidates. Conservative and UKIP candidates were the oldest, Scottish National Party and Plaid Cymru the youngest. The best gender balance was achieved by the Liberal Democrats (six females, six males) and Labour (seven females, twelve males); the worst was by UKIP (no females, twelve males) and the Conservatives (two females, 25 males). There was some resentment among female Conservatives about the party's poor record and apparent indifference to the gender issue. As pointed out above, most successful candidates had been incumbents (63 out of 78); 14 had previously been Westminster MPs. The vast majority were university educated (all Conservative and Labour candidates, ten out of twelve Liberal Democrats), although just four out of twelve UKIP candidates were university educated. Large concentrations of Conservative, Labour and Liberal Democrat candidates had previously worked

Table 5.5 Characteristics of successful 2004 EP candidates

	Total	Female	Ethnic	Mean age	Sitting MEP	Education			Occupation				
						University	Oxbridge	Law	Government	Academia	Business	Media	Other
Conservative	27	2	1	54	26	27	9	2	9	1	11	1	2
Labour	19	7	2	50	19	19	4	0	8	3	0	1	5
UKIP	12	0	0	55	3	4	0	0	2	1	6	1	2
Lib Dem	12	6	1	51	10	10	5	3	5	2	1	1	0
Green	2	2	0	49	2	2	0	0	2	0	0	0	0
SNP	2	0	0	42	1	2	0	1	0	0	1	0	0
PC	1	1	0	45	1	1	0	0	0	1	0	0	0
Others	3	2	1	53	1	3	0	1	1	0	0	0	1

in government service. Almost half of all Conservative and UKIP candidates had business backgrounds. The law, the media and academia were relatively poorly represented.

The results: apathy and antipathy

Continental comment focused on four aspects of the elections. The first was the shockingly low turnout in five of the ten new member states. Overall turnout in the 25 member states was 45.6%. In the ten new member states it was just 26%: in Slovakia turnout was just 16.9%; in Poland it was 20.87%; in the Czech Republic, Estonia and Slovenia it was well under 30% (see Table 5.6). No longer could the United Kingdom be considered as an isolated case of indifference, apathy or antipathy. However, whilst the UK could be portrayed as a country whose electorate had gradually become disillusioned, what could be made of countries which had only just become member states? The charitable explanation was a form of electoral fatigue. The more pessimistic

Table 5.6 Evolution of turnout rates in the member states, 1979–2004

Member state	1979	1984	1987	1989	1994	1995	1996	1999	2004
DE	65.7	56.8		62.3	60.0			45.2	43.0
FR	60.7	56.7		48.7	52.7			46.8	42.7
BE	91.4	92.2		90.7	90.7			91.0	90.8
IT	84.9	83.4		81.5	74.8			70.8	73.1
LU	88.9	88.8		87.4	88.5			87.3	90.0
NL	57.8	50.6		47.2	35.6			30.0	39.3
UK	32.2	32.6		36.2	36.4			24.0	38.9
IE	63.6	47.6		68.3	44.0			50.2	59.7
DK	47.8	52.4		46.2	52.9			50.5	47.9
EL		77.2		79.9	71.2			75.3	63.4
ES			68.9	54.6	59.1			63.0	45.1
PT			72.4	51.2	35.5			40.0	38.7
SE						41.6		38.8	37.8
AT							67.7	49.4	42.4
FI							60.3	31.4	41.1
CZ									28.3
EE									26.9
CY									71.2
LV									41.3
LT									48.4
HU									38.5
MT									82.4
PL									20.9
SI									28.3
SK									16.9
Average EU	63.0	61.0		58.5	56.8			49.8	45.6

Source: European Parliament.

pointed out that if such trends continued they would inevitably favour fringe and extreme parties.

A second much-commented aspect was the strong anti-incumbent vote. With the exceptions of Spain and Greece, where new governments had recently been formed, rebuffs were delivered to ruling parties and coalitions throughout the European Union. Here was graphic confirmation of the 'second-order' thesis; this was not one pan-European election, but 25 second-order national elections. 'Regrettably,' as outgoing EP President Pat Cox put it, 'Europe is too absent from European elections in East and West.'

A third aspect was the performance of far-right and Eurosceptical parties. With the exception of the Austrian far-right Freedom Party of Jörg Haider, which lost four out of its five seats, the far right consolidated its position through such parties as the French Front National and the Flemish Belgian Vlams Blok. Similarly, with the exception of Jens-Peter Bonde's Danish June Movement (which won just one seat), Eurosceptical parties significantly increased their representation: for example, the UK Independence Party (eleven); the League of Polish Families (ten); the Swedish June list (three); the Dutch Christian Union (two).

A fourth aspect of the results was the fragmentation of political representation through the proliferation of MEPs representing smaller, fringe parties or single issues. Chapter 3 remarked on the large number of micro-parties and independents. In the event, around 11% of the UK electorate voted for parties or independent candidates that didn't win a seat.

A realignment?

The 2004 European elections confirmed the dominant place of the centre-right, already announced in the 1999 European elections; the EPP-ED political group in the European Parliament gained the highest percentage of seats, and the share of the Liberals rose (see Table 5.7). Once the dust had settled, most political commentators homed in on this, together with a concommitant decline in voter support for the left, as the most significant aspect of the 2004 European elections. The last rounds of general elections in the 'old' EU member states had brought a series of shifts to the political right throughout Europe. Seven of the 15 governments shifted in composition from left to right (Austria, Denmark, France, Greece, Italy, Netherlands, Portugal). Internal shifts to the right within ruling coalitions occurred in four of them (Belgium, Finland, Luxembourg, Netherlands). By early 2004 only three member states had preserved the dominance of centre-left parties in government (Britain, Germany and Sweden) and even here, commentators argued, there had been internal shifts to the right in the parties' policy orientations, in the style of Tony Blair's 'Third Way'. It was this apparent realignment that led the leader of the European Parliament's EPP-ED Group, Hans-Gert Poettering, to insist that the nomination for the Presidency of the European Commission had to reflect this orientation.

Table 5.7   Overall results in the 25 member states

Country	EPP-ED	PES	ALDE	Greens/EFA	EUL/NGL	Ind/Dem	UEN	NA	Total
BE	6	7	6	2	0	0	0	3	24
CZ	14	2	0	0	6	1	0	1	24
DK	1	5	4	1	1	1	1	0	14
DE	49	23	7	13	7	0	0	0	99
EE	1	3	2	0	0	0	0	0	6
EL	11	8	0	0	4	1	0	0	24
ES	24	24	2	3	1	0	0	0	54
FR	17	31	11	6	3	3	0	7	78
IE	5	1	1	0	1	1	4	0	13
IT	24	16	12	2	7	4	9	4	78
CY	3	0	1	0	2	0	0	0	6
LV	3	0	1	1	0	0	4	0	9
LT	2	2	7	0	0	0	2	0	13
LU	3	1	1	1	0	0	0	0	6
HU	13	9	2	0	0	0	0	0	24
MT	2	3	0	0	0	0	0	0	5
NL	7	7	5	4	2	2	0	0	27
AT	6	7	0	2	0	0	0	3	18
PL	19	8	4	0	0	10	7	6	54
PT	9	12	0	0	3	0	0	0	24
SI	4	1	2	0	0	0	0	0	7
SK	8	3	0	0	0	0	0	3	14
FI	4	3	5	1	1	0	0	0	14
SE	5	5	3	1	2	3	0	0	19
UK	28	19	12	5	1	11	0	2	78
Total	268	200	88	42	41	37	27	29	732

Source: European Parliament.

But some commentators argued that a deeper political realignment could be discerned: 'The protest vote was cast not simply against incumbents, but against a certain political culture. This being a rejection of the system of governance (the state) and of policy-making (the parties), which had become the norm in Europe since World War II' (Azmanova, 2004). Such commentators point to a combination of modern social trends and the effect these have had on voters' perceptions: physical insecurity (terrorism, crime, diseases such as SARS and BSE); immigration; political crisis and democratic deficit (mismanagement, corruption); and economic slowdown and employment insecurity. According to this thesis, such charismatic anti-system political figures as Pim Fortuyn in the Netherlands and Robert Kilroy-Silk in the UK belong to a new political trend, a response to a generalised phenomenon of what in French would be called '*usure de pouvoir*':

> Decades of conservative-socialist governmental cohabitation, and the continuing loss of ideological distinctions between centre-left and centre-right developed a professionalized political establishment, that had elite policy-making at its base with in-bred compromise and consensus, increased bureaucratization, and an absence of political debate or involvement of civil society. (Azmanova, 2004)

If this analysis is correct, then the 2004 European elections in the United Kingdom were part of a generalised trend, evident throughout Europe.

One of the least commented aspects of the 2004 results is set out in Table 5.8: almost 6 million votes were invalid. In Italy, one-tenth of all votes cast were invalid. It is difficult to analyse these figures, which are provided on the European Parliament's website (<www.elections2004.eu.int/ep-election/sites/

Table 5.8   Valid and invalid votes, 2004

Country	Date	No. of voters	%	Votes	Valid votes	Invalid votes
BE	13 June	7,552,240	90.81	6,857,986	6,489,991	367,995
CZ	11/12 June	8,283,485	28.32	2,346,010	2,332,862	13,148
DK	13 June	4,012,663	47.90	1,921,541	1,894,346	27,195
DE	13 June	61,682,394	43.00	26,523,104	25,783,678	739,426
EE	13 June	873,809	26.83	234,485	232,230	2,255
EL	13 June	9,909,955	63.40	6,283,525	6,122,548	160,977
ES	13 June	34,706,044	45.10	15,666,507	15,512,282	154,209
FR	13 June	51,518,582	42.76	17,752,582	17,167,379	585,203
CY	13 June	483,311	71.19	350,387	334,268	16,119
LV	12 June	1,397,736	41.34	577,879	572,981	4,898
LT	13 June	2,654,311	48.38	1,284,050	1,207,070	76,980
HU	13 June	8,046,247	38.50	3,097,657	3,075,450	20,729
MT	12 June	304,283	82.37	250,691	245,722	4,969
NL	10 June	12,168,878	39.30	4,777,121	4,765,677	11,444
AT	13 June	6,049,129	42.43	2,566,639	2,500,610	66,029
PL	13 June	29,986,109	20.87	6,258,550	6,091,531	167,019
PT	13 June	8,821,456	38.60	3,404,782	3,270,116	134,666
SI	13 June	1,628,918	28.30	461,879	435,869	25,938
SK	13 June	4,210,463	16.96	714,508	701,595	12,913
FI	13 June	4,227,987	39.40	1,666,932	1,656,584	10,348
SE	13 June	6,827,870	37.80	2,584,464	2,512,069	72,395
IE	11 June	3,131,540	58.80	1,841,335	1,780,786	60,567
IT	12/13 June	49,854,299	73.10	33,597,496	32,460,082	3,137,414
LU	13 June	214,318	89.00	209,689	192,185	17,504
UK	10 June	44,157,400	38.83	17,146,559	17,007,703	138,856

Source: European Parliament.

en/results1306/turnout_ep/index.html>) without further information. Not all invalid votes were necessarily 'spoilt ballot papers' in the sense of a protest, but it is significant that in Italy there was until recently a legal obligation to vote. Presumably, a significant number of the 6 million European voters who bothered to turn out but spoilt their ballot papers sought to register some sort of protest against the establishment.

The new Parliament meets for the first time

The newly elected Parliament met in plenary session for the first time in Strasbourg, 19–22 July 2004. The weeks leading up to the Parliament's constituent plenary sessions are traditionally a period of intense political bargaining and this occasion was no exception.

As seen above, the EPP-ED was confirmed as the largest group in numerical terms, but its 268 members fell some way short of an absolute majority and the group was from the outset badly split, with the 'ED' (British Conservative) part resolutely opposed to the Constitutional Treaty (an issue on which the two sides had agreed to differ).

The PES Group remained the second largest grouping within the Parliament, but its 200 membership represented less than a third of the EP's overall membership and also fell some 68 votes short of the EPP-ED. If the PES Group's influence was weakened, so was the influence of the British Labour Party's contingent within it. The United Kingdom's 19 MEPs were only the fourth-largest national contingent, behind the French Parti Socialiste (31), and the Spanish PSOE (24) and German SPD (23).

Much political speculation focused on the creation of a new centre-grouping, the Group of the Alliance of Liberals and Democrats for Europe (ALDE), bringing together the UK's twelve Liberal Democrats with 76 other MEPs from 18 other member states (see Tables 5.7 and 5.9). Graham Watson, the outgoing leader of the old ELDR Group, rapidly emerged as the leader of the new grouping. Very early ambitions to capture a sufficient part of the centre ground so as to be able to rival the two main groupings had given way to a more pragmatic ambition to act as power-broker, and in the early days of the new Parliament much attention was focused on whether the ALDE would be able once again to freeze the PES Group out by forging a 'technical agreement' with the EPP-ED, at least over the election of Parliament's President. Curiously, this speculation seemed to pass most of the British media by.

Many insiders had always argued that the EPP-ED – ELDR deal which had led to Pat Cox's election had much to do with the uninspiring nature of the PES Group's candidate, the venerable but also aged Portuguese warhorse, Mario Soares. They also pointed to the fact that the old EPP-ED/PES 'technical agreement' had continued to function, if informally, in the 1999–2004 Parliament, despite the EPP-ED's preference for Pat Cox.

Table 5.9   Political groups in the European Parliament (July 2004)

Group		No. of members
EPP-ED	Group of the European People's Party (Christian Democrats) and European Democrats	268
PES	Socialist Group in the European Parliament	200
ALDE	Group of the Alliance of Liberals and Democrats for Europe	88
Greens/EFA	Group of the Greens/European Free Alliance	42
EUL/NGL	Confederal Group of the European United Left – Nordic Green Left	41
Ind/Dem	Independence and Democracy Group	33
UEN	Union for Europe of the Nations Group	27
NI	Non-inscrit members	33

Source: European Parliament.

The esoteric nature of these calculations seemed much removed from the themes of the June electoral contest, and some jaundiced commentators argued that this in itself was symptomatic of a Parliament that had somehow become more concerned with internal power plays and patronage calculations than with the genuine expression of the electorates' wishes.

It is true that a mixture of exogenous factors (treaty-based majority requirements prime among them) had encouraged the Parliament to create mechanisms such as the 'technical agreement' because, without them, it would simply be unable to wield the powers – both budgetary and legislative – that it had been given. It is true, too, that the sheer scale of the work and activities undertaken by the Parliament had made it difficult for its members to spend as much time as they would perhaps like in their constituencies and with their voters. But if, as some critics maintained, the Parliament's previous evolutionary trend was technocratic and Brussels-based, the discussions and negotiations between the political groups in June–July 2004 clearly indicated that the potential for a new sort of relationship with the European electorate had appeared.

Following the 1999 European elections, the discussions could perhaps best have been characterised as mainly about internal tactics and external presentation. But following the 2004 elections, the discussions were more overtly political. Slowly, but surely, the Parliament seemed to be edging away from consensual searches for workable alliances and towards more politicised majorities. If, as will be seen, the larger groups eventually shied away from such a politicised majority in the context of the election of the President, it did not mean that the underlying politicisation had been dissipated. Indeed, as this study went to press the Parliament was clearly divided in its attitude towards the Lisbon Strategy on classic left–right lines – the June/July 2004 discussions had provided a taster for the political debates ahead.

Thus, in late June it became plain that the EPP-ED and PES Groups would prefer to revive their old technical agreement, whereby the PES Group would put forward its preferred candidate for the President for the first half of the new Parliament, and the EPP-ED for the second half. This arrangement suited the EPP-ED leader, Hans-Gert Poettering, who would thus continue to lead the largest political grouping until the beginning of 2007. Graham Watson did not yet give up. Through press interviews, particularly with the Italian media, he seemed to offer the possibility of a five-year Poettering Presidency in return for a technical agreement which, presumably, would have brought the new ALDE Group a disproportionate amount of patronage.

But by early July the agreement between the two largest groups seemed to have been signed and sealed. Hans-Gert Poettering would be President from early 2007 through to June 2009. In return, the PES Group's preferred candidate, Josep Borrell, would be President until December 2006. In effect, the ALDE was frozen out. It was a sign of the British Labour contingent's declining clout that its proposed candidate for the Presidency, Terry Wynn, failed to be selected by the group. This had nothing to do with Mr Wynn's qualities (and, as an outgoing and much-respected President of the Budget Committee, these were generally recognised), but was more a reflection of numerical strength and, above all, general disapproval on the left of the British Labour government's stance over Iraq.

The UK's two Green MEPs, two SNP MEPs and the Plaid Cymru MEP once again joined their forces within the Group of the Greens/European Free Alliance, while Sinn Féin's Bairbre De Brún joined various communist, former communist and left socialist parties in the Confederal Group of the European United Left/Nordic Green left.

The UK Independence Party ran into minor problems in early July, when it became known through a *Daily Telegraph* article that one of its new members, Mr Ashley Mote, was facing nine counts of alleged housing benefit fraud. The party acted swiftly by removing the Whip 'because Mr Mote did not inform the party of this situation before, during or immediately after the campaign'. Mr Mote continued to sit in the Parliament, but as an Independent.

On 21 July another UKIP MEP, Godfrey Bloom, courted some controversy with his remark that 'no self-respecting small businessman with a brain in the right place would ever employ a lady of child-bearing age'. A member of the EP's women's rights committee, Mr Bloom told journalists he wanted to deal with women's issues because 'I don't think they clean behind the fridge enough ... I am here to represent Yorkshire women who always have dinner on the table when you get home. I am going to promote men's rights.'

Meanwhile, UKIP had joined forces once again with Jens-Peter Bonde's anti-Maastricht June Movement to form a new group, Independence and Democracy, which, with anti-European members from another nine member states, could muster 37 members – a not insignificant grouping.

From the outset there was tension and some contradiction between UKIP's official pronouncements and those of its new, high-profile recruit, Robert Kilroy-Silk. Hours after the European elections, when asked by journalists what he was going to do in the European Parliament, he replied: 'Wreck it – expose it for the waste, the corruption and the way it's eroding our independence and sovereignty.' 'I don't want to go to Brussels,' he continued. 'I don't want to be there. I don't want to spend time there.' And he had immediately to deny rumours that he wanted to replace the UKIP leader, Roger Knapman.

These pronouncements conflicted with those of the Party Chairman, Nigel Farage, when announcing that nine of UKIP's members would be sitting on parliamentary committees (though none would join parliamentary delegation trips abroad). Said Mr Farage: 'We will do everything we can to obstruct and delay legislation. That is a firm undertaking.' Mr Farage and his colleagues clearly planned to be active in the Parliament. Mr Kilroy-Silk just as clearly didn't.

Structures and offices

The Parliament's first task was to set up its own structures and elect its office holders. As seen above and in Chapter 1, the prime architects in this process are the political groups within the Parliament, and particularly the largest of them. Tables 5.7 and 5.9 described the seven groups and the membership of them. From the UK point of view, the most striking aspect of the new Parliament was the fragmentation of its representation among six different groups. In the early 1980s, thanks to the distortions of first-past-the-post and the small size of the Parliament, the British Conservatives had been able to form a sizeable political group almost alone. In the late 1990s, the British Labour contingent guaranteed it considerable power and influence within the PES Group, which was then the largest grouping within the Parliament. But in 2004 British representation was fragmented and none of its contingents, with the exception of the British Liberal Democrats, gave it much influence or patronage power.

Election of the President

The position of President of the Parliament brings together a curious mixture of formal powers and informal status. To some extent it is what the office holder makes of it, Pat Cox's use of his communication powers being a good example of this. But the position is also a symbolic demonstration of relative power within the Parliament. Pat Cox's election in 2002 is again a good example of this. At the same time, a little-known change to the Parliament's rules of procedure meant that the 2004 context would, for the first time, be by secret ballot. Given this, could the largest political groups deliver on their new-found agreement? Graham Watson's new ALDE Group suspected not, and on that basis put forward an attractive alternative candidate, Bronislaw Geremek, a historic and charismatic Solidarity figure, to stand against the altogether more low-key Catalan technocrat, Josep Borrell. During their campaigns, the two met in a public debate, with Pat Cox as convenor – an innovation designed to encourage public interest, but the results were inconclusive.

In reality, once the EPP-ED/PES deal had been done, Signor Borrell's election was a foregone conclusion, but the secrecy of the ballot box ensured that it was no walkover. A single round of voting was enough for Signor Borrell, always the favourite, to be elected, but some 80 votes from the EPP-ED/PES bloc were calculated to have 'defected' – almost certainly to the historic and respected figure of Bronislaw Geremek. (See Table 5.10.)

Table 5.10 The 2004–09 European Parliament elects its President

Candidates	Votes
Josep Borrell Fontelles (PES, ES)	388
Bronislaw Geremek (ALDE, PL)	208
Francis Wurtz (EUL/NGL, FR)	51
Number of votes cast	700
Spoilt/unfulfilled votes	53
Valid votes	647
Absolute majority required	324

Josep Borrell Fontelles was therefore elected as President for two and a half years

Source: European Parliament.

Participation in the Presidential election is traditionally high. No fewer than 700 of the Parliament's 732 members cast votes, though 53 ballot papers were considered spoilt (the UKIP MEPs symbolically tore up their ballot papers). The strong showing for Josep Borrell showed that, secret ballots notwithstanding, the political groups could deliver, at least in this context.

Election of the Vice-Presidents

Nowhere was the Parliament's well-oiled machinery for brokering deals between the political groups more in evidence than for the election of the 14 Vice-Presidents. The Independence and Democracy Group and the Union for Europe of the Nations Group facilitated the process by eschewing their right to put forward candidates, so that the other five groups were able to agree on a share-out of the posts on a d'Hondt basis (also taking into account the PES Group's almost certain occupancy of the post of President). As a result, only 14 candidates stood for the 14 posts and were elected by acclaim. (See Table 5.11.)

Two aspects of the table are noteworthy in the context of this study. The first is that the patronage benefits of maintaining an alliance with the Christian

Democrats had clearly paid off for the Conservatives, in the form of Edward McMillan-Scott's strong fourth place. Mr McMillan-Scott's showing also owed much to his high profile as a former leader of the British Conservatives in the EP and as a determined campaigner on such popular issues as abusive timesharing arrangements. The second is the absence of any British Labour Vice-President. David Martin had served with distinction as a Vice-President for ten years (from 1994 to 2004), but so weak was Labour within the PES Group, and so relatively weak was the PES Group within the EP, that neither the delegation nor the group could earmark a Vice-Presidency for a British Labour member this time around. The contemporaneous appointment of Briton David Harley as Secretary General of the PES Group could not reverse the impression of Labour's reduced status.

Table 5.11   Election of the Vice-Presidents

Candidate selected	Political group	Member state	No. of votes
1. Alejo Vidal-Quadras Roca	EPP-ED	ES	287
2. Antonios Trakatellis	EPP-ED	EL	253
3. Dagmar Roth-Behrendt	PES	DE	244
4. Edward McMillan-Scott	EPP-ED	UK	241
5. Ingo Friedrich	EPP-ED	DE	232
6. Mario Mauro	EPP-ED	IT	229
7. Antonio Costa	PES	PT	228
8. Luigi Cocilovo	ALDE	IT	223
9. Jacek Emil Sarysz-Wolski	EPP-ED	PL	214
10. Pierre Moscovici	PES	FR	209
11. Miroslav Ouzky	EPP-ED	CZ	189
12. Janusz Onyszkiewicz	ALDE	PL	177
13. Gérard Onesta	Greens/EFA	FR	167
14. Sylvia-Yvonne Kaufmann	EUL/NGL	DE	121

Members voting	693	
Blank/spoiled papers	26	
Votes cast	667	

Source: European Parliament.

Election of the Quaestors

The EP's five Quaestors are responsible for administrative and financial matters concerning members individually. The posts are not considered politically important, but they are part of the overall deal between the political groups. On this occasion six candidates were nominated for five posts, and it took three rounds of voting for all five posts to be filled. However, the ED's pragmatic agreement with the EPP again paid dividends when longstanding UUP MEP Jim Nicholson (EPP-ED, UK) was easily elected top of the first round. (See Table 5.12.)

Table 5.12 Election of the Quaestors

Result: Candidate elected	Political group	Member	No. of votes	Round in which elected
Jim Nicholson	EPP-ED	UK	389	First
Genowefa Grabowska	PES	PL	366	First
Astrid Lulling	EPP-ED	LU	265	Third
Godelieve Quisthoudt-Rowohl	EPP-ED	DE	285	Third
Mia De Vits	PES	BE	298	Third

First round:	
Voting	691
Spoiled votes	17
Valid votes	674
Majority required	338

Source: European Parliament.

Election of Committee Chairmen and Vice-Chairmen

Election of the Committee Chairmen and Vice-Chairmen is a more decentralised process, with elections held in the Committees themselves, but on the basis of prior agreements between the political groups. Table 5.13 lists UK office-holders in the 2004 European Parliament. The most striking aspect of the table is just how few British MEPs were elected as Chairmen and Vice-Chairmen. In part this decline could be ascribed to the effects of enlargement, but it was also a consequence of the fragmentation of British representation, with its consequent decline in British influence and patronage.

Approval of the President-Designate of the European Commission

As Chapter 1 recounted, the member states found it very difficult to find an acceptable candidate who would also be acceptable to an increasingly demanding European Parliament. Two developments made the situation potentially more fraught than had been the case in the past. First, the candidate could be nominated by a qualified majority of the member states (an innovation introduced by the Nice Treaty). Second, the vote in the Parliament would be secret (an innovation introduced by the Parliament itself, via its rules of procedure).

After a lengthy search, the European Council was able to propose José-Manuel Barroso and on Thursday 22 July the former Portugese Prime Minister was formally endorsed as the new President of the European Commission, winning 413 of the 711 votes cast, with 251 against, 44 abstentions and 3 spoiled ballots. According to the *Financial Times*, Mr Barroso owed his comfortable majority to his projection of 'the image of a pragmatic consensus builder and strong communicator at a time when the EU faces growing voter

Table 5.13 UK office-holders in the 2004 European Parliament

Position/office	Conservative	Labour	Liberal Democrat	Green/SNP/Plaid Cymru	UKIP
EP Vice-President	Edward McMillan-Scott				
Quaestor					
Committee Chairs	James Nicholson Giles Chichester (Industry, Research and Energy)	Philip Whitehead (Internal Market and Consumer Protection)			
Committee Vice-Chairs	Geoffrey Van Orden (Foreign Affairs) John Purvis (Economic and Monetary Affairs) Charles Tannock (Human Rights)	Michael Cashman (Petitions)	Emma Nicholson (Foreign Affairs) Elspeth Attwooll (Regional Development)		
Group Presidents			Graham Watson (ALDE)		
Inter-Parliamentary Delegations	Jonathan Evans (Chair, US) Neil Parish (Chair, Australia and New Zealand) Charles Tannock (Vice-Chair, Ukraine)	Neena Gill (Chair, South Asia) Terry Wynn (Vice-Chair, Australia and New Zealand)	Diana Wallis (Chair, EEA) Andrew Duff (Vice-Chair, Turkey)		
ACP-EU Joint Assembly		Glenys Kinnock			

apathy and a leadership deficit'. Despite the secret ballot, a majority of PES Group, Greens and Communists were reported to have voted against Barroso, chiefly because of his support for the US-led war in Iraq and the tough austerity policies he imposed in Portugal as Prime Minister.

But many PES Group MEPs, notably from the UK and Spain, were said to have joined the EPP and the centrist ALDE in supporting a candidate who had, after all, been unanimously nominated by EU leaders. The 58% support was not as broad as the 77% which the centre-left Romano Prodi had won in 1999, but more convincing than the grudging endorsement earned by centre-right former Luxembourg Prime Minister Jacques Santer in 1994, with less than 50%.

British Commissioner

After months of speculation, on Thursday 22 July British morning newspapers reported that Mr Blair was telling colleagues that he had offered the position of the UK's sole Commissioner to Peter Mandelson. The decision was bound up in broader speculation about a reshuffle of the government team, which was widely expected to be announced on the same day. As the day wore on, however, none of the usual activity accompanying a reshuffle had materialised, and journalists were intrigued to learn that Mr Blair had left for his Sedgefield constituency. Rumours circulated about rows in Downing Street, with alleged visits from the Chancellor and the Foreign Secretary determined to ward off a third revival of Mandelson's Cabinet career – but also of his appointment as Commissioner (the presentation of such a dual choice was an excellent example of the Prime Minister's tactical nous). By the evening, Sky News and ITN were reporting that Peter Mandelson had been appointed, but a Downing Street spokesman continued to insist that he 'didn't recognise' that position. Ironically, the BBC's *News at Ten* bulletin ran the Mandelson appointment as a major news story. The EP's approval of Mr Barroso came much further down the running order and was covered only very briefly.

Europe speaks ... the June Inter-Governmental Conference

'Europe speaks', declared a *Times* editorial, going on to ask 'But will its political leaders listen?' (15 June 2004). The newspaper acknowledged a strong anti-incumbency tendency in the results but, juxtaposing the low turnout and strong performances for Eurosceptical parties with the forthcoming crunch talks on the draft European Constitution, the paper argued that the Heads of State or Government had to stop talking 'in a language of their own' and return to first principles. For the paper, this meant vetoing the draft Constitution and concentrating on basic reform: 'the reformers have spoken,' it argued, 'but they are still not being heard'. The message was echoed by other more Eurosceptical publications; notably, the *Sun* asked in characteristically straightforward fashion: 'Are you deaf?'

Mr Blair was clearly not deaf, but on 18 June he nevertheless signed up to the Constitutional Treaty, arguing that he had won a good deal for the United Kingdom, and that all of the 'red lines' that the government had drawn remained intact. Many political commentators were sceptical of this claim, but others pointed out that in France the Constitutional Treaty was criticised for containing too many concessions to the Anglo-Saxon model. *The Economist* was perhaps the most notable of a number of publications that called for European voters to 'reject the new constitutional treaty and demand something better' (26 June).

Some 17 million people, out of a total registered electorate of 44 million, voted in the June 2004 European elections. Had the elections mattered? As they rapidly faded from view, it became apparent that any effect they might have had would be further 'smudged'. On 24 June Tony Blair called two snap by-elections (for 15 July) for the Westminster seats of Leicester South and Birmingham Hodge Hill, two Labour seats vacated respectively by the death of Jim Marshall and the departure of Terry Davis for the position of the Council of Europe in Strasbourg.[8] Speculation rapidly mounted. Would Labour hold on? Would the Liberal Democrats break through? Would the Conservatives maintain their position as the chief threat to Labour? The European elections were forgotten.

Appendix 5.1: Summary of EP election results and UK MEPs elected

Table 5.14 European Parliament election results at regional level, Great Britain[a]

	Con	Lab	LDem	UKIP	SNP/PC	Others	Total
Votes:							
North East	144,969	266,057	138,791	94,887		135,787	780,491
North West	509,446	576,388	335,063	257,158		437,108	2,115,163
Yorks and Humberside	387,369	413,213	244,607	228,666		299,346	1,573,201
East Midlands	371,359	294,918	181,964	366,498		191,964	1,406,703
West Midlands	392,937	336,613	197,479	251,366		258,640	1,437,035
East	465,526	244,929	211,378	296,160		292,231	1510,224
London	504,941	466,584	288,790	232,633		392,501	1,885,449
South East	776,370	301,398	338,342	431,111		360,196	2,207,417
South West	457,371	209,908	265,619	326,784		188,735	1,448,417
Wales	177,771	297,810	96,116	96,677	159,888	89,424	917,686
Scotland	209,028	310,865	154,178	78,828	231,505	192,413	1,176,817
Great Britain	4,397,087	3,718,683	2,452,327	2,660,768	391,393	2,838,345	16,458,603

Table 5.14   continued

	Con	Lab	LDem	UKIP	SNP/PC	Others	Total
Share of Vote:							
North East	18.6%	34.1%	17.8%	12.2%		17.4%	100%
North West	24.1%	27.3%	15.8%	12.2%		20.7%	100%
Yorks and							
Humberside	24.6%	26.3%	15.5%	14.5%		19.0%	100%
East Midlands	26.4%	21%	12.9%	26.1%		13.6%	100%
West Midlands	27.3%	23.4%	13.7%	17.5%		18.0%	100%
East	30.8%	16.2%	14.0%	19.6%		19.4%	100%
London	26.8%	24.7%	15.3%	12.3%		20.8%	100%
South East	35.2%	13.7%	15.3%	19.5%		16.3%	100%
South West	31.6%	14.5%	18.3%	22.6%		13.0%	100%
Wales	19.4%	32.5%	10.5%	10.5%	17.4%	9.7%	100%
Scotland	17.8%	26.4%	13.1%	6.7%	19.7%	16.4%	100%
Great Britain	26.7%	22.6%	14.9%	16.2%	2.4%	17.2%	100%
Change 1999–2004:							
North East	8.8%	–8.1%	+4.3%	+3.3%		+9.2%	
North West	–11.3%	–7.2%	+4.1%	+5.6%		+8.8%	
Yorks and							
Humberside	–12.0%	–5.1%	+1.1%	+7.4%		+8.5%	
East Midlands	–13.1%	–7.6%	+0.2%	+18.5%		+2.0%	
West Midlands	–10.6%	–4.6%	+2.5%	+11.6%		+1.0%	
East	–11.9%	–8.9%	+2.0%	+10.7%		+8.1%	
London	–5.9%	–10.3%	+3.7%	+6.9%		+5.6%	
South East	–9.3%	–6.0%	+0.0%	+9.8%		+5.4%	
South West	–10.1%	–3.6%	+1.9%	+11.9%		–0.1%	
Wales	–3.4%	+0.6%	+2.3%	+7.4%	–12.1%	+5.3%	
Scotland	–2.0%	–2.3%	+3.3%	+5.4%	–7.5%	+3.0%	
Great Britain	–9.1%	–5.4%	+2.2%	+9.2%	–2.2%	+5.2%	
Seats:							
North East	1	1	1				3
North West	3	3	2	1			9
Yorks and							
Humberside	2	2	1	1			6
East Midlands	2	1	1	2			6
West Midlands	3	2	1	1			7
East	3	1	1	2			7
London	3	3	1	1		1	9
South East	4	1	2	2		1	10
South West	3	1	1	2			7
Wales	1	2			1		4
Scotland	2	2	1		2		7
Great Britain	27	19	12	12	3	2	75

[a] Percentages have been rounded to the nearest decimal point.

Source: Electoral Commission.

Table 5.15   UK MEPs, by party (and region and round elected)

Party	Region	Round elected
Conservative:		
Richard Ashworth	SE	8
Robert Atkins	NW	8
Christopher Beazley	E	6
John Bowis	Lon	4
Philip Bradbourn	WM	5
Philip Bushill-Matthews	WM	1
Martin Callanan	NE	2
Giles Chichester	SW	7
Nirj Deva	SE	3
Den Dover	NW	2
James Elles	SE	6
Jonathan Evans	Wa	2
Daniel Hannan	SE	1
Malcolm Harbour	WM	7
Chris Heaton-Harris	EM	4
Roger Helmer	EM	1
Caroline Jackson	SE	4
Timothy Kirkhope	Y & H	2
Edward McMillan-Scott	Y & H	6
Neil Parish	SW	1
John Purvis	Sc	7
Struan Stevenson	Sc	3
Robert Sturdy	E	4
David Sumberg	NW	5
Charles Tannock	Lon	7
Geoffrey Van Orden	E	1
Theresa Villiers	Lon	1
Labour:		
Michael Cashman	WM	2
Richard Corbett	Y & H	5
Robert Evans	Lon	9
Glyn Ford	SW	1
Neena Gill	WM	6
Mary Honeyball	Lon	5
Richard Howitt	E	3
Stephen Hughes	NE	1
Glenys Kinnock	Wa	1
David Martin	Sc	1
Linda McAvan	Y & H	1
Arlene McCarthy	NW	4
Claude Moraes	WM	2
Eluned Morgan	Wa	4
Peter Skinner	E	5
Catherine Stihler	Sc	4
Gary Titley	NW	1
Philip Whitehead	EM	3
Terry Wynn	NW	7

Table 5.15   continued

Lib Dem:		
Elspeth Attwooll	Sc	5
Chris Davies	NW	3
Andrew Duff	E	3
Fiona Hall	NE	3
Chris Huhne	SE	10
Saj Karim	NW	9
Sarah Ludford	Lon	3
Liz Lynne	WM	4
Bill Newton Dunn	EM	6
Emma Nicholson	SE	4
Diana Wallis	Y & H	3
Graham Watson	SW	3
Plaid Cymru:		
Jill Evans	W	3
SNP:		
Ian Hudghton	Sc	2
Alyn Smith	Sc	7
UKIP:		
Gerard Batten	Lon	6
Godfrey Bloom	Y & H	4
Graham Booth	SW	2
Derek Clark	EM	5
Nigel Farage	SE	2
Robert Kilroy-Silk	EM	2
Roger Knapman	SW	6
Ashley Mote	SE	7
Mike Nattrass	WM	3
Jeffrey Titford	E	2
John Whittaker	NW	6
Tom Wise	E	7
DUP:		
Jim Allister	NI	1
Sinn Féin:		
Bairbre De Brún	NI	2
UUP:		
Jim Nicholson	NI	3

Source: Electoral Commission.

Notes

1. In contrast to 1999 the votes were, because of simultaneous local elections, counted in local authority areas and not in constituencies (except in Scotland where there were no local elections). This handicaps exact comparisons with 1999.
2. The nearest miss was in Scotland where, with 892 more votes, Labour would have got a third seat, instead of the Conservatives holding on to a second one. In the North East the Liberal Democrats secured representation, denying Labour a second seat by 5,764 votes. In the West Midlands the Earl of Bradford came within 5,116 votes of getting a second seat for UKIP. The West Midlands was also the region in which the BNP (with 0.8 of a winning vote) came closest to winning a seat, although Simon Darby was four times farther away than the Earl of Bradford.
3. Mr Bell and Mr Herron saved their deposits; 39 party lists forfeited theirs.
4. As a consequence of the 2002 Electoral Fraud (Northern Ireland) Act, voters were required to produce photographic identification at polling stations. The 2004 Electoral Commission report pointed out that a high number of people had turned up at the polls without such ID.
5. For an account of the mechanics of voting on Gibraltar, see Electoral Commission (2004b, pp. 61–3).
6. Roy Perry, James Provan and Lord Stockton (Con) and Bill Miller (Lab).
7. Jacqueline Foster, Ian Twinn and Richard Balfe (Con) and David Bowe, Barbara O'Toole and Mark Watts (Lab).
8. Curiously, Chris Heaton-Harris, who had only just been re-elected as a Conservative MEP, was the party's candidate for Leicester South.

6
Reflections

The paradox of a consequential non-event

The chapters in this study, together with the statistical Appendix, offer strong confirmation to the image of this particular European contest as a 'second-order' national election. Yet it *was* a national election, with all that this implied for expenses and activities. What, then, did it mean for British politics? At one level, the election was clearly a dry run, a dress rehearsal for the first-order General Election that was generally expected for the spring of 2005. The experiences of all of the parties would be fed back into their calculations on how to maximise their tactical advantages and how to hone their campaigning machinery.

At another level, the 2004 European elections confirmed and perhaps accelerated a number of underlying trends in British politics.

The ever-decreasing turnout of recent years was checked, but not the flight from the main parties. The decline in two-party dominance was proceeding even faster in voting for Strasbourg than for Westminster, as Table 6.1 demonstrates.

A concomitant trend was the fragmentation of political representation and, as Chapter 5 showed, a consequent weakening in the overall impact of British representation in the European Parliament (a phenomenon well known to the French). This is perhaps more pronounced in the European elections where, as Chapter 3 described, proportional representation has led a large number of micro-parties and individuals to stand, not in search of a seat, but to make a point or to pass a message.

Another noticeable trend was the increased concentration on negative campaigning. Attacks on an opponent's integrity and competence are as old as electioneering. But the Labour Party's single-minded focus on the political record and alleged limitations of Michael Howard seemed to exceed all precedent. The Conservatives too were exceptionally reluctant to reveal new policies or talk about much except the misguidedness of the Labour government. Even the Liberal Democrats, ostensibly the most positively pro-European of parties, made little of Europe as an issue. The Greens were the exception that proved the rule. The ultimate in negative messages was, surely, UKIP's simple and effective 'NO' slogan.

Table 6.1   The decline in the vote of the two largest parties
(Conservative plus Labour percentage share of national vote)

General Elections	%	European elections	%
1955	96.1		
1964	87.5		
1974	76.8		
		1979	80.0
		1984	75.9
1987	74.6		
		1989	72.2
1992	77.7		
		1994	69.5
1997	73.9		
		1999	61.8
2001	58.4		
		2004	49.3

Source: Butler and Butler (2000).

Consequences for the parties and their leaders

Labour

The Labour Party lost the election; its share of the national vote was the lowest since 1910. Yet it emerged almost content. Things could have been so much worse. Despite all the premature obituaries written about his Premiership, Tony Blair emerged resilient, buoyed by an almost universal expectation that Labour would win the 2005 General Election, confirmed by all the current opinion polls. There could be no doubt of Tony Blair's survival until after that event. With his position thus consolidated, he felt able to announce on 30 September that he would continue throughout the next Parliament, though not beyond.

Tony Blair had transformed the strategic and tactical landscape of the 2004 European elections with his 20 April announcement of his conversion to a referendum, a switch that greatly helped Labour in the short term, even though it did grave damage to Mr Blair's reputation for consistency. It was, as Peter Riddell observed in *The Times*, a tactical victory but a strategic defeat for the leader who had said in 1997 that putting Britain at the heart of Europe was, for him, central.

The tactical advantage went beyond Britain's shores, strengthening Mr Blair's hand in the June Inter-Governmental Conference and effectively ensuring that the government secured all of its negotiating positions. It also had other consequences for Mr Blair's fellow Heads of State or Government; it was not long before President Chirac had to concede a referendum for the French people.

Back home, Mr Blair's U-turn was one more contribution to the great debate over the issue of 'trust'. All politicians had become increasingly mistrusted: Tony Blair's conduct over Iraq was made a central symbol of that feeling.

In the aftermath of the election, Mr Blair showed his strength by appointing Alan Milburn to take charge of Labour's campaigning in place of Gordon Brown, and by appointing the brilliant but controversial Peter Mandelson to be Britain's sole Commissioner in Brussels. Mr Blair's reported attempt to bring Mr Mandelson back into the British Cabinet was regarded as a sign of his renewed confidence.

Had Mr Blair, as a *Financial Times* article argued, 'missed his chance to lead in Europe'? Was he, as the same newspaper's editorial argued, 'The lost leader?' What none could deny was that Mr Blair had survived a 'wobbly' period in his leadership and emerged strengthened.

Conservatives

Among the party leaders, the most energetic European election campaign was that of Mr Howard. On the opening day of his campaign he travelled from Manchester to Edinburgh to Cardiff. Thereafter, he ranged the country in his 'Battle bus', visiting all eleven regions at least once. He also flew to Gibraltar – the only leader to do so. There was a positive and optimistic 'buzz' at the outset of his campaign, even if Labour had already 'shot his fox' by acceptance of a referendum on the Constitutional Treaty. A carefully calculated 'grid' had been elaborated to ensure a higher regional profile. A series of pronouncements and interviews meant that Mr Howard could take personal encouragement from the fact that his old 'something of the night' image had largely gone, to be replaced by the image of a more sensitive man, the son of persecuted refugees.

Yet by the end of the campaign there was a sense of fatalism among Conservative supporters and activists, a generalised feeling of a missed opportunity and of failed promise, a belief that the party's leader had a glass jaw. How had this happened? The account set out in Chapter 5 gave some clues. The launch of Mr Howard's campaign was undermined by allegations of abuses of the European Parliament's expenses system by two Conservative MEPs. Thereafter, Mr Howard's regional campaign was badly overshadowed by the media's increasing fascination with the UK Independence Party and Robert Kilroy-Silk, and his reaction to the UKIP 'threat' was widely perceived as being clumsy and wrong. (As one UKIP insider put it, 'It was clearly so counter-productive that we thought it had to be a subtle ploy.')

The bad news for Mr Howard continued after the elections, with subsequent opinion polls demonstrating that he had failed to dent Labour's lead. During the campaign former minister John Redwood was brought into the fray, ostensibly, it was thought, to woo potential Tory UKIP voters back into the fold. But Mr Redwood's pronouncements upset the pro-European wing of the party and when, in a hasty reshuffle immediately after the elections, Mr Redwood was brought back onto the Shadow front bench, the pro-European wing was even more upset.

The cumulative impression given – the lack of a 'Plan B'; the 'cranks and political gadflies' episode; the appearance of John Redwood; and the hasty reshuffle not to mention an unhelpful 'Bagehot' article in *The Economist* – was of a casting around, of a leader who was not steady under fire, of a leader who had somehow failed to secure good strategic advice. Whether true or not, this was the enduring impression given by the media coverage during and immediately after the elections. At least it suggested that Labour's negative campaigning had in part worked.

Mr Howard had worked hard, combining energetic campaigning with the forensic skills and wit already apparent in his Commons appearances, and he could have expected better. But structural weaknesses undermined his strengths. For example, the benefits of his determined regional campaign were undermined by his party's national strategy. As one candidate pointed out, in the South West the real enemy was the Liberal Democrats, and yet the national campaign focused only on Labour.

Again, the Conservatives (and, more passionately, the SNP) were clearly onto something in making the Common Fisheries Policy (CFP) into a campaign issue. But after a few days of campaigning it became clear that the Tories' policy was, as one insider put it, 'insufficiently thought through'. Journalists, no doubt prompted, had soon realised that the CFP could only be renegotiated if the other member states agreed to open such negotiations, and that unilateral withdrawal without negotiations would be tantamount to unilateral withdrawal from the EU itself. Naturally, this prospect enraged the Tory Europhiles. In the end, however, the CFP issue was overshadowed by the Labour government's 'red lines' and the UK Independence Party's straight 'NO'.

Wisdom is always easy with hindsight. Was the party's mid-April optimism misplaced? What had gone wrong? Some party insiders wondered whether, once the UKIP bandwagon had taken off, Mr Howard would not have been better advised to abandon the regional campaign in favour of a more centralised approach, concentrating on the national media and ensuring a single message. Whatever, the party seemed unable to make an impression, and the leader-writers seemed unable to make up their minds. Was the party in crisis? Was it in decline? As their Labour opponents had reasoned, the Conservatives could ill afford to destabilise their fourth leader in seven years, and there was no doubt that Michael Howard would take them into the expected spring 2005 General Election. But six months after the European elections, Michael Howard's Conservatives were in a worse position in the opinion polls than under Iain Duncan Smith.

Liberal Democrats

Clearly, Charles Kennedy's shrewd tactics had paid off and so, it seems, had his underlying strategy. Mr Kennedy displayed energy in the campaign and guile in his tactics, thus consolidating his leadership. But the Liberal Democrats were lucky in the way that their local election gains in the North East and the North West came early in the announcements of results. The local elections were a 'victory', and portrayed as such by a media looking for some sort of sensation. The European elections, in which the party came fourth (after UKIP) and got barely half the percentage it had received in the local elections, was clearly a disappointment, despite the gain of two seats. Nevertheless, the enduring impression of 'super Thursday' was of a strong Liberal Democrat performance, and this impression was carried over into the by-election campaigns for Birmingham Hodge Hill and Leicester South, with media speculation on further sensational wins for the Liberal Democrats.

It has long been said that Britain has moved from two-party politics to two-and-a-half-party politics. Perhaps June 2004 saw it creeping towards two-and-three-quarter-party politics. In local and regional politics the Liberal Democrats had now become major players, even though in numbers remaining far from replacing the Conservatives as the principal party of opposition.

There were two possible reasons for concern about the Liberal Democrats' performance. First, the party's stance on Iraq clearly detached a large number of Muslim votes from Labour. Yet it remained to be seen whether Muslim voters would stay with the Liberal Democrats or whether, more pragmatically, they would return to Labour, from whence most of them had come. Second, as the split-ticket voting between the local and the European elections clearly demonstrated (see the statistical Appendix), the Liberal Democrats continued to have difficulty in resolving a central paradox; the leadership is plainly more Euro-enthusiastic than the party's grassroots support.

United Kingdom Independence Party

By its own declared intentions well in advance of the elections, the UK Independence Party met its campaign targets. The Kilroy-Silk bandwagon clearly gave them a late bonus, but so did Mr Blair's decision on a referendum. Had Labour still been insisting that a referendum was not necessary, the Conservatives would have been able to stick to their preferred game plan of 'a referendum on a referendum', and therefore would have leaked less votes to UKIP. But as the glow of their election success faded, the party's strategists had several hard questions to ponder.

First, it was clear that UKIP had very effectively siphoned off disaffected Conservative voters, but it was not at all clear that these voters would remain.

Indeed, there was every probability that most of them would return to the Conservative fold for a General Election.

Second, was UKIP going to remain just a 'single issue' part? If it did so, the first problem would be exacerbated, unless the Party took a strategic decision to restrict itself to contests on the European issue. In the period immediately after the European elections the party issued conflicting messages about its intended behaviour in Tory marginal seats. Would it act as a spoiler to force the European issue? Meanwhile, the interest Godfrey Bloom's sexist pronouncements generated strongly indicated the need for the party to adopt at least a rudimentary palette of policy positions on other issues, particularly given the decision to take up parliamentary committee positions.[1]

Third, although the party did not implode, as its critics predicted or hoped, it did begin to fray at the edges; Ashley Mote and then Robert Kilroy-Silk had both effectively left within a few weeks of the elections. ('You're all barmy', Mr Kilroy-Silk was reported to have said as he stormed out. 'Kilroy was here', quipped a 28 October *Guardian* editorial.) The risk of 'implosion' was linked to the problem of leadership. It was not very long before the party's new star was involved in very public speculation about whether he would replace the less charismatic Roger Knapman, and when it became apparent that this would not happen, it became equally apparent that it would only be a matter of time before Mr Kilroy-Silk left. Perhaps, inwardly, this was what the party's leadership had hoped for, but the exit of their star act risked damaging their attractiveness.

Fourth, though the party strenuously denies linkage of any sort with the far right, it clearly did act to some extent albeit inadvertently as a lightning conductor drawing off potential BNP support. In effect, the UKIP has the same tactical problem with the BNP that the Conservatives have with the UKIP. Whilst both must necessarily distance themselves, they know that some of their support may drift further right, particularly in a second-order election. Should such support be alienated or disowned (viz. Mr Howard's 'cranks and political gadflies')? Clearly, the more Mr Blair is able to occupy the political centre ground, the more pronounced this problem becomes for the right.

As this study was going to press, the Electoral Commission released information on party expenditure (see Table 6.2) which revealed an important, if not vital, element in the UK Independence Party's success. It spent £2,361,754 on campaign costs – over a third more than the Labour Party. The party spent £1.59 million on advertising, £320,218 on leaflets and £228,000 on market research and advertising. This expenditure was reported to have been largely funded by the Yorkshire businessman, Paul Sykes (£1.44 million), and a Kent businessman, Alan Bown (£513,000).

The Greens

The Greens could breath a sigh of relief. They had retained their two seats in Strasbourg – against the psephologists' expectations, if not their own,

Table 6.2 Party expenditure on the European elections campaign[a]

Party	Expenditure
Conservative Party	£3,130,266
UK Independence Party	£2,361,754
Labour Party	£1,707,224
Liberal Democrats	£1,188,691
Green Party	£404,058
Respect	£243,599
British National Party	£228,813
Scottish National Party	£93,304
English Democrats	£61,466
Plaid Cymru	£37,150
Scottish Green Party	£37,083
Forward Wales	£19,031
Scottish Socialist Party	£20,090
Alliance for Green Socialism	£12,236
Countryside Party	£11,976
The Common Good	£10,937

[a] Only parties spending more than £10,000 are listed.

Source: Electoral Commission.

and they thus had confirmation that their tactics of concentrating heavily on their heartlands had been correct. However, the June 2004 elections had sent a mixed message. In the London Mayoral elections, for example, the Greens had trailed the BNP.

The Greens' relief was tinged with great sadness. On 9 July Mike Woodin, one of the party's two Principal Speakers, a longstanding Oxford City Councillor and second on the Party's list for the South East, died after a long illness. He was just 38. His friend and colleague Caroline Lucas declared that: 'Mike was one of the driving forces behind the Green Party's resurgence over the last few years.' He had happily survived long enough to see the Greens retain their Strasbourg position.

Respect

The Respect coalition's electoral performance was something of an anti-climax even though George Galloway had reinforced his position as a minor national figure. The coalition's creation had occurred with a great deal of passion, particularly in opposition to the ongoing Iraq conflict, but somehow the party's campaign never really took off. Whatever electoral specificity it may have had was mainly lost from view as the Liberal Democrats soaked up most of the protest vote – at least as far as the local elections were concerned.

The BNP

Did the BNP have the potential to break through and win one or more Strasbourg seats? As Table 6.3 and the statistical Appendix show convincingly, the answer must be 'Yes'. The 10 June impact of the BNP was considerable – if modest by the major parties' standards. The party took two seats on the Greater London Assembly and, as seen above, won more votes than the Greens in the London Mayoral election. In the European elections the party came close enough – 22,000 votes away from a seat in the West Midlands. Table 6.3 shows just how close the BNP came in four regions.

Table 6.3   BNP 'near misses' in the 2004 European elections

Region	Last elected MEP (%)	BNP (%)	Gap (%)
North West	7.9 (2nd, Lib Dem)	6.4	1.5
West Midlands	9.1 (3rd, Con)	7.5	1.6
Yorks & Humberside	12.3 (2nd, Con)	8.0	4.3
East Midlands	12.9 (1st, Lib Dem)	6.5	6.4

Source: Electoral Commission.

From the very outset, the government considered the weakening of the BNP's potential through higher turnout as a strong reason for the experiment for all-postal ballot voting. But in the event BNP support actually rose in two of the four all-postal ballot regions. Nor was there a correlation between strong UKIP performances and weaker BNP votes. Why, then, did it not win one or more seats, as its Continental *confrères* had clearly expected? There are no obvious answers. But what should be noted is that some 880,000 British voters considered the BNP to be a respectable recipient for their votes.

Scotland, Wales and Northern Ireland

In Scotland and Wales the existential crisis of the national parties continued, as Table 6.4 demonstrates. The SNP leader, John Swinney, felt obliged to resign. Though his resignation was attributed to the party's poor showing in the European elections (he had vowed to overtake Labour and, quite simply, didn't), political analysts pointed to the underlying conflict between Mr Swinney's position and 'fundamentalists' who believed that the SNP should focus on the objective of total independence. To general surprise, Mr Swinney was replaced by his predecessor, Alex Salmond, who had previously let it be known that he was not interested in taking up the leadership cudgels again.

In Northern Ireland the transition from Revd Ian Paisley and John Hume, the charismatic grandees of the previous generation, and the arrival of Sinn Féin (in both the North and the South of Ireland) was as expected.

Table 6.4   The declining nationalist vote in Scotland and Wales

	Turnout	Con (%)	Lab (%)	Lib Dem (%)	SNP (%)	UKIP (%)	Other (%)
Votes in Scotland 1999–2004:							
1999 Sc Pmt	57.2	15.5	34.0	12.6	27.6	0.0	10.3
1999 Europe	24.7	19.8	28.7	9.8	27.2	1.3	13.3
2001 GE	58.2	15.6	43.9	16.4	14.3	0.1	9.7
2003 Sc Pmt	49.0	15.6	29.4	11.8	20.9	0.6	21.7
2004 Europe	30.6	17.8	26.4	13.1	19.7	6.7	16.4
Votes in Wales 1999–2004:							
1999 W. Assem	46.1	16.5	35.5	12.5	30.6	0.0	4.8
1999 Europe	28.1	22.8	31.1	8.2	29.6	3.1	4.5
2001 GE	61.6	21.0	48.6	13.8	14.3	0.9	1.4
2003 W. Assem	38.2	19.5	38.3	13.3	20.5	2.9	5.5
2004 Europe	41.4	19.4	32.5	13.1	17.4	10.5	9.7

Source: Electoral Commission.

The mechanics

Proportional representation

Many UK MEPs looked back longingly to the old days with single-member constituencies. But it was also widely realised that, as an irrevocable Treaty-based commitment, PR for European elections was there to stay. Moreover, PR was now established in differing forms in elections in Scotland, Wales, Northern Ireland and London, and was currently being extended to local government in Scotland.

The closed-list system was unlikely to be changed. It clearly entrenched the re-election of incumbents. The main parties would be reluctant to open the door to the sort of public intra-party warfare that an open-list system could be expected to produce.

On the other hand, it was probable that the parties would look again at their selection methods. There were complaints about the composition of the audiences at certain Conservative hustings. There were objections to the pro-incumbent reselection rules in the Labour and Liberal Democrat Parties. But there was no sign after the election of any upswelling of indignation that would lead to any significant change.

Postal voting

In a campaign that lacked highlights the problems associated with postal voting produced the longest running story. Yet despite minor problems about issuing the ballots on time, postal voting was generally adjudged a success. It certainly increased turnout – but not, despite folklore to the contrary, strongly to any partisan advantage. There were stories of abuse, sometimes in nursing homes, for example, but more often among inner-city ethnic communities. Vigorous police investigations initially failed to produce any significant number of genuine abuses, though at the time of writing formal investigations and at least one court case were still under way.

The limited hiccups over the postal vote, highlighted by the Electoral Commission, gave the Deputy Prime Minister, John Prescott, an excuse to abort the all-postal referendums on Regional Assemblies promised for the North West and for Yorkshire and Humberside and, as the disastrous results in the surviving North East region referendum showed, he was well advised to do so.

More generally, the European elections saw a continuation in the trend for the electorate to opt to vote by post (3.9% in the 2001 General Election; 8.3% for the 2004 European elections). Overall, 37.4% of the UK electorate was issued with a postal vote.

Simultaneous elections

In 2003 it had been decided to postpone for a year the local elections in Wales to avoid their coinciding with the Welsh Assembly elections due on 1 May 2003. But a year later the government chose to delay for a month the local elections in England and Wales, due on 7 May 2004, so that they should coincide with the European elections due on 10 June. Moreover it was widely expected that the next General Election would be called for 5 May 2005 so that they would coincide with the local elections due on that date. The motive for holding elections simultaneously is plainly to increase turnout, and increased turnout is generally held to help Labour, although the degree to which it does so is probably exaggerated.

The media

In its December 2004 report, the Electoral Commission pointed to the sporadic and broken nature of media reporting of the European elections. It also underlined the fact that 'apathy' had in itself become a media story – so much so that the BBC deliberately 'rationed' its programmes to one 'apathy story' each. But it was acknowledged that the media could not be held to blame for distraction or indifference when the European elections were run alongside others and whilst the business of government and Parliament continued at full pace. As previous Nuffield Studies have pointed out, part of the problem lies in a misunderstanding about the inter-relationship between Westminster and Strasbourg politics – they are, after all, part of the same continuum. That understanding will only come when it is positively recognised and argued by British domestic politicians, whereas, as this account has shown, the party leaders and spokesmen chose to concentrate primarily on domestic issues, largely to the exclusion of European policy issues.

Discouraging prospects?

The sixth set of European elections in the United Kingdom gave much food for thought. Turnout was higher, but still, by the standards of General Elections, low. Relative awareness was certainly lower than for the other elections held at the same time (see Electoral Commission, 2004b). Eurosceptical and xenophobic parties performed well. A vote in the EP on a censure motion during the election campaign (on the Commission's handling of the 'Eurostat' affair) passed largely unnoticed – a huge irony in the light of subsequent events. The Common Statute saga was rolled over into the new European Parliament – and would presumably dog that Parliament just as much as it had dogged its predecessor. The strong Eurosceptical showing in several member states seemed to have little, if any, consequences for their governments in the 17–18 June Inter-Governmental Conference.

The strengthened UK Independence Party was regarded by Continental politicians as something of a curiosity but also as a symbolic reminder of the UK's increasingly Eurosceptical bent. All seemed agreed that this was not a one-off.

Meanwhile, the other British political parties were unsure how to deal with it. One Labour MEP, Richard Corbett, drafted a pamphlet, published by Britain in Europe (<www.britainineurope.org.uk/.ten/articles/theres-something-about-ukip>), in which he argued that 'There can be little doubt that many people lent UKIP their vote, as Robert Kilroy-Silk himself said, because of UKIP's views on immigration, rather than out of a clear understanding of the party itself.' This argument was inevitably weakened once Mr Kilroy-Silk had effectively left the party, and the internet enabled UKIP to hit back at Mr Corbett with counter-accusations (see, for example <www.ukip-ynl.org.uk/news.htm>). Other Labour Party members set up a 'UKIP watch' website (<http://ukipwatch.org/>) in order to monitor its activities. Attempts to portray UKIP members as 'wreckers' seemed strengthened in the autumn, when in a full plenary session of the Parliament Mr Farage alleged that one of the nominated Commissioners, Frenchman Jacques Barrot, had had a criminal conviction. British members were swift to condemn Mr Farage but were obliged rapidly to change tack when it became apparent that the allegation was true. Mr Barrot received a suspended jail term in a party funding case in 2000, but it was automatically erased by a 1995 Presidential amnesty. Under French law, no reference may be made to such a sentence, which carries no criminal record. Mr Barrot, of the centre-right Union for a Popular Movement, was never barred from public office.

In terms of European politics, the fragmentation of British representation has, inevitably, led to less influence and patronage. The contingent of British Labour MEPs had been losing influence from the 1999 elections onwards. (Some saw the unexpected resignation of Alan Donnelly as an early symptom of this decline.) But after the 2003 invasion of Iraq the European Parliamentary

Labour Party was effectively sent to Coventry by other PES Group members, and it was not until the autumn controversy surrounding Mr Rocco Butiglione and the investiture of the new Barroso Commission that the EPLP, which refused Tony Blair's demands that it should vote for the new Commission, was able to win back some political kudos. The Tories remain split and the softer, wetter side of the party enjoys some benefits of patronage through its pact with the EPP, but has little real political influence.

Meanwhile, new political issues were already looming on the horizon: the future financing of the enlarged European Union; the future of the UK's budgetary rebate; the question of Turkish membership. Nearer home, thoughts were turning to the pending General Election; the UK Presidency in the second half of 2005; and the probable 2006 Referendum on the European Constitution.

For the European Parliament, the messages were mixed, but not encouraging. Was it simply to be condemned to being the 'Power without the glory' (*Bulletin*, 3 June 2004). Was it, as *The Economist*'s 'Charlemagne' wrote, 'A Crucible – or a Zoo?', where 'odd behaviour is the only thing that stirs interest in the European Parliament'? (24 July 2004).

Previous Nuffield Studies have suggested 'winners' and 'losers'. In terms of domestic politics, this study has described the strange alchemy of British politics that seemed to reverse the situation of the two main party leaders in a matter of weeks. In closing, however, this study limits itself to a simple observation. If, as Mr Blair professed at the outset of his Prime Ministership in 1997, his greatest goal was to resolve the UK's problematic relationship with the EU, then undoubtedly he was a loser. As a MORI poll/FPC pamphlet cogently argued, there was a strong risk that any referendum held on the Constitution would be turned into a referendum on his leadership. In the space of seven years Tony Blair had gone from being the European cause's greatest champion to its greatest liability. This must surely be one of modern British politics' greatest ironies.

Coda

The June 2004 European elections had had a low profile and they faded rapidly from the public's consciousness. But they did not disappear without trace. They were a nationwide contest, and they brought together the same political parties that would, very probably within a year, contest a General Election. As such, they gave a clear indication as to the likely winner. They also gave the first hints of political mortality of one of the most successful British Prime Ministers in recent history, exacerbated the Conservative Party's existential crisis and gave fresh succour to the permanent optimists of the British political system, the Liberal Democrats. Last, but by no means least, they demonstrated graphically the sea-change in the attitude of the British electorate towards the European integration process and gave a glimpse of some of the sharp rocks lurking underneath.

Note

1. A 6 June 2004 double-paged spread in the *Mail on Sunday* publishing various allegations about Nigel Farage's parliamentary lifestyle made little impact, but the allegations and counter-allegations made by previous party officials, including Dr Alan Sked and Dr Richard North, probably did add to the impression of a party at risk of implosion.

Appendix: An Analysis of the Results

John Curtice, Stephen Fisher and Michael Steed

Introduction

As Chapter 1 set out, European elections have long struggled to fulfil the aims of their advocates. Relatively few voters go to the polls. Those who do vote appear inclined to use them as an opportunity to express their views about domestic politics, typically by recording their dissatisfaction with the incumbent government, rather than as a chance to say what kind of Europe they would like. They may also consider it an occasion to have an apparently harmless flutter with a minor party (Reif and Schmitt, 1980; Reif, 1985a). As a result of these characteristics, European elections have been dubbed mere 'second-order' contests.

Britain has not been immune from this pattern. Turnout has consistently been lower in European elections than it has in any of the country's domestic contests. In four out of the five elections held between 1979 and 1999 it was also lower than in any other member of the European Union. With the exception of the 1979 election, which occurred just a month after the election of a new Conservative government, support for the governing party has always been lower than it was at the previous General Election. Meanwhile the Greens had unprecedented success in coming third in votes in the 1989 European elections, while in the 1999 election, the first to be fought under a system of proportional representation, nearly one in five votes were cast for parties not represented at Westminster.

Yet certain features of past European elections in Britain give some pause for thought. Why have the Liberal Democrats and their predecessors, always in opposition and relatively small but also the most pro-European of Britain's political parties, averaged just 12% of the vote in European elections held between 1979 and 1999 when their average share of the vote in General Elections over the same period has been as high as 17% and in local elections as high as 28%? Why was it that the United Kingdom Independence Party, which wishes Britain to leave the European Union, emerged as the most successful of the non-Westminster parties in 1999? In short, parties with distinctive stances on Europe appear to have done particularly well or particularly badly in European elections. Perhaps attitudes towards Europe do matter to some degree in European elections, albeit perhaps it has been people's views about Britain's relationship with Europe that affect behaviour rather than any perception of what the European Parliament should be doing for Europe as a whole (Steed, 2002, 2004).

Meanwhile, low turnout can no longer be regarded as a peculiar feature of European elections. At the General Election in 2001 turnout was lower than at any previous contest since 1918, while recent local and devolved elections have also registered record low turnouts. Mindful of these figures, as well as the turnout of just 23.1% at the European elections in 1999, the government took two steps to try and encourage more voters to participate. The first was to hold an all-postal ballot in four of the eleven regions into which Britain is divided for the purposes of European elections; such ballots had already proved successful in raising turnout at recent local elections (Electoral Commission, 2003a). The second step was to postpone local and London

Mayoral and Assembly elections that were due to be held in May so that they coincided with the European vote. While low by most standards, turnout in local elections has usually been higher than in previous European elections; the measure also helped avoid any danger of voter fatigue as a result of being asked to vote twice in little more than a month.

This then leaves two important questions. To what degree did the 2004 European election register the public's mood about Europe, and to what extent did it reflect debates about domestic politics? In so far as it reflected either, what does it tell us about the British public's attitudes towards Europe or about the state of the country's domestic politics? How successful were the measures that were adopted at this election to increase turnout and what longer-term lessons can be drawn about their utility in future elections, either European or domestic? These are the basic questions tackled in this appendix. After introducing how we set about our analysis, there are three main sections. First we look at the pattern of turnout both to assess the impact of the government's attempts to increase turnout and to ascertain how inclined the public were to vote in these elections once the effect of those attempts are put to one side. Second, we look at the pattern of support for those parties not currently represented at Westminster in order to assess what appears to have motivated their supporters. Third, we then examine how we can best account for the fortunes of those parties that are currently represented at Westminster, including looking at the impact of the pattern of support for non-Westminster parties. After then briefly considering how the pattern of party support was rewarded by the electoral system, we finally consider what appear to be the answers to our two key questions.

Data and methods

As in 1999, Great Britain was divided into eleven separate regions for the purposes of allocating seats. With one minor exception – the addition of Gibraltar to the South West region – these regions were exactly the same as the ones used five years ago.[1] However, in England and Wales at least, the count was conducted local authority by local authority rather than, as in 1999, constituency by constituency. Only in Scotland was the count conducted once again by constituency. As local authority boundaries do not correspond to constituency boundaries, this makes it difficult to compare the pattern of voting at this election with either that at the last General Election in 2001 or the previous European election in 1999 at anything other than the level of the eleven regions.

The task is not, however, an impossible one. By following a rule that so long as there is a 95% or higher correspondence between the boundary of one or more local authorities and one or more constituencies, we have been able to delineate 164 separate 'areas' in England and Wales where we can compare the result at this election with that in previous elections. Much of our analysis is based on these areas together with the 72 Scottish constituencies.[2] As the size of these areas varies substantially, in all of our analyses every area has been weighted by the size of its electorate.

However, not all of our analyses look at how voting changed since 1999 or 2001. We are also sometimes simply interested in how a party's support or turnout varied in 2004. For this purpose we simply examine how voting varied across the 380 English and Welsh local authorities together with the 72 Scottish constituencies. These analyses too are weighted by the size of the electorate in each counting unit.[3]

Turnout

More people opted to vote in these European elections than had done in any previous European election in Great Britain. True, at 38.2%, Britain remained near the bottom of the turnout league: amongst the 15 longer-standing members of the European Union, only Sweden recorded a lower turnout.[4] It nevertheless represented a stark contrast to the record low turnouts recorded in a number of domestic contests since 1997. Did this mean that the widespread concern that recent low turnouts indicated that Britain's voters were becoming increasingly disengaged from politics had in fact been misplaced? Or might it perhaps simply have been the result of the introduction of all-postal ballots and the holding of local elections on the same day?

There is no doubt that all-postal ballots and coincident local elections helped to increase the turnout. First, as we can see in Table A.1, turnout was just under 6 points higher where all-postal ballots were held than it was where a traditional ballot was held. Amongst those places where a traditional ballot was held, turnout was up to 4 points higher where a local election was also taking place than where it was not, though holding a local election appears to have made rather less difference where an all-postal ballot was conducted.

Table A.1   Turnout by type of ballot and presence/absence of local election[a]

| | Type of Ballot | | | |
| | Traditional | | Postal | |
Local Election[b]	% voted	change since 1999	% voted	change since 1999
None	33.5	+7.9	41.3	+19.0
Some	36.9	+11.3	42.9	+20.4
Everywhere	37.8	+14.8	41.8	+23.5
All	36.4	+11.8	42.0	+21.7

[a]   Table based on 'areas' as defined above.

[b]   Local election: None = no local election held in any of the component local authorities in that area; Some = local election held in some local authorities but not in others; Everywhere = local election held in all of the component local authorities. The London Mayoral and Assembly election is regarded as a local election.

This, however, is to underestimate seriously the impact that all-postal ballots and local elections had on turnout. The four regions where all-postal ballots were held were amongst the five regions with the lowest level of turnout in 1999. Equally, those parts of England where local elections were held consisted disproportionately of the urban half of the country, where turnout is always lower. In short, both measures were deployed in those parts of the country where voters are usually less inclined to vote. To assess their impact properly we should therefore look at how much turnout increased since 1999 rather than simply at the level of turnout.[5]

By this measure, holding an all-postal ballot had a dramatic impact. Turnout rose by as much as 10 points more where such ballots were held than it did where traditional ballots were conducted. While this is a somewhat smaller gap than had been evident in many of the previous experiments with all-postal ballots in local elections (Electoral Commission, 2004a, p. 30), it still confirms the broad message of those experiments that all-postal ballots can make a significant difference to turnout in low-profile elections.[6]

Meanwhile, holding a local election appears to have added about 7 points to the turnout where a traditional ballot was held and nearly 5 points where an all-postal ballot was conducted. So local elections also proved to be an important added incentive that brought an extra 1 in 20 or so voters to the polls.

The apparent importance both of all-postal ballots and of coincident local elections in raising the turnout was starkly illustrated in the one region, Scotland, where no local elections were held anywhere and where a traditional ballot was held. Turnout rose by just 6 points, far less than in any region in England and Wales. In fact, this increase was markedly lower than what was manifest in those parts of England where there were no elections and a traditional ballot was held; here turnout rose by just under 10 points (9.8%).

Two rather contradictory implications could be drawn from this contrast. On the one hand, it might suggest that the existence of a more high-profile local election campaign in much of England had a spillover effect on the turnout in those English districts where local elections were not being held. In that case, the gaps in Table A.1 rather understate the impact of local elections on the turnout.

On the other hand, perhaps turnout in Scotland was depressed for other reasons; after all, there had been a relatively high profile Scottish Parliament election just twelve months earlier. In that event, the first column of Table A.1 might overstate the impact of coincident local elections on the turnout in those areas where a traditional ballot was held, while in addition the final row might overstate the impact of holding a postal ballot. If we exclude Scotland from the table, then amongst areas with a traditional ballot the difference between the turnout where local elections were held everywhere and those where they were held nowhere falls to 5 points, the same gap as in those areas where an all-postal ballot was conducted. At the same time, the apparent impact of holding an all-postal ballot also falls somewhat, though it still stands at as much as 9 points.

Whatever the exact size of the overall impact, holding local elections appears to have made more of a difference in certain kinds of areas than others.

First, it appears to have had more impact in urban areas than in rural ones. The difference in the increase in turnout between those areas with no elections and those with local elections everywhere was around 2 points higher in more urban areas than in more rural ones, irrespective of whether a traditional or an all-postal ballot was held.[7]

Second, local elections also appear to have had rather more impact in those areas where a relatively low proportion of the population had a degree. Here, too, there is a persistent gap in the increase in turnout of just over 2 points. Turnout tends to be relatively low in all kinds of elections both in urban areas and in those with a low proportion holding a degree. But their rather greater readiness to turn out where a local election was held suggests that the pulling power of European elections for people in these areas is particularly low.[8]

There is also some evidence that the impact of an all-postal ballot may have varied a little from one kind of area to another. These ballots appear to have had somewhat more impact on the turnout in those places with a relatively large proportion of routine workers than they did elsewhere. This can be seen in Table A.2 which indicates that the difference in the increase in turnout between those places where an all-postal ballot was held and those where a traditional ballot was conducted was a point or two more in those areas with a relatively large proportion of people in routine manual occupations.[9] Still, this gap is undoubtedly small relative to the apparent impact of all-postal ballots in general and does not suggest that such ballots radically alter the kind of people who are more likely to vote in elections (see also Curtice et al., 2004). In particular, despite claims during the campaign that those living in Asian communities may have been put under undue pressure to return their postal ballots, there is no evidence that turnout increased particularly markedly in those all-postal areas with a relatively large proportion of those who consider themselves to come from an Asian background.

Table A.2   The differential impact of all-postal ballots

| | Change in % voting since 1999 Proportion in routine occupations[a] | |
	Low	High
No local elections:		
Traditional Ballot	+9.1	+6.2
All-Postal Ballot	+18.5	+19.2
Difference	*9.4*	*13.0*
Some local elections:		
Traditional Ballot	+11.3	+11.0
All-Postal Ballot	+20.3	+20.5
Difference	*9.0*	*9.5*
Local elections everywhere:		
Traditional Ballot	+14.7	+15.4
All-Postal Ballot	+22.3	+24.3
Difference	*7.6*	*8.9*

[a] Proportion in routine occupations: High = more than 10% of those aged 16–74 in routine manual occupations; Low = more than 10%.

However, the use of all-postal ballots and the holding of coincident elections were not without partisan consequence. Both were held in areas that were disproportionately Labour in sympathies. The impact of the government's choice of where to hold all-postal ballots can be seen if we assume that turnout was 9 points lower in those regions where an all-postal ballot was held (as our analysis suggests would have happened if a conventional ballot had been held) but that the parties' share of the vote was the same as it actually was. Under this assumption, Labour's share of the national vote would have been 0.4 points lower, while that of the Conservatives' would have been 0.2 points higher.

Meanwhile, the additional impact of holding coincident elections can then be estimated by assuming that turnout would have been 5 points lower in those local authorities where local elections were held (including London), while the share of the vote won by each party was unchanged. This scenario reduces Labour's share of the national vote by another 0.3 points, and adds another 0.2 points to the Conservative tally.[10] Thus, even if we reckon that they had no impact on the share of the vote won by each party in the places where they were used,[11] in combination all-postal ballots and coincident local elections helped add 0.7 points of the vote to Labour's national tally while costing the Conservatives 0.4 points, thereby easing Labour's difficulties a little.[12]

Nor were all-postal ballots and coincident local elections implemented without some apparent confusion. In the four all-postal regions, no less than 1.9% of ballot papers were rejected before being included in the count, while of those included in the count 0.35% more were deemed to be spoilt in these regions than were elsewhere. Spoilt votes were also more common where coincident local elections were held, and especially so where voters were being asked to place more than one cross on the ballot paper in an all-out local council election at the same time as only putting one cross on their European ballot paper. While some people may well have only wanted to vote in their local elections – indeed, where both were held more people cast a valid vote in the local elections than did in the European election (Rallings and Thrasher, 2004b) – it is notable that the incidence of both spoilt and rejected papers was highest in places with relatively high numbers of young people and people without educational qualifications, groups who have less interest in and knowledge of politics (Bromley and Curtice, 2002; Norris, 2002; Parry et al., 1992) and thus are most likely to be confused by more complex voting arrangements.

While all-postal ballots together with local elections may have helped increase turnout, they were not solely responsible for the increase since 1999. As we have seen, turnout still rose by nearly 8 points where neither local elections nor all-postal ballots were held and, indeed, by 10 points where those circumstances pertained in England. If, as seems not unreasonable, these figures can be regarded as a measure of what would have happened across the country as a whole in the absence of local elections and any all-postal ballots, it would appear that turnout would still have been between 31% and 33%, in line with the 32% turnouts recorded in the first two European elections in 1979 and 1984, suggesting that the underlying propensity of the electorate to vote in European elections returned to a level that is normal or typical of European elections.[13] While this hardly indicates a dramatic new interest in matters European amongst the British public, it does appear to signal that the recent marked decline in turnout in general may have begun to be reversed.

The outsiders

We now turn to the first of the two questions that we posed at the beginning of this appendix, that is, to what extent did attitudes towards Europe make a difference? One of the supposed symptoms of a second-order contest, voting for minor parties, was much in evidence. No less than a third of the vote was cast for parties that are not currently represented in the House of Commons, while the two parties that dominate the Commons benches, the Conservatives and Labour, between them won less than half the vote for the first time since the advent of the modern party system.

But the most successful of those parties not currently represented in the House of Commons, the United Kingdom Independence Party (UKIP), was no ordinary minor party. Rather, it was a party for whom Europe, and in particular its wish that Britain should withdraw from the European Union, was its *raison d'être*. It won 16.2% of the vote, up 9.2% from its 7.0% in 1999. It not only beat the Liberal Democrats for third place but also surpassed the previous best performance by a non-Westminster party in a European election, the 14.9% won by the Greens in 1989.

As Table A.3 shows, the party tended to win a particularly high share of the vote in those local authorities where a large proportion of people are self-employed or are aged over 65 and which are located outside the country's urban centres. Even when we allow for this pattern, which operated throughout the country, the party still did particularly well in the southern half of England. Indeed, it did best of all in island and peninsular communities on the south and east coasts of England, areas traditionally popular with older people and where self-employment is relatively common; indeed, the party won no less than 28.8% across Devon and Cornwall, topping the poll. Past survey research suggests that these are just the kinds of patterns one would expect if those voting UKIP were expressing an antipathy towards the European Union.[14] That antipathy is of course often rooted in a strong sense of feeling British or English, sentiments whose relative weakness in Scotland and Wales helps explain UKIP's much lower vote there.

Table A.3 UKIP support, by region and social character of local authority

	% vote UKIP					
	% self-employed[a]		*% aged 65 plus*[b]		*% in agriculture*[c]	
	Low	*High*	*Low*	*High*	*Low*	*High*
Scotland/Wales	7.0	9.3	6.9	8.5	6.6	8.7
North of England[d]	12.7	14.6	12.7	13.9	12.6	13.9
South & Midlands	17.9	22.6	18.5	22.9	17.6	22.5

[a] % self-employed: Low = less than 7.5% of those aged 16–74 in self-employment either as a non-professional small employer or own-account worker; High = more than 7.5%.

[b] % aged 65 plus: Low = less than 16.5% of the population aged 65 or more; High = more than 16.5%.

[c] % in agriculture: Low = less than 1% of those aged 16–74 employed in agriculture (urban); High = more than 1% (rural).

[d] The North of England comprises the three northernmost regions of England. The South & Midlands comprises the rest of England.

The UK Independence Party's vote had displayed much of this character in 1999. But it was even more evident in 2004. As Table A.4 shows, not only was the party's vote higher in areas with more small businessmen, more older people and in more urban areas, but it also increased more in such places between 1999 and 2004. At the same time, as can be seen from Table 5.14 (p. 172), UKIP's strongest advance was in the South and Midlands of England outside London. UKIP's success was, it seems, founded on its ability to recruit those of a Eurosceptic disposition into its ranks even more successfully than it had done five years previously.[15]

Table A.4 UKIP support in 1999 and 2004, by social character of area[ab]

	% vote UKIP					
	% self-employed		*% aged 65 plus*		*% in agriculture*	
	Low	*High*	*Low*	*High*	*Low*	*High*
1999	5.8	8.7	6.2	8.0	5.7	8.0
2004	13.8	19.8	14.7	18.2	13.1	18.7
Change	*+8.0*	*+11.1*	*+8.5*	*+10.2*	*+7.4*	*+10.7*

[a] For definitions see Table A.3.

[b] This table is based on England only.

A key ingredient of that ability appears to have been the candidature of Robert Kilroy-Silk; that at least is the apparent implication of UKIP's performance in the region where he headed the party's list, the East Midlands. The party's vote rose there by 6.5 points more than it did anywhere else. In securing 26.1% of the vote, Mr Kilroy-Silk's list not only outperformed the party's list in the South West, the region where the party had done best in 1999, but came within a whisker of coming top in the region. It was a performance that provided an object lesson to Britain's other political parties, some of which were still accommodating themselves to fighting elections under a multi-candidate list system; it showed how placing a well known popular candidate at the head of a party's list can increase its vote. Even in a closed party list system the popularity of individual candidates can still make a difference (Curtice and Steed, 2000b).[16]

UKIP was far from being the only party not currently represented at Westminster to make a significant advance. Although it failed to win any seats, with 4.9% of the vote, the British National Party secured the highest share of the vote ever won by a far right party in a nationwide election in Britain. It thus built on the success it had secured in some Pennine towns in the 2001 General Election and in subsequent local elections. But while the BNP, like UKIP, would like to see Britain withdraw from the European Union, its defining characteristic is antipathy to immigration, particularly by those from non-white and non-Christian backgrounds. The geographical character of its vote reflected this very different appeal. As can be seen from Table A.5, the party did best in working-class constituencies where many lack educational qualifications; the kind of characteristics associated with illiberal views on social issues. It did not share UKIP's success amongst small business communities and older people in shire England, though it shared its relative weakness in Scotland.

Table A.5   BNP support, by social character of local authority[a]

| | % vote BNP | | |
	% routine manual workers[b]	% no educational qualifications[c]	% employed in agriculture[d]
Low	3.8	3.8	5.7
High	6.4	6.7	4.0

[a] This table is based on England only.
[b] % routine manual workers: Low = less than 10% of those aged 16–74 in routine manual occupations; High = More than 10%.
[c] % no educational qualifications; Low = less than 32% of those aged 16–74 have no educational qualifications; High = more than 32%.
[d] % in agriculture: Low = less than 1% of those aged 16–74 employed in agriculture (urban); High = more than 1% (rural).

Table A.5 does not, however, adequately identify the areas where the BNP secured its strongest support. As in recent local elections this was in a number of towns and cities in the north of England where there is a substantial ethnic minority population. The BNP won no less than 9.0% of the vote in the 20 local authorities in the north of England with the highest non-white populations, and especially those with substantial Asian ones. Its largest share of the vote (16.7%) was achieved in Burnley, the site of its most significant local election successes. This pattern of higher support in areas of ethnic concentrations was also apparent in the West Midlands. But the BNP was particularly unsuccessful in places in the south of England with high ethnic minority populations, most notably in London where the party won just 4.0% of the vote. It appears that the politicisation of racial tensions in Britain is at present very much confined to one part of the country. At the same time the relative success of the BNP in the north of England indicates that getting more people to vote through the use of all-postal ballots is not an effective way of limiting its success.

In contrast to UKIP and the BNP, the Greens did not make any significant advance at all on their 1999 vote of 6%. This though was still enough to enable them to retain their status as Britain's fifth largest party in European elections. The party did best where a relatively large proportion of the population had a degree as well as in local authorities with a relatively young population. This was if anything even more true than it was in 1999. Evidently the party continued to profit from the support of Britain's younger and better educated citizens, amongst whom concern about the environment and sustainability is greatest (Bryson and Curtice, 1998; Bromley and Curtice, 1999).

Much of the far left in England and Wales was brought together under the umbrella of the Respect coalition, led by the expelled Labour MP, George Galloway, and campaigning on a platform that emphasised opposition to Britain's involvement in the Iraq War. It made only limited headway, winning just 1.7% of the vote in England and Wales. In contrast, its nearest equivalent in Scotland, the Scottish Socialist Party, led by Tommy Sheridan, secured as much as 5.2% of the vote north of the border. But Respect's anti-war platform evidently had a strong appeal amongst the country's Muslim community. The larger the Muslim population, the more votes Respect secured; it won as much as 7.4% in those local authorities where over 10% of the population regard themselves as Muslim. The presence of other ethnic minorities also had a modestly positive impact on Respect's vote. As a result, the party's vote was far higher in the country's most ethnically diverse region, London; within London itself the party's highest votes were secured in the two boroughs, Newham (21.7%) and Tower Hamlets (20.8%), which between them have the largest ethnic minority and the largest Muslim population anywhere in Britain.

So if UKIP's advance was apparently an expression of views about Europe, votes cast for the other parties not currently represented at Westminster were less evidently a reflection of such views. Respect's advance, albeit a very limited one, was probably the product of discontent with the UK government's foreign policy. The BNP and the Greens meanwhile expressed the views of distinctive social and ideological communities that are largely not defined with reference to 'Europe'. The willingness of voters to vote for Respect, the BNP and the Greens might perhaps have been enhanced both by the use of a proportional electoral system and by a feeling that European elections do not matter. But even if this were the case, the distinctive social geography of their support suggests that their voters were not indulging in any ill-considered experimental whim, but rather were reflecting some important social and ideological divisions in British society.

The Westminster parties

A second classic symptom (if not a proof) of second-order elections, that governing parties lose votes, was very much in evidence at this election. With just 22.6% of the vote, Labour won a lower share of the vote than any previous British governing party had secured in a European election. Indeed, it was Labour's worst performance in a nationwide poll since it first started fighting elections on a widespread basis in 1918. Amongst governing parties across Europe, only the German Social Democrats and the Polish Social Democrats suffered a bigger reverse (–19.4%) compared with the last General Election.

Moreover, as in 1999, when the party won only 28.0% of the nationwide poll, Labour's vote fell most heavily in places where it usually had done relatively well (Curtice and Steed, 2000a). But there was also a striking difference between the pattern of Labour losses this time around and what happened in 1999. Then Labour's vote fell most heavily compared with the previous General Election in seats with a relatively large working class. It appeared as though 'traditional' Labour supporters were using the election to protest against the apparently less than traditional character of Tony Blair's government. This time, in contrast, Labour lost ground just as heavily in places where middle-class voters are relatively common.

These points are illustrated in Table A.6 which shows the pattern of the change in Labour's vote in England since 1999 and 2001 according to, first, how well Labour did in 1999, and second, the class composition of an area. Compared with 1999, let alone 2001, Labour's vote clearly fell more in places where it had more 1999 votes to defend (doubtless in part because in some places where the party is weak it simply had few votes left to lose). Compared with 2001 this happened largely irrespective of the class composition of the area. But in contrast, compared with 1999, Labour's vote actually fell more heavily in relatively middle-class areas; that is, the kind of place where Labour's vote had held up rather better five years previously.

Table A.6 Change in Labour vote since 1999/2001, by past Labour vote and class character of area[a]

% professionals and managers[b]	*Labour % vote 1999*			
	Less than 20%	*20–30%*	*30–40%*	*More than 40%*
Change in % vote since 1999:				
Low	−3.4	−5.5	−7.5	−10.2
High	−4.6	−7.2	−9.0	−11.5
All	−4.4	−6.9	−8.0	−10.6
Change in % vote since 2001:				
Low	−8.4	−20.9	−25.0	−27.5
High	−12.5	−19.2	−25.3	−24.7
All	−11.5	−19.5	−25.1	−26.7

[a] This table is based on England only.
[b] % professionals and managers: Low = less than 25% of those aged 16–74 in professional or managerial occupations, 2001 Census; High = more than 25%.

So it appears that Labour supporters in more working-class areas defected to an even greater extent than they had done five years earlier. But this time they were joined by those in more middle-class areas. These latter areas contain the kind of people to whom 'New Labour' rather than 'Old Labour' should have a particular appeal. It appears that their support for the party had now been significantly weakened.

If Labour found it relatively difficult to retain the support of one supposedly 'New Labour' constituency, it also had some particular difficulty in maintaining its support amongst a more traditional one. We have already noted the relative success of Respect in areas with large Muslim populations. It appears to have secured that support particularly at Labour's expense. As Table A.7 shows, even after we take into account Labour's prior strength, the party's vote fell rather more in those areas with a relatively high Muslim population. It is likely that some voters in these areas used the election as an opportunity to protest against the government's involvement in the war against Iraq.

Two parts of the country where Labour usually polls well, however, stayed relatively loyal to the party. In Wales, Labour's share of the vote was actually slightly higher than it had been in 1999. The 1999 election occurred just a month after the party received a severe drubbing in the Welsh Assembly election, a result that was then echoed in the outcome of the European election. The rather better Labour performance in the principality this time confirmed the impression given by the outcome of the 2003 Assembly election that the party has now recovered from the adverse effect of the allegations made in 1999 that the Labour leadership in London had attempted to exercise undue influence on who was to be Labour's leader in the Assembly. Meanwhile, Plaid Cymru's vote fell by no less than 12 points compared with 1999, dropping most in the South Wales valleys where it had performed particularly well in the Assembly and European elections of 1999.

Table A.7 Change in Labour vote since 1999, by past Labour vote and Muslim composition[a]

| % Muslim[b] | Change in % Labour vote since 1999 Labour % vote 1999 | | | |
	Less than 20%	*20–30%*	*30–40%*	*More than 40%*
Low	−4.4	−6.8	−7.5	−9.2
High	–	−8.2	−8.7	−12.8

[a] This table is based on England only.

[b] % Muslim: Low = less than 5% of the population identify themselves as Muslim; High = more than 5%.

In Scotland, Labour's vote fell less than it did in any region of England. Here, too, the party seems to have profited from a decline in support for the nationalists. Indeed, the SNP's vote fell below 20% in a nationwide contest for the first time since 1987. Given that the nationalist parties have usually done relatively well in European elections this was a particularly disappointing result for the SNP; it was the first time that the party's European vote was lower than it had been in the previous Westminster election. Within days, the leader of the party, John Swinney, had decided to resign (see Chapter 6).

The Liberal Democrats have long been regarded as a party of protest (Alt et al., 1977). At this election their opposition to the war in Iraq arguably left them rather better placed than the Conservatives to profit from any antipathy to Britain's military involvement. Dissatisfaction with the government certainly seems to have been part of the explanation for the 2 point increase in the party's support compared with 1999. As Table A.8 shows, the party made most progress compared with 1999 in just those places where Labour lost most ground – in places where Labour won more votes in 1999, and especially in areas with a relatively large Muslim community.

Table A.8 Change in Liberal Democrat vote since 1999, by past Labour vote and Muslim composition[a]

| % Muslim[b] | Change in % Liberal Democrat vote since 1999 Labour % vote 1999 | | | |
	Less than 20%	*20–30%*	*30–40%*	*More than 40%*
Low	+1.0	+1.6	+1.2	+3.4
High	–	+1.9	+3.4	+5.8
All	+1.0	+1.7	+2.1	+4.3

[a] This table is based on England only.

[b] % Muslim: Low = less than 5% of the population identify themselves as Muslim; High = more than 5%.

Despite apparently profiting from anti-government protest, this election once again demonstrated that European elections are relatively difficult terrain for the Liberal Democrats. As at every previous European election, the party's share of the vote was lower than it had been at the previous General Election. As in 1999, the party's vote was particularly down on its General Election score in those areas where it had done best in Westminster contests, with Labour the principal beneficiary, a pattern that confirms the importance of local campaigning and tactical anti-Conservative support to the Liberal Democrats' ability to win seats at a General Election.

Even more remarkable, however, was the contrast between the Liberal Democrat performance in the European election with that in the local elections held on the same day. Although local elections might be considered to be just as much a 'second-order' election as a European election (but see Heath et al., 1999) and thus just as much an opportunity to cast a protest vote against the government, the Liberal Democrats fared far better in the local elections. For example, across 66 provincial English councils where most of the component local election contests were fought by all three main parties, the Liberal Democrat share of the vote was on average no less than 12.5 points lower in the European elections than it was in the local elections.[17] While some of this difference reflects the fact that far more voters had the opportunity to vote for UKIP, the Greens, or some other smaller party in the European elections than they did in the local elections, the gap between the Liberal Democrats' European and local election performance was greater than that of the Conservatives (8 points) and Labour (a little under 4 points).[18] Evidently, many a voter willing to vote for the Liberal Democrats in local elections was then reluctant to support the party in European elections. This suggests that there is antipathy amongst some Liberal Democrat supporters to the party's relatively pro-European stance.

Meanwhile, in contrast to the Liberal Democrats, Britain's other opposition party, the Conservatives, suffered a drop in support compared with the previous European election, falling by as much as 9 points. This was the first time that support for the principal opposition party was down on its performance at the previous European election. The pattern of the Conservative drop was striking. In 1999 and 2001 the party had performed relatively well in areas with a relatively large proportion of older people and relatively few with a degree. These were just the kind of places where the emphasis given by the party's then leader, William Hague, to opposition to adoption of the euro and to a relatively conservative stance on moral issues and on social questions such as asylum seekers would be expected to be particularly attractive (Curtice and Steed, 2000a; Curtice and Steed, 2002). At this election, as Table A.9 shows, these were just the kinds of places where Conservative support fell most heavily.

Table A.9 Change in Conservative share of the vote, by social composition of area[a]

| | Change in % Conservative vote | | | | | |
| | *% with a degree*[b] | | *% aged 65 plus*[c] | | *% self-employed*[d] | |
	Low	High	Low	High	Low	High
Since 1999	−11.1	−9.1	−9.1	−10.9	−9.5	−10.5
Since 2001	−7.2	−6.5	−6.0	−8.0	−5.4	−9.1

[a] This table is based on England only.
[b] % with a degree: Low = less than 17% of those aged 16–74 have a degree; High = more than 17%.
[c] % aged 65 plus: Low = less than 16.5% of the population aged 65 or more; High = more than 16.5%.
[d] % self-employed: Low = less than 7.5% of those aged 16–74 in self-employment either as a non-profession small employer or own-account worker; High = more than 7.5%.

We can see too from Table A.9 that support for the Conservatives also fell somewhat more in areas with relatively large numbers of people in non-professional self-employment. Meanwhile, as Table A.4 showed, such areas, together with those with relatively large numbers of older people, were just the kinds of places where UKIP was most successful. This clearly suggests that one key reason why the Conservative vote fell was because the party lost support to UKIP. Perhaps the latter's more avowedly anti-European stance had more appeal for a largely Eurosceptic Conservative electorate than did the Conservatives' own more measured criticisms of the operation of the European Union.

The UK Independence Party undoubtedly prospered most in areas where the Conservatives have usually polled relatively well. UKIP's share of the vote rose compared with 1999 by only 5.2 points where the Conservatives won less than 20% of the vote in 1999, but by as much as 12.0 points where the Conservative tally had previously been over 45%. But if this meant that UKIP was winning votes from the Conservatives it should also be the case that the Conservative vote fell most where UKIP performed best. Table A.10 shows that this was indeed the case. Compared with 1999, the Conservative vote decreased by 4.5 points more in those places where UKIP's vote rose by more than 10 points than it did where UKIP's vote rose by less than 6 points. A similar analysis of the fall in Conservative support since 2001 produces an equivalent gap of no less than 8.5 points. However, the same table also suggests that, contrary to what was assumed by many commentators, UKIP's success did not just damage the Conservatives but also damaged the Liberal Democrats. Compared with 1999, their vote increased by 3.6 points less where UKIP's vote rose most, compared with where it rose least, while there is also a 5.5 point gap in an equivalent analysis of change since 2001.[19] In contrast, it is evident that a strong UKIP performance did not particularly hurt Labour at all.

Table A.10   Party performance, by UKIP performance

UKIP	Con	Lab	Lib Dem
Change in % share of vote since 1999:			
Up less than 6	−6.4	−7.1	+4.5
Up 6–8	−7.3	−5.6	+2.4
Up 8–10	−9.7	−6.0	+1.7
Up more than 10	−10.9	−6.7	+0.9
Change in % share of vote since 2001:			
Up less than 11	−1.0	−21.0	−1.1
Up 11–14	−4.9	−22.2	−2.4
Up 14–17	−7.7	−18.8	−4.7
Up more than 17	−9.5	−18.5	−6.6

The Conservatives suffered from the rise of UKIP, but so also did the Liberal Democrats, perhaps in not dissimilar measure. The latter's vulnerability to UKIP's Eurosceptic appeal would certainly appear to be consistent with its persistent difficulty in winning votes in European elections as compared with both local and General Elections. In any event, it looks as though we can conclude that both of Britain's main opposition parties lost some votes at least because of hostility towards Europe amongst those who might otherwise have been expected to support them.[20] In contrast, Labour's woes appear to have little to do with Europe; it seems to have been vulnerable to mid-term protest voting, not least over Iraq.

The electoral system

As in 1999, the use of a regional d'Hondt method of proportional representation produced an outcome that could only be described as approximately proportional. This can be seen in Table A.11 which compares the proportion of the vote won by each party in Great Britain with the proportion of seats that each party won under the current system together with what would have happened if various alternative forms of proportional representation had been in place. As is typical of what happens when the d'Hondt divisor is used and the country is divided up into a number of different regions, the Conservatives as the largest party secured a substantially higher proportion (9.3%) of seats than it did votes. At the other end of the spectrum, the Greens were again under-represented, while the BNP failed to win any seats at all despite winning nearly 5% of the vote.

Table A.11   Outcome under alternative electoral systems

			% seats Method of allocation			
	% vote	Actual	Modified Sainte-Laguë	Pure Sainte-Laguë	National PR[a]	1999 seats
Con	26.7	36.0	34.7	30.7	28.0	32.1
Lab	22.6	25.3	24.0	24.0	24.0	29.8
UKIP	16.2	16.0	17.3	17.3	17.3	16.7
Lib Dem	14.9	16.0	17.3	17.3	16.0	15.5
Green	6.2	2.7	2.7	5.3	6.7	2.4
BNP	4.9	0.0	0.0	2.7	4.0	0.0
Respect	1.5	0.0	0.0	0.0	1.3	0.0
SNP	1.4	2.7	2.7	1.3	1.3	2.4
PC	1.0	1.3	1.3	1.3	0.0	1.2
Others	4.9	0.0	0.0	0.0	0.0	0.0
Deviation[b]	–	15.4	14.7	9.2	6.3	15.0

[a]   National PR assumes use of the d'Hondt method of allocation.
[b]   Deviation is the sum of the differences between % votes and % seats divided by two.

The reduction in the number of seats from 84 to 75 (leaving Northern Ireland's three seats to one side) together with their reallocation between the regions to bring them in line with their current electorates proved particularly costly for the Labour Party. Despite coming second in votes they were only slightly over-represented in seats. This was because Labour was unfortunate enough to be runner-up for the last seat in no less than seven of the eleven regions (a fate that in contrast did not befall the Conservatives anywhere). If, however, each region had had the same number of seats as it did in 1999, in six of these regions Labour would have secured the extra last seat, an outcome that, as the last column of Table A.11 shows, would have ensured that Labour was significantly over-represented. Nevertheless, as we would expect from previous research on electoral systems (Lijphart, 1994), having more seats as in 1999 would still have resulted in a slightly more proportional outcome, as measured by the index of deviation (Loosemore and Hanby, 1971).

Even greater proportionality would, however, have been achieved if either a different system of allocating seats or a national rather than a regional list system had been used. In allocating seats to regions for this election, the Electoral Commission decided after a process of consultation to use the Sainte-Laguë (or Webster) method of allocation, the most proportional of the divisor methods of allocating seats (Electoral Commission, 2003b; McLean and Mortimore, 1992). If this same method had also been used to allocate seats to votes, the level of disproportionality would have been cut by just over a third. Meanwhile, as previous research would lead one to expect (Lijphart, 1994), changing from a regional to a national list system would have produced an even more proportional result than would switching the method of allocation.[21]

However, one of the criticisms that is sometimes levelled at highly proportional electoral systems is that they can make it too easy for extremist parties to secure representation (Hermens, 1941), though it might be noted that the BNP has been able to secure some representation under the plurality rule in recent local elections (Electoral Reform Society, 2004). Table A.11 indicates that the BNP would indeed have secured representation if either the Sainte-Laguë method of allocation had been used or if a national list system had been operating. However, as implemented in some Scandinavian countries, Sainte-Laguë has been modified to make it rather more difficult for a party to secure its first seat (Carstairs, 1980), and this modification[22] would in fact have been sufficient to deny the BNP representation, albeit at the expense of losing almost all the increase in proportionality that the use of Sainte-Laguë would otherwise have produced. Equally, under a national list system, the introduction of a requirement that a party win 5% of the vote before being allocated any seats would also have been enough, albeit only just enough, to deny the BNP any representation.

Conclusion

We have addressed two main questions in this appendix. The first was to consider whether the outcome simply reflected domestic considerations or whether people's views about Britain's relationship with Europe also made a difference. The second was to assess the impact of the use of all-postal ballots and coincident local elections on the turnout.

People's views about Europe did appear to make a difference at this election. The success of UKIP was concentrated in just those kinds of places where the public is more likely to hold critical views about Europe. In securing this result the party appears to have been particularly successful in appealing to a section of the electorate that at the last European election had been attracted to the Conservatives by that party's Eurosceptical stance. At the same time, UKIP appears also to have won votes that might otherwise have been secured by the Liberal Democrats, who once again found European elections particularly difficult terrain; indeed, the party did much less well than it did in local elections held on the same day.

In short, this election served to register the significantly Eurosceptic mood of the British public at present (European Commission, 2004a; Evans, 2003). That same public also demonstrated its relative disinterest in matters European. Although more people voted than in any previous European election, once the impact of all-postal ballots and coincident local elections is allowed for, it appears that turnout simply returned to the norm for European elections, a norm that would still have left Britain at the bottom of the turnout league amongst the 15 older member states of the European Union. Also, the fact that around 5% more people reckoned it was worth voting if a local election was held locally confirms that what happens in Brussels is still thought to be of less import by many people than what happens in their local town hall.

Domestic politics also played a role. The fall in Labour support appears to have had little to do with its stance on Europe and much to do with dissatisfaction with the performance of the government amongst its previous supporters. Part of that dissatisfaction appears to have been engendered by opposition to Britain's involvement in Iraq, most clearly demonstrated by Labour's losses and gains for both the Liberal Democrats and Respect in areas with a large Muslim population. And while people might be more willing to vote for smaller parties in European elections, especially now that a system of proportional representation is in place (albeit one that still discriminates significantly against smaller parties), at the same time the differences in the pattern of support for those parties suggests that each of them was mobilising distinct strands of domestic public opinion.

Moreover, the election has demonstrated two important developments in British domestic politics. The first is that dissatisfaction with the Labour government may no longer be concentrated amongst the party's more traditional working-class supporters but is now to be found amongst its more middle-class supporters as well. In contrast to 1999, Labour struggled to win votes in more middle-class areas as well as in more working-class ones. But defeat for Labour in 1999 was followed by a second large majority in 2001. Whether Labour's losses this time around again prove to be no more than a classic 'second-order' protest remains to be seen.

The second important development is that the decline in turnout that was first registered after the 1997 General Election appears for the time being at least to have been substantially reversed. After we take into account the use of all-postal ballots and coincident local elections, voters seemed as inclined to vote in this election as they had been in most European elections between 1979 and 1994. This would seem to corroborate the claim that recent low turnouts have been the product of political circumstance rather than any growth of apathy on the part of the electorate, a situation that in part at least may have disappeared with the vanishing of Labour's large opinion poll lead over the Conservatives (Bromley and Curtice, 2002).

At the same time the election confirmed that the use of all-postal ballots can increase turnout in low-profile elections substantially, although the effect was somewhat lower than in most previous local election pilots. The greater use of postal voting does come at some cost, that is, an increase in apparently inadvertently spoilt ballots, while the Electoral Commission detected some public antipathy to being required to vote by post, an antipathy that led the Commission to conclude that all-postal ballots of the kind deployed to date should not be held in future (Electoral Commission, 2004a). But it would appear that if politicians do wish to increase the turnout in low-profile elections, then they will still wish to introduce a procedure that makes it likely that most people opt to vote by post.

On the experience of this election they may also be inclined to ensure that future European elections coincide with local elections. Doing so also appears to result in rather more spoilt ballots, particularly when voters are asked to cast different numbers of votes on different ballot papers. But perhaps a more serious objection is that if a European election coincides with local elections in some places but not in others, one party could secure some partisan advantage. Measures that make it easier for all voters to vote may be thought desirable, but those that encourage some rather than others to do so are clearly more debatable.

Acknowledgement

We are deeply indebted to Philip Mitchell for assistance in developing the database of 'areas' used in this appendix.

Notes

1. Gibraltar is excluded from our analysis throughout. The outcome in Northern Ireland is also not included here.
2. Of these 164 areas, 40 comprise a single constituency, 62 comprise 2 or 3, and 62 comprise 4 or more. Only in 4 cases (Tyne & Wear, 13 constituencies; Birmingham, 11; Humberside, 10; and a group of 4 boroughs in the east of Greater Manchester, 10) do they comprise 10 or more seats.
3. It should also be noted that the outcome of the election in Scotland and Wales is sufficiently distinctive in a number of respects that our analyses of what happened in 2004 or of change since previous elections are sometimes confined to local authorities or areas in England. This is indicated in the relevant tables.

   Information on the social characteristics of 'areas' and local authorities comes from the 2001 Census (Office for National Statistics, 2003a, 2003b).
4. Thanks to a 51.2% turnout in Northern Ireland, turnout in the United Kingdom as a whole was 38.9%, just enough in fact to overtake Portugal (38.7%) as well.
5. This appears to have been a point that was insufficiently appreciated by the Electoral Commission in its assessment of the impact of the all-postal ballots on turnout in 2004. Although it reported the difference between the change in turnout since 1999 in the four pilot regions and elsewhere as well as the level of turnout in 2004, more emphasis is given to the latter (Electoral Commission, 2004a, pp. 6, 29–30). Note that in contrast to the Commission, our figures for turnout exclude invalid votes.
6. One likely explanation for the lower impact was the fact that voters were required to return a countersigned declaration of identity, a requirement that had been dispensed with in a number of previous all-postal ballots.
7. Urban areas are defined as those with less than 1% of those aged 16–74 employed in agriculture. Rural areas are the remainder. Note that the results of this and other analyses in this appendix of differences between urban and rural areas are confirmed if, where it is possible, we use a measure of population density rather than percentage employed in agriculture. The findings reported in this paragraph are also supported by more formal multivariate analysis in which both percentage employed in agriculture and percentage with a degree are entered as interval level variables.
8. It might have been thought that turnout would have increased particularly sharply in those areas where an all-out local election was held, and thus overall control of the council was more evidently at stake. Of this, however, there is no sign.
9. As we might anticipate if we exclude Scotland from this table, the difference where no local elections were held falls to 10.0 in areas with a relatively high proportion of those in routine occupations, but this is still higher than the equivalent figure of 8.6 for those areas with a relatively low proportion of routine manual workers.
10. We have seen that all-postal ballots appear to have had a slightly greater impact in areas with relatively high numbers of people in routine occupations, while coincident local elections did so in more urban areas with relatively low proportions of people with a degree. All of these characteristics are associated with a higher

Labour vote, so the figures in this paragraph in fact probably slightly underestimate the advantage that Labour derived.

11. In practice we have been unable to uncover any systematic evidence that higher turnouts advantage one party over another.

12. Under our assumptions, the use of all-postal ballots could not of course have made any difference to the outcome in seats, as in each case postal ballots were held across a whole region. But in the regions in England outside London, coincident local elections were held in some parts of a region but not others. As coincident local elections differentially increased the turnout in predominantly Labour areas, their use could potentially have helped Labour win a seat. In practice Labour did not win the last seat in any region and so it is unlikely that holding coincident local elections helped Labour win any seats. But there evidently is some possibility that a party might derive a partisan advantage in seats if a future European election were to be held at the same time as local elections in some local authorities within a region but not in others.

13. We should note that this was the first European election at which, even in an area where a traditional ballot was being held, any voter could vote by post on demand. Early evidence suggests that nearly 1 in 10 voters were registered to vote by post, compared with 1.3% in 1999, and that such voters were around 30% more likely to have voted (Electoral Commission, 2004a; Rallings and Thrasher, 2000). If it were the case that in the absence of postal voting on demand the level of turnout amongst these voters would have been the same as that amongst the rest of the electorate, then this 30% increase could have been responsible for at least 2 points of the increase in turnout in places with a traditional ballot. This would then suggest that the underlying propensity of the electorate to vote is still not quite at the levels of 1979 and 1984. However, it seems likely that those who have made the effort to register by post consist disproportionately of those who are inclined to vote anyway, and thus the net contribution of postal voting demand to the level of turnout in places with traditional ballots was rather less than 2 points.

14. For example, according to the 2003 British Social Attitudes survey, 24% of those aged over 65 would like Britain to leave the European Union while only 7% of those aged under 35 take that view. Equally, 27% of those in non-professional self-employment want Britain to withdraw, more than any other occupational group. On the geographical distribution of attitudes towards Europe see Curtice (1996).

15. Indeed, the resulting geographical concentration of its support means that UKIP could well win seats in the Commons should it repeat its performance at this election in a UK General Election.

16. We might also note the relative success of two independent candidates. Martin Bell, a former television reporter who was elected Independent MP for Tatton in 1997, won 6.3% of the vote in the Eastern region, performing particularly well in the two counties on which his campaign was focused, Norfolk (9.3%) and Suffolk (8.2%). Meanwhile, Neil Herron, a greengrocer who was once convicted for refusing to use metric weights and measures, won 5.1% of the vote in the North East and no less than 16.5% in his home city of Sunderland. No doubt Mr Herron also tapped into Eurosceptic sentiment; it is certainly noticeable that UKIP's vote increased less in the North East than in any other region of Britain.

17. Note that in a minority of cases there was no local election in a small number of wards in the local authority.

18. A similar but much smaller difference can also be observed in London where the smaller parties did fight the 'local' Mayoral and Assembly election as well as the European election. The Liberal Democrats' share of the European vote was 1.6 points lower than on the Assembly list vote and 3.1 points lower than on the constituency vote. That these differences are smaller probably reflects the fact that the Liberal Democrats also find it more difficult to win votes in London Assembly elections than they do in local borough elections in the capital. The party won as much as 20.6% of the votes cast in the 2002 London Borough elections, nearly 4 points higher than on the London-wide Assembly vote, despite not fighting all the wards.

19. The impact of UKIP's success on the Conservatives' performance can also be seen if we compare the outcome in the local and the European elections. We can divide a set of 66 provincial English councils where most of the wards were fought by all three main parties, into two groups, those where UKIP's vote was at least 14 points higher in the European elections than in the local elections, and those where the gap was smaller. Amongst the former group, the Conservatives' share of the vote was as much as 12 points lower in the European elections than in the local elections, while amongst the latter it was only 5.2 points lower. Although at the same time this analysis only produces a 1.3 point difference in the Liberal Democrat performance in the two kinds of local authority, this appears to reflect the fact that those places where UKIP performed less well were often places where the Liberal Democrats are relatively strong in local elections; the local Liberal Democrat vote tended to fall off in the European elections in such places, irrespective of how well UKIP performed. We might also note that in London, where UKIP's share of the European vote was 3.9 points higher than its share of the list vote in the London Assembly election, the Conservatives' European tally was 1.7 points lower than its Assembly list vote, the Liberal Democrats' European vote 1.6 points lower, while Labour's share was just 0.3 points lower.

20. We should note, however, that the Conservatives in particular may also have suffered most from the advance of the BNP, whose appeal tapped into broader concerns about immigration rather than about Europe in particular. We have already seen that the BNP did particularly well and the Conservatives lost ground relatively heavily in places with high numbers of people with no educational qualifications. Meanwhile, the Conservative vote fell by 2.3 points more in areas where the BNP vote was up on 1999 by 3 points or more than it did in areas where the BNP advanced by less than that. The equivalent figure for Labour is only 0.6 points while the Liberal Democrats actually did slightly better where the BNP did relatively well.

21. Note that if both Sainte-Laguë and a national list system had been in place, the outcome would have been even more proportional. In particular, under this method of allocation Plaid Cymru would still have secured a seat.

22. This modification consists of using the divisors 1.4, 3, 5, and so on, rather than 1, 3, 5, and so on.

Bibliography

Alt, J., Crewe, I. and Särlvik, B. (1977), 'Angels in plastic: Liberal support in 1974', *Political Studies*, Vol. 25: 343–68

Azmanova, A. (2004), *Electoral Dynamics in Europe at the Beginning of the Century: A Right-Wing Alignment?*, European Policy Centre, Brussels

Ballinger, C. (2002), 'The Local Battle, the Cyber Battle', in D. Butler and D. Kavanagh, *The British General Election of 2001*, Palgrave Macmillan, Basingstoke

Blondel, J., Sinnot, R. and Svensson, F. (1994), *Institutions and Attitudes: Towards an Understanding of Low Turnout in the European Elections of 1994*, European University Institute, Working Paper No. 96/19, Florence

Blondel, J., Sinnot, R. and Svensson, F. (1998), *People and Parliament in the European Union: Participation, Democracy and Legitimacy*, Clarendon Press, Oxford

Bogdanor, V. (2004), 'The Eurosceptic Constitution', *E!Sharp*, September

Bowler, S. and Farrell, D.M. (1993), 'Legislator shirking and voter monitoring: impacts of European Parliament electoral systems upon legislator–voter relationships', *Journal of Common Market Studies*, Vol. 31, No. 1

Brockington, D., Rallings, C. and Thrasher, M. (2005), *Local Electoral Cycles and Turnout*, University of Plymouth mimeo

Bromley, C. and Curtice, J. (1999), 'Is There a Third Way?', in R. Jowell, J. Curtice, A. Park and K. Thomson (eds), *British Social Attitudes: The 16th Report: Who Shares New Labour Values?*, Ashgate, Aldershot

Bromley, C. and Curtice, J. (2002), 'Where Have All the Voters Gone?', in A. Park, J. Curtice, K. Thomson, L. Jarvis and C. Bromley (eds), *British Social Attitudes: The 19th Report*, Sage, London

Bryson, C. and Curtice, J. (1998), 'The End of Materialism?', in R. Jowell, J. Curtice, A. Park, L. Brook, K. Thomson and C. Bryson (eds), *British Social Attitudes: The 15th Report: How Britain Differs*, Ashgate, Aldershot

Butler, D. (1995), *British General Elections since 1945* (2nd edn) Blackwell, Oxford

Butler, D. and Butler, G. (2000), *Twentieth Century British Political Facts, 1900–2000*, Macmillan, Basingstoke

Butler, D. and Kavanagh, D. (1997), *The British General Election of 1997*, Macmillan, Basingstoke

Butler, D. and Kavanagh, D. (2002), *The British General Election of 2001*, Palgrave Macmillan, Basingstoke

Butler, D. and Marquand, D. (1980), *European Elections and British Politics*, Macmillan, London

Butler, D. and Rose, R. (1960), *The British General Election of 1959*, Macmillan, London

Butler, D. and Westlake, M. (1995), *British Politics and European Elections 1994*, Macmillan, Basingstoke

Butler, D. and Westlake, M. (2000), *British Politics and European Elections 1999*, Macmillan, Basingstoke

Carstairs, A. (1980), *A Short History of Electoral Systems in Western Europe*, Allen and Unwin, London

Coleman, S. (ed.) (2002), *2001: Cyber Space Odyssey: The Internet in the UK Election*, Hansard Society, London

Coleman, S. and Spiller, J. (2003), 'Exploring new media effects on representative democracy', *Journal of Legislative Studies*, Vol. 9, No. 3, Autumn

Corbett, R. (2004a), *The EU Constitution in Fact and Fiction – A Response to Gisela Stuart*, Labour Movement for Europe, Leeds

Corbett, R. (2004b), *The New European Union Constitution: 1. What it Says; 2. What it Changes; 3. Exploding the Myths*, Britain in Europe, London, Autumn

Corbett, R., Jacobs, F. and Shackleton, M. (2003a), *The European Parliament* (5th edn), John Harper, London

Corbett, R., Jacobs, F. and Shackleton, M. (2003b), 'The European Parliament at fifty: a view from the inside', *Journal of Common Market Studies*, Vol. 41, No. 2, April

Cowles, M. Green and Dinan, D. (eds) (2004), *Developments in the European Union*, Palgrave Macmillan, Basingstoke

Cox, M. (2003), 'When trust matters: explaining differences in voter turnout', *Journal of Common Market Studies*, Vol. 41, No. 4, September

Curtice, J. (1996), 'One Nation Again?', in R. Jowell, J. Curtice, A. Park, L. Brook and K. Thomson (eds), *British Social Attitudes: The 13th Report*, Dartmouth, Aldershot

Curtice, J., Boon, M. and Rustin, M. (2004), *Public Opinion and the 2004 Electoral Pilot Schemes*, Electoral Commission, London

Curtice, J. and Steed, M. (2000a), 'Appendix: An Analysis of the Results', in D. Butler and M. Westlake, *British Politics and European Elections 1999*, Macmillan, Basingstoke

Curtice, J. and Steed, M. (2000b), 'And now for the Commons? Lessons from Britain's first experience with proportional representation', *British Elections and Parties Review*, Vol. 10: 192–215

Curtice, J. and Steed, M. (2002), 'Appendix 2: The Results Analysed', in D. Butler and D. Kavanagh, *The British General Election of 2001*, Palgrave Macmillan, Basingstoke

Dalton, R., McAllister, I. and Wattenburg, M. (2002), 'The Consequences of Party Dealignment', in R. Dalton and M. Wattenburg (eds), *Parties Without Partisans*, Oxford University Press, Oxford

Dehousse, F., Coussens, W. and Grevi, G. (2004), *Integrating Europe: Multiple Speeds – One Direction?*, European Policy Centre, Working Paper No. 9, Brussels, April

Denver, D. and Hands, G. (1997), 'Turnout', in P. Norris and N. Gavin (eds), *Britain Votes 1997*, Oxford University Press, Oxford

Denver, D. and Hands, G. (2004), 'Exploring variations in turnout: constituencies and wards in the Scottish Parliament elections of 1999 and 2003', *British Journal of Politics and International Relations*, Vol. 6, No. 4: 527–42

Denver, D. and McAllister, I. (1999), 'The Scottish Parliament elections 1999: an analysis of the results', *Scottish Affairs*, Vol. 28

Department for Constitutional Affairs (2004), *Voters & Voting Insight Project: Phase 1 Report*, 7 September

Dunleavy, P., Margetts, H. and van Heerde, J. (2004), 'Political Alignments in the 2004 London Elections'. Paper presented to EPOP conference, Oxford University, September

Electoral Commission (2002), *Modernising Elections*, Electoral Commission, London, July

Electoral Commission (2003a), *The Shape of Elections to Come*, Electoral Commission, London, August

Electoral Commission (2003b), *Distribution between Electoral Regions of UK MEPs*, Electoral Commission, London

Electoral Commission (2004a), *Delivering Democracy? The Future of Postal Voting*, Electoral Commission, London

Electoral Commission (2004b), *The 2004 European Parliamentary Elections in the United Kingdom – The Official Report*, Electoral Commission, London, December

Electoral Reform Society (2004), *Burnley and the BNP and the Case for Electoral Reform*, Electoral Reform Society, London

Engstrom, M. (2002), *Rebooting Europe: Digital Deliberation and European Democracy*, Next Generation Democracy No. 4, Foreign Policy Centre and the British Council, London

European Commission (2004a) *Eurobarometer 61, Spring 2004 (First Results)*, European Commission, Brussels

European Commission (2004b) *Eurobarometer 61: Public Opinion in the European Union*. Available at <http://europea.eu.int/comm/public_opinion>

European Commission (2004c) *Flash Eurobarometer: Post European Elections 2004 Survey*, European Commission, Brussels

Evans, G. (2003), 'Will We Ever Vote for the Euro?', in A. Park, J. Curtice, K. Thomson, L. Jarvis and C. Bromley (eds), *British Social Attitudes: The 20th Report*, Sage, London

Farrell, D.M. and Scully, R. (2003a), 'Life Under List: British MEPs' Attitudes to Electoral Reform'. Paper presented to the annual EPOP meeting, Cardiff, September

Farrell, D.M. and Scully, R. (2003b), 'Electoral reform and the British MEP', *Journal of Legislative Studies*, Vol. 9, No. 1, Spring

Foreign & Commonwealth Office (2004), *White Paper on the Treaty Establishing a Constitution for Europe*, CM 6309, September

Franklin, M. (2001), 'European Elections and the European Voter', in J. Richardson (ed.), *European Union: Power and Policy Making*, Routledge, London

Franklin, M., van der Eijk, C. and Oppenhuis, E. (1996), 'The Motivational Basis of Participation in European Elections, 1979–94: The Case of Britain', in C. Rallings et al. (eds), *British Elections and Parties Yearbook 1995*, Frank Cass, London

Gabel, M. (2003), 'Public support for the European Parliament', *Journal of Common Market Studies*, Vol. 41, No. 2, April

Gagatek, W. (2003), 'The British Conservative Party and the Group of the European People's Party – An Analysis of the History and Present Shape of Difficult Relationships'. Unpublished paper, Warsaw

Galloway, D. (2001), *The Treaty of Nice and Beyond*, Sheffield University Press, Sheffield

Galloway, D. (2004), 'Variable Geometry in the Council', in M. Westlake and D. Galloway (eds), *The Council of the European Union*, John Harper, London

Geddes, A. (2004), *The European Union and British Politics*, Palgrave Macmillan, Basingstoke

Gill, M., Atkinson, S. and Mortimore, R. (2004), *The Referendum Battle*, Foreign Policy Centre and MORI, London, September

Gitelson, A. and Richard, P. (1983), 'Ticket-splitting: aggregate measures vs. actual ballots', *Western Political Quarterly*, Vol. 36: 410–19

Grant, C. (2004), 'The peculiarities of the British', *CER Bulletin*, Issue 37, August/September

Grothe, T. (2003), 'The Struggle for a Common Statute of MEPs – An Analysis of Decision-Making in the European Union from a Rational Choice Institutionalist Perspective'. Unpublished MA thesis, College of Europe, Bruges

Hanmer, M. and Traugott, M. (2004), 'The impact of voting by mail on voter behaviour', *American Politics Research*, Vol. 32, No. 4: 375–405

Hare, D. (1993), *The Absence of War*, Faber and Faber, London

Hayward, J. (ed.) (1995), *The Crisis of Representation in Europe*, Frank Cass, London

Heath, A., McLean, I., Taylor, B. and Curtice, J. (1999), 'Between first and second order: a comparison of voting behaviour in European and local elections in Britain', *European Journal of Political Research*, Vol. 35: 389–414

Hermens, F. (1941), *Democracy or Anarchy? A Study of Proportional Representation*, University of Notre Dame Press, Notre Dame, Ind.

Hix, S. (2004), 'EU balance of power shifts to the right', *E!Sharp*, September

Hix, S., Kreppel, A. and Noury, A. (2003), 'The party system in the European Parliament: collusive or competitive?', *Journal of Common Market Studies*, Vol. 41, No. 2, April

Hix, S. and Lord, C. (1997), *Political Parties in the European Union*, Macmillan, Basingstoke

Hix, S. and Marsh, M. (2004), *Predicting the Future: The Next European Parliament*, Burson-Marsteller, Brussels

Hix, S. and Scully, R. (eds) (2003), 'Special Issue: The European Parliament at Fifty', *Journal of Common Market Studies*, Vol. 41, No. 2, April

Hix, S., Raunio, T. and Scully, R. (2003), 'Fifty years on: research on the European Parliament', *Journal of Common Market Studies*, Vol. 41, No. 2, April

House of Commons Library (1999), *European Parliament Elections – 1979 to 1994*, Research Paper 99/57, June

House of Commons Library (2000a), *The Political Parties, Elections and Referendums Bill – Electoral Aspects*, Research Paper 00/1, January

House of Commons Library (2000b), *The Political Parties, Elections and Referendums Bill – Referendums and Broadcasting*, Research Paper 00/3, January

House of Commons Library (2002), *The European Parliament (Representation) Bill*, Research Paper 02/78, December

House of Commons Library (2003a), *Combining Local Elections, Greater London Authority Elections and European Elections in 2004*, Standard Note SN/PC/1994, June

House of Commons Library (2003b), *Measures to Address Low Turnout*, Standard Note SN/PC/2051, August

House of Commons Library (2003c), *Electoral Performance of Far-Right Parties in the UK*, Standard Note SN/SG/1982, September

House of Commons Library (2003d), *The European Parliamentary and Local Elections (Pilots) Bill*, Research Paper 03/76, October

House of Commons Library (2004a), *All-Postal Voting*, Standard Note SN/PC/2882, October

House of Commons Library (2004b), *The Draft Single European Currency (Referendum) Bill*, Standard Note SN/PC/2851, January

House of Commons Library (2004c), *The European Parliamentary and Local Elections (Pilots) Bill: Recent Developments*, Standard Note SN/PC/2806, March

House of Commons Library (2004d), *Proposals for a Referendum on the New European Constitution*, Standard Note SN/PC/3604, May

House of Commons Library (2004e), *European Parliament Elections 2004*, Research Paper 04/50, June

House of Commons Library (2004f), *The Electoral Commission*, Standard Note SN/PC/3127, July

House of Commons Library (2004g), *Referendums for Regional Assemblies*, Standard Note SN/PC/2922, July

Independent Commission on Proportional Representation (2003), *Interim Report*, Constitution Unit, School of Public Policy, University College London

Independent Commission on Proportional Representation (2004), *Changed Voting, Changed Politics: Lessons of Britain's Experience of PR since 1997* (final report), Constitution Unit, School of Public Policy, University College London

Inglehart, R. (1997) *Modernization and Postmodernization: Cultural, Economic and Political Change in 43 Societies*, Princeton University Press, Princeton

Jackson, N. (2003), 'Vote Winner or Nuisance? E-mail and British MPs' Relationships with Their Constituents'. Paper delivered to the 2003 Political Studies Association annual conference (available at <www.psa.ac.uk/cps/2003G-L.htm>)

Jackson, N. (2004), 'Political Parties, Their E-Newsletters and Subscribers: "One Night Stand" or a "Marriage Made in Heaven"'. Paper presented at the PSA, University of Lincoln, April [f. 148]

Jansen, T. (2001), *Pan-European Political Parties*, European Essay No. 14, Federal Trust, London

Johansson, K.M. (2002), 'The Christian Democrat coalition and the quest for European Union', *Journal of Common Market Studies*, Vol. 40, No. 5, December

Johnston, R.J. and Pattie, C.J. (2002), 'Campaigning and split-ticket voting in new electoral systems: the first MMP elections in New Zealand, Scotland and Wales', *Electoral Studies*, Vol. 21: 583–600

Judge, D. and Earnshaw, D. (2003), *The European Parliament*, Palgrave Macmillan, Basingstoke

King, S. (2004), *The Impact of Electoral System Change on UK Candidate Selection*, School of Public Policy, London

Kurpas, S., Incerti, M. and Crum, B. (2004), *Preview of the 2004 European Parliament Elections – Results of an EPIN Survey of National Experts*, European Policy Institute Network, Working Paper No. 11, Brussels, May

Lamoureux, F. (2004), *Draft Constitution: Why a 'Rear Guard' Should be Established*, Research Paper for Notre Europe, Paris

Leonard, M. and Arbuthnot, T. (2002), *Next Generation Democracy*, Foreign Policy Centre and the British Council, London

Lijphart, A. (1994), *Electoral Systems and Party Systems: A Study of Twenty-Seven Democracies, 1945–1990*, Oxford University Press, Oxford

Loosemore, J. and Hanby, V. (1971), 'The theoretical limits of maximum distortion: some analytic expressions for electoral systems', *British Journal of Political Science*, Vol. 1: 467–77

Mair, P. (1995), 'Political Parties, Popular Legitimacy and Public Privilege', in J. Hayward (ed.), *The Crisis of Representation in Europe*, Frank Cass, London

Marquand, D. (1979), *Parliament for Europe*, Jonathan Cape, London

Marshall, B. and Lloyd, B. (2004), 'Making the Case for Politics: Report on Work of the Electoral Commission'. Paper presented to EPOP conference, Oxford University, September

Maurer, A. (1999), *What Next for the European Parliament?*, Federal Trust, London

Maurer, A. (2003), 'The legislative powers and impact of the European Parliament', *Journal of Common Market Studies*, Vol. 41, No. 2, April

McLean, I. and Mortimore, R. (1992), 'Apportionment and the Boundary Commission for England', *Electoral Studies*, Vol. 11: 293–309

Morgan, R. and Steed, M. (eds) (2003), *Choice and Representation in the European Union*, Federal Trust, London

Morrison, J. (2003), 'The last ballot box', *Prospect*, December

Norman, P. (2003), *The Accidental Constitution*, Gazelle Press, London

Norman, P. (2004), 'The rise and rise of Euroscepticism', *E!Sharp*, September

Norris, P. (2002), *Democratic Phoenix: Reinventing Political Activism*, Cambridge University Press, New York

Office for National Statistics (2003a) *Census 2001: Report for Parliamentary Constituencies*, The Stationery Office, London

Office for National Statistics (2003b) *Census 2001: Key Statistics for Local Authorities in England and Wales*, The Stationery Office, London

Parry, G., Moyser, G. and Day, N. (1992), *Political Participation and Democracy in Britain*, Cambridge University Press, Cambridge

Peterson, J. and Shackleton, M. (eds) (2002), *The Institutions of the European Union*, Oxford University Press, Oxford

Rallings, C. and Thrasher, M. (1998), 'Split-Ticket Voting at the 1997 British General and Local Elections – An Aggregate Analysis', in D. Denver et al. (eds), *British Elections and Parties Review 1998*, Frank Cass, London

Rallings, C. and Thrasher, M. (2000), *British Political Facts 1832–1999*, Ashgate, Aldershot

Rallings, C. and Thrasher, M. (2001), 'Measuring the level and direction of split-ticket voting at the 1979 and 1997 British general and local elections: a survey-based analysis', *Political Studies*, Vol. 49, No. 2: 323–30

Rallings, C. and Thrasher, M. (2004a), 'Not All "Second-Order" Contests are the Same – Turnout and Party Choice at the Concurrent 2004 Local and European Parliament Elections in England'. Unpublished paper.

Rallings, C. and Thrasher, M. (2004b), 'Voters Don't Need Political Scientists and Political Scientists Shouldn't Jump to Conclusions!' Paper presented at the annual meeting of the specialist group of the Political Studies Association on Elections, Public Opinion and Parties, Oxford University, 10–12 September

Raunio, T. (2002), 'Political Interests: The European Parliament's Party Groups', in J. Peterson and M. Shackleton (eds), *The Institutions of the European Union*, Oxford University Press, Oxford

Reif, K. (1985a), 'Ten Second Order Elections', in K. Reif (ed.), *Ten European Elections: Campaigns and Results of the 1979/81 First Direct Elections to the European Parliament*, Gower, Aldershot

Reif, K. (1985b), *Ten European Elections: Campaigns and Results of the 1979/81 First Direct Elections to the European Parliament*, Gower, Aldershot

Reif, K. (1997), 'Reflections: European elections as member state second-order elections revisited', *European Journal of Political Research*, Vol. 31: 115–24

Reif, K. and Schmitt, H. (1980), 'Nine second-order national elections: a conceptual framework for the analysis of European election results', *European Journal of Political Research*, Vol. 8: 3–44

Richardson, J. (ed.) (2001), *European Union: Power and Policy Making*, Routledge, London

Rittberger, B. (2003), 'The creation and empowerment of the European Parliament', *Journal of Common Market Studies*, Vol. 41, No. 2, April

Rose, R. (2004), 'Turnout for the European Parliament: A Comparative Perspective'. Paper delivered to an Electoral Commission/DEMOS seminar, London, 15 September

Rovny, J. (2004), 'Conceptualising party-based Euroscepticism: magnitude and motivations', *Collegium*, No. 29, Bruges

Scully, R. and Farrell, D.M. (2003), 'MEPs as representatives: individual and institutional roles', *Journal of Common Market Studies*, Vol. 41, No. 2, April

Smith, J. (1995), *Voice of the People: The European Parliament in the 1990s*, Royal Institute of International Affairs, London

Steed, M. (2002), 'Choice, Representation and European Elections', in R. Morgan and M. Steed (eds), *Choice and Representation in the European Union*, Federal Trust/Kogan Page, London

Steed, M. (2004), *The European Parliament and the British People: 2004*, European Essay No. 30, Federal Trust, London, May

Stuart, G. (2003a) *The Making of Europe's Constitution*, Fabian Ideas 609, Fabian Society, London

Stuart, G. (2003b), 'We have to tear it up and start again', *Guardian*, 17 December

Taggart, P. and Szczerbiak, A. (2004), 'Supporting the European Union? Euroscepticism and the Politics of European Integration', in M. Green Cowles and D. Dinan (eds), *Developments in the European Union*, Palgrave Macmillan, Basingstoke

Thomsen, S.R. (1987), *Danish Elections 1920–79: A Logit Approach to Ecological Analysis and Inference*, Politica, Aarhus, Denmark

Thomsen, S.R., Berglund, S. and Worlund, I. (1991), 'Assessing the validity of the logit method for ecological inference', *European Journal of Political Research*, Vol. 19: 441–77

Waller, R. (1980), 'The 1979 local and general elections in England and Wales', *Political Studies*, Vol. 28, No. 3: 443–50

Ware, L., Borisyuk, G., Rallings, C. and Thrasher, M. (forthcoming), 'A new algorithm for estimating voter turnout when the number of ballot papers issued is unknown', *Electoral Studies*

Weiler, J.H.H. (1999), *The Constitution of Europe*, Cambridge University Press, Cambridge

Westlake, M. (1994), *A Modern Guide to the European Parliament*, Pinter, London

Westlake, M. (2001), *Kinnock: The Biography*, Little, Brown, London

Westlake, M. and Galloway, D. (2004), *The Council of the European Union*, John Harper, London

Wynn, T. (2004), 'The EU Budget: Public Perception and Fact'. Unpublished paper, Brussels

Index